The Complete Guide to
MERCURY DIMES

Second Edition

by
David W. Lange

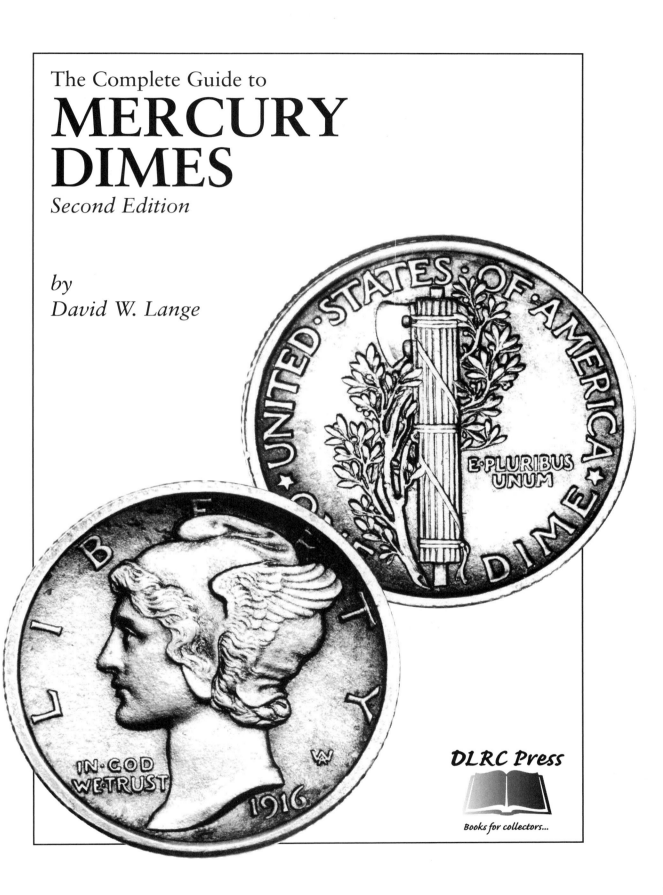

DLRC Press

Books for collectors...

In memory of Joseph F. Rust,

who passed too soon.

DLRC Press

Books for collectors...

Virginia Beach, Virginia
(800) 776-0560 ✳ info@davidlawrence.com

www.davidlawrence.com

Printed in the United States

Acknowledgements

The principal photography for this book was performed by Tom Mulvaney. His work includes the obverse and reverse photos of each date/mint combination, the error gallery, the grading guide and numerous close-up photos. Additional photographs were taken by Bob Everett (deceased), Bill Fivaz, J. T. Stanton, Alan Herbert, Arnold Margolis, Cathy Dumont, Douglas A. Mudd, Monique Schalk and David W. Lange.

The layout and typesetting were performed by John Feigenbaum and Kim Ludwig at DLRC Press.

A special thanks goes to the following professionals who shared their insight in reviewing the author's manuscript for the original edition of this book, as well as providing other useful comments: Bill Fivaz, Phelps Dean Witter and the late Norman Talbert.

Among those who lent items from their collections or inventories for inclusion in this book were Gary Acquistapace, Ken Barr, Peter K. Beane, Pete Bishal (deceased) , Eugene Bruder, Michael L. Chambers, Jim Checkovich, Mark W. Clark, Douglas C. Daniels, Bill Fivaz, Peter F. Hamilton, Kenneth R. Hill, Ralph Huntzinger, Jonathan K. Kern, John McIntosh, Tom Miller, David & Ginger Pike, Vic Rollo, Gerald Singer, J. T. Stanton, Sam Thurman, Fred Weinberg and David Woloch.

Others who provided supplemental information and reference materials or who shared their unique knowledge of this series include John F. Bergman (deceased), Auctions by Bowers & Merena, Gerald L. Kochel, J. P. Martin, Ron Miller (deceased), Darrel Neidigh, Andrew W. Pollock III, Joel Rettew, Sr., Thomas J. Rosario and Robert A. Weinman (deceased).

Thanks go also to the following institutions which furnished historical photographs and/or information: Smithsonian Institution National Museum of American History, Washington, DC; American Numismatic Association Library, Colorado Springs, CO; National Archives and Records Administration, College Park, MD; the Denver Public Library and the San Francisco Public Library.

A special thanks goes to Wayne T. De Cesar, who guided the author's research efforts at the National Archives and Records Administration, and to Richard Doty, who provided photographs of and insight about Mercury Dimes in the National Numismatic Collection.

The following organizations permitted information to be reprinted from their publications: Whitman Publishing, LLC. — *A Guidebook of United States Coins*, by R. S. Yeoman; Numismatic Guaranty Corporation of America — *NGC Census*; Professional Coin Grading Service — *PCGS Population Report*; CDN, Inc. — *The Coin Dealer Newsletter and Monthly Summary*; Amos Press — *Coin World* and *The Numismatic Scrapbook Magazine*; The American Numismatic Association — *The Numismatist*.

FOREWORD to the First Edition

by Bill Fivaz

The world situation was worrisome at best in 1916, and things were changing rapidly in Europe. Changes were occurring in this country as well, and many people look upon 1916 as one of the most significant years in numismatics.

Gone were the three virtually identical Liberty bust designs by Charles E. Barber on the dime, quarter and half dollar, replaced by the beautiful neo-classic representations of this figure by Adolph Weinman on the dime and half, and by Hermon MacNeil on the quarter. All three were tied together by the fact that, for the first time, their designs were not similar for each denomination; all three stood on their own as true and lasting works of art.

Weinman's Winged Liberty Head design for the smallest of these denominations is covered in detail by David W. Lange in this book, and I urge all readers to take a few minutes to read the pages leading up to the date analysis. These pages present a well-researched look at Weinman and his model, Elsie Kachel Stevens, and give one an excellent overview of the politics at that time in so far as getting new coin designs approved is concerned. Public acceptance of the coin is also well documented, and sections on *Pattern Coins*, *Mint Errors* in the series, *Proof Coinage* and *Grading* will be of significant interest to the reader.

David's *Date-and-Mint Analysis* is superbly done, covering all the essentials necessary for the collector, and the enlarged photos of each date taken by Tom Mulvaney are an excellent reference tool. Mintage figures, known varieties (most of which are illustrated), rarity factors and values from 1945 to the present for most grades offer a meaningful "track record" for each issue.

Readers will find the author's "Comments" section at the end of each listing of enormous wealth. Here he analyzes the strike characteristics, discusses full-band availability, and offers insights into other factors that may impact the coinage for that particular year and mint.

David has obviously done his homework, and the manner in which his information is presented is logical, accurate and easy to follow. This excellent book, on one of this nation's most popular coin series, certainly deserves a special place in one's numismatic library.

Author's Foreword
Special to the Second Edition

The original edition of this book was published in 1993, which now seems a lot longer time ago than it really is. So much has happened in these dozen years that it's difficult to know where to start.

The Complete Guide to Mercury Dimes was a follow-up effort to a similar book I wrote on Buffalo Nickels published the previous year. Both works were initiated by the late coin dealer David Lawrence Feigenbaum, proprietor of David Lawrence Rare Coins. He had already established a series of Complete Guide books with his own publications exploring the dimes, quarters and halves of 1892-1916. Dave loved the Barber coins, and it was seemingly inevitable that he would be the one to write standard references on these series.

In a conversation with him in 1991, Dave revealed to me that he was seeking authors to write similar volumes on each of the popular USA coin series. When he asked me for my thoughts regarding possible authors, I gave him several names, but we didn't discuss the matter again for some months. When I then asked him how the project was going, he said he had people lined up to do books on the Seated Liberty coin series, but he was particularly concerned about finding someone for Buffalo Nickels. Impulsively, I told him that I could probably do as good a job with that title as most numismatic writers, and to my surprise he agreed.

Though I'd been a columnist and feature writer in numismatics for several years, I had never written a complete book. This was new territory for me. In addition, I was not then, nor am I now, a specialist in any one USA coin series. I have my favorites, but I've always been a generalist who likes to maintain a working knowledge of all series. Nevertheless, my Buffalo Nickel book was good enough for me to segue into a similar reference on Mercury Dimes. Both books were well received, though the revised edition of my Buffalo Nickel book, published in 2000, proved to be vastly superior to the first.

Since 1993 the hobby has lost a good friend in Dave Lawrence, who succumbed to ALS, or Lou Gehrig's Disease, just a few years ago. Son John Feigenbaum has taken over both the coin business and its publishing arm, DLRC Press, and David Lawrence Rare Coins is now a bigger player in the retail market than Dave ever imagined. John was the one who did the layout for the DLRC books, and he now serves as publisher.

The Complete Guide to Mercury Dimes was followed by a similar volume on the Lincoln Cent series, which, due to the extended period covered, was a much longer and more difficult book to prepare. Though published by another company, it is quite compatible with the DLRC books. In addition, I've written a few other books since then, a couple of which are awaiting publication as this is written. With this experience came increased confidence, and I was determined to do an improved edition of the Mercury Dime book when the appropriate time arrived. *The Complete Guide to Mercury Dimes* has now been out of print long enough that those desiring a new edition are probably equal in number to those new to the hobby who have never heard of it at all.

Shortly after the first edition of this title was published, I joined Numismatic Guaranty Corporation as its Director of Research. While that role involves a wide variety of activities, the bottom line is that I've had the chance to view a lot more coins than I did previous to writing the first edition. This increased exposure has prompted an expansion of the date-and-mint study of each issue, including the proofs. While there are no "new" Mercury Dimes since 1993, there is a lot more known about them. This is partly the result of an additional twelve years of certified grading and encapsulation, as well as the building and dispersal at auction of several important Mercury Dime collections.

New to this edition is a chapter on the history of collecting Mercury Dimes. Indeed, history is at the core of this book, and the story of this coin's inception and development has been greatly expanded. This was made possible through time spent performing research at the National Archives and Records Administration in College Park, Maryland. While many will collect a coin series just for the appeal of the coins themselves, I truly believe that a real appreciation of any series comes only with knowledge of the coins' history and the ability to place each piece in its cultural and economic context.

My own collection of Mercury Dimes, which included a number of plate coins from this book, was sold intact not long after publication of the first edition. Veteran collectors know all too well that the real fun of collecting is in the hunt. When completion is achieved, disinterest often follows. While I remain interested in all USA coins, as well as most world issues, there was nothing more to add to my set of Mercury Dimes. Nor could I afford to upgrade the About Uncirculated pieces to Mint State.

The passion for collecting remains, however, and I've recently assembled a new set of these coins in well worn condition. Building a matched set of problem-free coins, ones having completely original surfaces and similar toning, is quite a challenge, even in the grades of Very Good through Very Fine. Adolph Weinman's little dime is a simply beautiful design, and it appeals to me in all grades. Worn coins also free one from the worry of preservation, as such pieces are quite safe in most coin albums. Indeed, it was the empty holes of a coin album that beckoned to me as a child, while I searched through every conceivable source of coins just to fill one more. It seems I've come full circle with this series, now buying the very same sort of pieces I used to seek from pocket change some 40 years ago.

David W. Lange
Sarasota, Florida
May, 2005

Introduction

There are numerous reasons why people become coin collectors. Many inherit their interest from a parent or some other relative; a few are introduced to the hobby by a friend or co-worker. Children are natural collectors, and coins may be among the countless items hoarded briefly and then passed on as interests change. In recent decades, ever greater numbers of collectors have come from within the ranks of the investors, persons who were surprised to discover that there is more to money than simply making money.

Whatever one's age or background, there must be something about the hobby of numismatics that enables a person to stick with it through a lifetime. This something is very likely to be a particular coin which speaks to the imagination as an object of beauty and human interest. It may be a silver stater of Ancient Greece; it may be a bronze sestertius of the Roman Empire; it may be a gold sovereign of Victorian England. For the typical American collector, this coin is quite often the Winged Liberty Dime. We know it better as the "Mercury" Dime.

Coined by the millions from 1916 through 1945, Mercury Dimes remain a familiar image in the hobby, although long vanished from everyday circulation. Nearly two generations have passed since these beautiful little silver pieces were known to every American, and it is only we collectors who now derive benefit from their charm. These coins, the work of Adolph A. Weinman, were widely hailed on their debut in 1916, a rare accomplishment among United States coin designs. Being generally suspicious of change, particularly that initiated by the federal government, Americans nevertheless took the youthful Miss Liberty to their hearts and shed no tears over the passing of her matronly predecessor.

The image of a youthful female adorned with wings, symbolizing "liberty of thought," was new to United States coinage. There were, however, historical precedents in the Ancient World. In the coinage of Bithynia, King Prusias II is portrayed with a winged diadem, while silver denarii of the Roman Republic frequently included the familiar portrait of a winged Roma.

Bronze coin of Bithynia, depicting King Prusias II with a winged diadem, 183-149 B.C.
(Courtesy of Stephen M. Huston)

Winged head of Roma on a silver denarius issued by C. Terentius Lucanus, circa 147 B.C.

Aluminum two francs coin of French Equatorial Africa, portraying Marianne with winged head. Dated 1948, designed by Louis Bazor

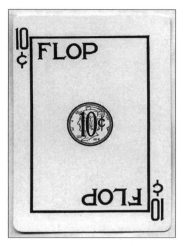

The Mercury Dime appears on a playing card of the 1920s produced by the Coin Card Company of Water Valley, MS and Memphis, TN

The use of a winged-head figure may have varied in meaning from one culture to another, but such imagery was compelling, and it recurs even in more modern coinage of the Old World. Typical of many coins minted by France for its African colonies is the two-francs piece of French Equatorial Africa dated 1948. The youthful Marianne, symbol of the French Republic and the ideological equivalent of our goddess Liberty, is depicted in a manner nearly identical to the American dime. She wears the flowing hair, the *pileus* (liberty cap) and the petite wings seen on Weinman's dime of 1916. There was a certain justice in France's copying of this artist's design, as many have commented that Adolph Weinman's half dollar (also created in 1916) was largely a reworking of the French silver coins then in circulation.

As charming as the winged portrait of Miss Liberty may have been, the coin's reverse, though skillfully rendered, became a source of some consternation. In 1916, the fasces was nothing more than an ancient symbol of authority dating from the glory of Rome. It was thus entirely acceptable on an American coin. Three years later, however, the followers of Benito Mussolini seized upon this image as their symbol for a new order in Italy. By 1922 they had achieved their goal, and the fasces would thence forward be associated with tyranny and mob rule. Protests over its continued use on a United States coin were initially few in number, but they grew as the Nazis too asserted their power in Germany.

In retrospect, it seems that America's entry into World War II would have required that the fasces be removed immediately from our ten-cent piece, as the war was basically a struggle against international fascism. Instead, the United States Mint was so overwhelmed with the rapid increase in demand for fresh coinage that it couldn't possibly undertake any design changes for the duration of the war. By 1945, when coinage of the Mercury Dime was finally brought to a conclusion, the crusade against fascism had already been won. Ultimately, it was not any perceived fault with the coin's imagery which caused it to be terminated, but rather the desire to honor a fallen leader. President of the United States Franklin D. Roosevelt had died during the final months of the war. As he was so closely associated with the March of Dimes campaign to end polio, this denomination was selected to host his portrait beginning in 1946.

Thus, the Mercury Dime was replaced at the three U. S. mints by the Roosevelt Dime. With hundreds of millions having been coined during World War II

Miss Liberty was recruited to appear on this pin from the 1939 March of Dimes campaign

alone, the Mercury Dime remained a familiar item for another twenty years. It was not until the complete disappearance from circulation of all silver coins during the late 1960s that Weinman's beautiful young lady faded entirely from public consciousness.

Neutron irradiated dimes were a popular souvenir back when Americans were still excited about living in the "Atomic Age." Several varieties are known.
(Courtesy of Bill Fivaz)

The old Mercury Dime still makes an appearance from time to time. This souvenir gaming token dated 1991 depicts a 1944 dime and an undated Peace Silver Dollar
(Courtesy of Gary Acquistapace)

Today, only collectors remember and cherish these little dimes. Within the non-numismatic population, a few persons of sufficient age may yet recognize a Mercury Dime when shown one. By and large, however, people have short memories for the coins which have passed their way. Given the number of Americans who cannot positively identify Roosevelt on the current dime, it's safe to say that very few outside of the coin hobby know of Weinman's masterwork.

As we numismatists assemble and enjoy our collections, we must also remind ourselves that we are simply the curators of a revolving museum, one in which each collector is but the temporary owner of his or her coins. As we ultimately pass from this world, and our collections are dispersed, others will come to know the pleasure that we've taken in our time from collecting and studying Mercury Dimes. This book was written for those who desire to do both of these things, now and in the future.

2004 high-relief tribute to the Mercury Dime coined by the Gallery Mint Museum

Table of Contents

CHAPTER 1

History of the Series

*

The Design

*

Adolph A. Weinman

*

Elsie Kachel Stevens

History of the Mercury Dime Series

"a new design may, therefore, be adopted in 1916 . . ."

The coinage Act of September 26, 1890 amended Section 3510 of the Revised Statutes of the United States to read in part:

> The Director of the Mint shall have power, with the approval of the Secretary of the Treasury, to cause new designs or models of authorized emblems or devices to be prepared and adopted in the same manner as when new coins or devices are authorized. But no change in the design or die of any coin shall be made more often than once in twenty-five years from and including the year of the first adoption of the design, model, die, or hub for the same coin...[1]

At a meeting of the New York Numismatic Club in December of 1914, a letter was read from prominent New York City coin dealer and general critic of all matters numismatic, Thomas L. Elder, in which Elder drew the club's attention to this provision of the law and urged that a movement be started to create new designs for the fractional silver coinage of the United States. As reported by *The New York Times* December 11, Elder, a member of the club's Executive Committee, was urging that a special committee be appointed to petition the government for "more artistic designs."[2]

In detailing the changes made to the gold coinage beginning in 1907, Elder went on to observe that, "after all the attempts of our Government to improve our coinage, the most abominable products of our mints, the half dollar, the quarter, and the dime, remain. The figure of Liberty on the coins is a mere caricature. The head, as it appears at present, is an insult both to the Goddess of Liberty and to the beauty of American womanhood."

What the Treasury Department may have thought of Elder's commentary is not recorded, but it is evident that the club's petition seeking new designs for the fractional silver pieces made its way to the right party. An undated memorandum was sent in January of 1915 from Frederic P. Dewey* to Assistant Treasury Secretary William P. Malburn, in which Dewey listed the first year of coining and the names of the artists for each of the denominations then current. Armed with this information, Malburn then wrote on January 18 to his boss, Treasury Secretary William Gibbs McAdoo:

From the accompanying memorandum of the Acting Director of the Mint you will observe that the present silver half dollar, quarter dollar and dime were changed in 1892, and a new design may, therefore, be adopted in 1917 [7 corrected by hand to 6]. This can be done any time in the year, and, therefore, if you desire, a design may be made and coinage commenced on January 2 of that year.[3]

Written in Malburn's hand at the bottom of this memo is the notation, "Secy says take this up later," to which McAdoo further added, "W.P.M. - Let the Mint submit designs before we try anybody else - ." Finally, the memo bears an additional notation indicating that it was received by Acting Director Dewey on March 14, 1915.

It's surprising that Treasury Secretary William G. McAdoo would take a more than bureaucratic interest in the nation's coinage, which could easily have gone on with the same staid, Victorian Era designs, but then this was a time of great vitality in the nation. It was the Progressive Age, and there existed a widespread movement toward reform in both government and the economy. The White House was occupied by an idealistic individual, educator Woodrow Wilson, and a general sense of public advancement in terms of health and morality pervaded much of American society. While some of the reforms enacted during that decade would prove to be double-edged swords, such as the prohibition of alcohol sales and consumption, with its resulting crime wave,

---

*Dewey was the U. S. Mint's Assayer, but he was serving temporarily as Acting Director. The former Director, George E. Roberts, had left office the previous November, and his replacement had not yet reported.

there was a general improvement in the quality of life for most Americans.

This movement toward reform had a great influence on the arts, as well. It was in 1910 that the federal Commission of Fine Arts was created to oversee all aspects of design in government projects. While this role was not extended to coinage design officially until 1921, the Commission was informally consulted on such matters almost from its inception, as we shall see.

It was during the administration of President Theodore Roosevelt (1901-09) that the nation's chief executive first took an active role in the process of coin design. His initiative resulted in several of our finest coin types, including the four new gold coins introduced in 1907-08 and the familiar Lincoln Cent which, in modified form, is still being coined today. This spirit of artistic improvement carried over within the Treasury Department under Roosevelt's successor, William H. Taft, and his administration produced the glorious Indian Head and Buffalo Nickel in 1913, considered by many numismatists to be the USA's finest coin type.

It seemed clear enough from a reading of the 1890 law that the three fractional silver denominations of dime, quarter dollar and half dollar were now eligible for new designs, but Assistant Secretary Malburn wanted to be certain before proceeding with the project. He wrote to Solicitor of the Treasury Lawrence Beel on April 14, 1915 seeking a legal opinion:

> The facts being that, as shown by the Annual Report of the Director of the Mint, 1891, p. 71, the present designs for our subsidiary silver coins were adopted in 1891, while, as shown by the Catalogue of Coins in the Philadelphia Mint, pp. 62, 67 and 72, no coins of these designs were issued until 1892; I would thank you for your opinion as to whether it would be lawful and in accordance with Sec. 3510 R. S., as amended

September 26, 1890, (Stat. L., 26 484) to adopt new designs and issue coins therefrom in 1916. It seems to me that new coins could be issued in 1916.[4]

The Solicitor responded by memorandum three days later that these coins were indeed eligible for new designs. By this time the new Mint Director, Robert Wickliffe Woolley, had assumed office at the Mint Bureau in Washington, DC. He was quickly apprised of the coin design initiative, and he wrote to Philadelphia Mint Superintendent Adam M. Joyce on April 14:

> The Secretary of the Treasury is very anxious that the work on designs for the silver half and quarter dollar and dime, for coinage in 1916, be begun as soon as Mr. Barber conveniently can do so. Of course, the Panama medal, etc., have right of way. Will you please take this matter up with him and I will see you on my return from the Pacific coast.[5]

Woolley was going west to inspect the installation of new equipment at the San Francisco Mint for the coining of commemorative issues for the Panama-Pacific International Exposition, including the novel and massive fifty-dollar pieces. The subject of these coins occupied much of the Mint's correspondence during the latter months of 1914 and the first months of 1915, and it was quite an undertaking.

It was clearly the intention at this stage to have U. S. Mint Chief Engraver Charles E. Barber submit models for the new coins of 1916, though McAdoo's addendum to the memo of January 18, quoted above, suggests that this was merely a procedural consideration. Beginning in 1907 Barber's designs had been rejected repeatedly in favor of those furnished by outside artists, but it was in keeping with tradition and respect for his position that he was given the first opportunity.

The selection and refinement of designs for

the Panama-Pacific coins, as well as technical obstacles to coining the fifty-dollar pieces, provided enough drama for the Mint that the subject of new fractional silver coins for 1916 was put aside for several months. It was not until October of 1915 that the trail of correspondence picks up again. On the 6th, Director Woolley wrote to Charles Barber at the Philadelphia Mint, "You are hereby authorized and directed to come to Washington on Friday, October 8th, for conference with this Office in connection with coin designs."[6]

It is not clear from this letter whether Barber had already prepared his models but, in any event, they would ultimately prove to be unsatisfactory. While technically proficient and extremely knowledgeable in all aspects of coining technology, Charles Barber was simply too much a Victorian in his artistic taste. Grounded in the classical art that dominated much of the 19th Century, all of Barber's creations reflected this fashion which, by the early 20th Century, was quite at odds with the realistic trend in art. His coin designs included the very ones which were now to be replaced, and it appeared doubtful that he would achieve any artist breakthroughs.

Born in England in 1840, Charles E. Barber immigrated to America thirteen years later with his family. Father William Barber was a skilled engraver who assumed the role of Chief Engraver of the U. S. Mint in 1869, following the death of longtime predecessor James B. Longacre. The elder Barber was assisted in this capacity by son Charles, who succeeded his father as Chief Engraver upon William's death in 1879. By 1915 Charles Barber has outlived nearly everyone of his generation at the Mint, with the notable exception of fellow Englishman and longtime rival, Assistant Engraver George T. Morgan. It was Morgan who would finally succeed Barber as Chief Engraver when the latter passed away, two years later.

"I beg that you suggest the names of artists who are capable of undertaking this work."

The Act of September 26, 1890, which permitted the adoption of new coin designs after 25 years of use, also made provision for the temporary employment of artists not directly associated with the Mint. This had been the desperate response of Congress to the coin designs of that period, which even then were perceived as staid and antiquated. It would also prove to be Barber's undoing with respect to the circulating coinage, though he, along with Morgan, still enjoyed a near monopoly on the designs of commemorative coins and medals.

A curious aside to the search for new designs is that it drew the attention of one such outside artist who had already scored a hit at the Mint. On November 27, 1915 Director Woolley responded to a letter sent him by Victor D. Brenner, designer of the Lincoln Cent:

> I beg to acknowledge the receipt of your letter of the 24th instant relative to new designs for the subsidiary coins. The series of designs now in this Bureau have been called to my attention. No steps have yet been taken looking to the submission of designs by outside artists.[7]

In a break with the longstanding tradition of utilizing similar designs for each of the silver denominations, a practice inherited from Europe, the Treasury Department opted to go with unique compositions for the three different coins. Once Barber had submitted his models, Mint Director Woolley wrote to the Chief Engraver on December 1, "You are hereby authorized and requested to visit Washington to attend a meeting of the Fine Arts Commission at eleven o'clock, Friday, December 3, 1915, on business connected with coin design."[8] It's likely that Barber already anticipated the outcome of this meeting. Indeed, Woolley, in a letter dated December 2 and ini-

The Complete Guide to Mercury Dimes

tialed by McAdoo, signaled their intention to the Commission of Fine Arts:

> A period of twenty-five years having nearly elapsed since the adoption of the designs of the half-dollar, quarter dollar and one-dime pieces, it becomes the privilege of the undersigned, under the law, to consider new designs for these coins, and I have the honor to invite the distinguished cooperation of the Fine Arts Commission in performing this important and difficult task.
>
> I take pleasure in submitting to you a number of tentative designs prepared by the Engraver of the Philadelphia Mint and ask for your early criticism thereof.
>
> Should you deem it necessary to call for other sketches I beg that you suggest the names of artists who in your opinion are capable of undertaking this work.[9]

Note that Woolley and McAdoo asked for the names of specific individuals, rather than suggesting an open design competition. In the Mint's only previous experience with a public competition, the results had been less than satisfactory. Seeking new designs to replace Christian Gobrecht's seated figure of Liberty on the silver coins, in 1891 the Mint announced a contest in which all artists were invited to participate. To sculptors of established worth, however, both the remuneration and the submission period seemed inadequate. A boycott of the competition by all qualified parties resulted in the Mint receiving a couple of hundred amateurishly rendered sketches from would-be artists of no merit. To the great satisfaction of Charles Barber, Mint Director Edward O. Leech had had no alternative but to proceed with the Chief Engraver's own submissions.

For the new silver coins of 1916, Director Woolley and Treasury Secretary McAdoo seemed inclined to hold a limited competition, the terms of which were as yet uncertain. The creation of the Commission of Fine Arts in 1910 made this undertaking more desirable than had been the case previously. Charged with the overseeing of all governmental art projects, the Commission was composed of several individuals from within the various arts. It members were highly respected, and in later years the Commission's

approval would come to be sought in the finalizing of all coin designs. As noted previously, however, in 1915 its participation was merely a courtesy.

In its meeting of December 3, 1915 the Commission hosted Woolley and Barber as it reviewed the latter's models. The minutes of this meeting reveal that a misinterpretation of the 1890 law had led the participants to believe that a redesign of the fractional silver coins was not optional, but rather mandatory:

> Twenty-five years having nearly elapsed since the adoption of the present designs of half-dollar, quarter-dollar and one-dime pieces, under the law coins with new designs will have to be issued... Mr. Woolley stated that before going to an outside designer the Mint had their designer, Mr. Barber, prepare a number of preliminary designs which he had brought with him, and laid before the Commission. Mr. Barber was present in consultation. Considerable discussion ensued. Mr. Woolley, after leaving the meeting, returned at one o'clock the following day and lunched with the Commission. During the luncheon the details of the problem were again discussed with him.[10]

It's significant that Woolley returned alone to meet with the Commission the following day, as the subject of this second meeting was no doubt the unsuitability of Barber's models.

In a cover letter to Woolley dated December 9, 1915 the Commission's Secretary and Executive Officer, Colonel William W. Harts, relates that a sub-committee had been appointed to work with the Mint in the matter of new designs for the three silver pieces. The committee was chaired by sculptor Herbert Adams and also included painter Edwin Howland Blashfield, both of whom signed a December 8 letter addressed to Director Woolley, which Colonel Harts enclosed with his own. The Adams/Blashfield letter makes reference to three sculptors who were selected by the sub-committee as candidates for design submissions, observing that "they all realize the great educational value of a beautiful coinage, and appreciate the honor bestowed upon an artist asked to design a coin which is to be seen by millions of people every day." The letter went on to further extol their candidates' virtues:

From what I know of these men, I felt that they would naturally attack the problem in a practical manner, and I found on talking with them that each of them agrees with me that the only logical way to approach such a problem would be to go to the Mint, study the methods of manufacture and learn the practical requirements, at the very start. I believe each of these men has the artistic ability to produce a design which will be a credit to the administration, and that they would be practical in adapting their work to the requirements of modern coinage.[11]

These artists had been contacted only informally about their willingness to participate in an invitational competition, and it was requested of Woolley that the three not be told of the Commission's recommendation. The difficulties and compromises experienced in the creation of acceptable coin models and in dealing with the Chief Engraver were well known to most American sculptors; they had heard the horror stories related by Augustus Saint-Gaudens, James Earle Fraser and Victor D. Brenner, all of whom had had to overcome the road blocks put in their paths by Barber. Bearing this in mind, and not wishing to frighten these artists away, Adams had discreetly inquired of the three candidates their inclination to cooperate with the Mint. Woolley replied to Colonel Harts on December 18:

> I beg to acknowledge the receipt of your letter of December 9th relative to new designs for the subsidiary coins, and transmitting an informal letter received from Mr. McAdam [sic], stating that he had talked with each of the three sculptors mentioned in his letter as to their willingness to cooperate with the Mint on the practical side, if asked to submit designs.
>
> Your wish that the sculptors be not informed that their names were suggested by the Commission will be complied with gladly.
>
> My conference with the members of the Commission was pleasant and satisfactory and I wish to thank you personally for your courtesy to me. [12]

The three sculptors suggested by the Commission included Hermon Atkins MacNeil and Adolph Alexander Weinman, both of New York City, and Albin Polásek of Chicago. The first two are, of course, quite well known to collectors of United States coins, as they were ultimately successful in having their designs selected for the coinage of 1916. Polásek, however, is a name that does not ring a bell with American coin enthusiasts, as all of his sculpting achievements were outside of the numismatic arena.

A native of Moravia (now part of the Czech Republic), Polásek was born in 1879 and came to American at an early age. A student of the Pennsylvania Academy, he ultimately rose to become an instructor at the prestigious Art Institute of Chicago. His most notable works are busts of prominent Americans of his own time, including architect Charles F. McKim and financier J. P. Morgan.[13]

After evidently conferring with Secretary McAdoo, Woolley, on December 22, sent identical letters to all three artists:

> I desire to confer with you relative to the submission of a new design for the subsidiary coins of the United States, and would appreciate a call on me at the United States Assay Office, 24 Pine Street, New York, next Monday at 12, noon.[14]

Woolley then wrote to Herbert Adams that same day:

> I beg to thank you sincerely for conferring with Messrs. McNeil [sic], Weinman and Polasek, and to say that I have asked each of these gentlemen to meet me, at different hours, on Monday next in New York. It will be my pleasure to keep you advised as to the progress being made.[15]

A few days later Woolley wrote to Superintendent Joyce at the Philadelphia Mint on the 27th, informing him of the latest developments:

> I beg to inform you that Mr. Albion Polasek [sic], Mr. Norman A. McNeil [sic] and Mr. Adolph Weiman [sic], all of New York, have been commissioned to submit designs for the new subsidiary coins. Mr. Polasek will probably call on you tomorrow, Mr. McNeil on Wednesday and Mr. Weiman some time early next week. Please introduce them to Mr. Barber and request him to give them all possible information regarding the practical side of coin designing. I have assured them that all inquiries will be cheerfully responded to, and that in their efforts to create the best possible design they will receive from Mr. Barber and others at the Philadelphia Mint at all times hearty co-operation.[16]

It's plainly evident that Woolley had been told of Barber's past history in obstructing the work of outside artists, and he was determined that these new participants would be handled with greater care. It's not clear from the correspondence whether, at that point in the process, the three sculptors each knew of the others' involvement. Woolley, in his correspondence with each individual, omitted the names of the other two. Typical is this December 28 letter to Weinman, identical to those sent to MacNeil and Polásek, in which the terms of the competition are outlined:

> Following our talk of December 27th at the United States Assay Office, New York, with regard to new designs for subsidiary coins of the United States, I beg to commission you to submit designs under the following conditions:
>
> First. That all requirements of law relating to dimensions, designs, devices and legends shall be complied with.
>
> Second. That you are to submit several designs before April 13, 1916, and it is understood that under no circumstances will this time limit be extended.
>
> Third. That if, after the submission of a reasonable number of designs, none, in the opinion of the Secretary of the Treasury and the Director of the Mint, is considered suitable, you will be paid the sum of $300 in complete and full satisfaction of your services.
>
> Fourth. That if the Director of the Mint, with the approval of the Secretary of the Treasury, decides to adopt one of your designs you are to be paid the sum of $2,000. upon acceptance, it being understood that you are to supply the Mint at your own expense with a satisfactory working model.
>
> I beg to state in this connection that it is the intention of the Secretary of the Treasury and the Director of the Mint to ask the advice of the Commission of Fine Arts as to the suitability and appropriateness of the designs submitted by you.
>
> I shall be pleased to be advised at the earliest possible moment whether or not the above conditions are accepted by you.[17]

There was a lot riding on the outcome of this design search, and Woolley wanted to avoid a repeat of the disappointing 1891 episode. In this mission he had strong allies within the Commission of Fine Arts, as revealed in his letter of December 29 to Herbert Adams:

> Colonel Harts called on me yesterday and showed me a telegram which he had just received from you. This morning he called again with Mr. Charles Moore, Chairman of the Commission of Fine Arts, and brought your letter of December 28th. I took pleasure in explaining to them just what I had said to Messrs. McNeil [sic], Polasek and Weinman, and showed them the attached copy of my letter to each. Both of these gentlemen agreed that the arrangement as I understand it has due regard for the ethics of the Society of Sculptors, is fair to the sculptors commissioned, and safeguards the interests of the Government.
>
> I tried to make clear to Messrs. McNeil, Polasek and Weinman that each was to submit designs suitable for the three subsidiary coins - the half-dollar, quarter-dollar and dime - and that the Secretary of the Treasury and myself reserve the right to accept one, two or three, or to reject all, - the excellence and appropriateness of the designs to be the determining factor in reaching a decision.
>
> I have gone somewhat into the history of the selection of other designs of coins and medals and find that almost invariably there has been competition; in this particular case I feel that there is no competition because each man has an opportunity to get his design accepted, regardless of the merits of the work of another.[18]

There were still some questions in the minds of the three sculptors, and a letter from Woolley to Adolph Weinman dated January 4, 1916 is fairly typical. In it the Director informs Weinman that his request for a commission of just a single coin denomination cannot be honored. Woolley further advises him that all submitted designs will be used as the Director and the Secretary determine, though the reverse of the quarter dollar and half dollar must have an eagle, while that of the dime will have no eagle.[19]

The Philadelphia Mint, c. 1969
(Historic American Buildings Survey, Library of Congress)

Whatever misgivings these three artists may have had were set aside, and a number of designs were submitted in competition with those of Charles Barber. After examining about fifty sketch models, Treasury Secretary McAdoo and Mint Director Woolley selected three pairs which presented approximations of the coins ultimately struck for circulation. Writing to Weinman on February 28, Woolley informed him that his designs had been selected for both sides of the dime and the half dollar and for the *reverse of the quarter*.[20] At some point a clarification was reached in which the quarter dollar was to be the work of Hermon MacNeil exclusively.

As nearly everyone had anticipated, Barber's designs were not among those chosen. Woolley informed the Chief Engraver of the competition's outcome in a letter dated March 8, 1916:

> I beg to advise you that selections have been made from a large number of designs submitted for the proposed new subsidiary silver coins. The models submitted by Mr. Adolph Weinman have been chosen for the Half Dollar and the Dime, and the designs submitted by Mr. Hermon MacNeil have been determined upon for the Quarter Dollar.
>
> It is understood that satisfactory working models are to be delivered to the Mint not later than May 1st, 1916, and they are to conform in all respects to the requirements of the Mint.
>
> In advising you of the decisions reached I beg to express the appreciation of the Secretary of the Treasury and myself of the very beautiful designs submitted by you, and to thank you for your deep interest in the matter.[21]

Numismatists may be able to judge for themselves the merits of Barber's work. His submissions for the design competition of 1916 were displayed in a public hallway at the Philadelphia Mint as enlarged photo plaques at least as recently as 2000, though, with the Mint presently closed to informal tours, viewing them may be a bit of a challenge.

On the same day that Barber was informed his designs would not be used, the Mint distributed a press release announcing the new coins:

> Within the next few months the Treasury will begin coinage of new half-dollars, 25-cent and 10-cent pieces. Designs of these coins must be changed by law every twenty-five years and the present twenty-five year period ends with 1916. The designs for the new coins have not been completed and the dies will not be ready for at least two months. It is expected that dies for the new coins will be shipped to the San Francisco Mint about May 1st.[22]

The numismatic community was naturally delighted at the prospect of new coin issues, but the Mint was not particularly forthcoming. Soliciting further details about the new designs, Editor of *The Numismatist*, Frank G. Duffield, wrote to the Director and was told by him, "the Department has no available information in regard to them."

As we now know, Adolph Weinman produced a charming profile bust of the youthful goddess Liberty wearing a cap surmounted by wings. To this obverse was paired a reverse design featuring a Roman fasces around which was wrapped the olive branch of peace. While described in official correspondence as the Winged Head Liberty type, it acquired, almost immediately upon its release circulation, the misnomer "Mercury Dime."

Woolley sent a letter to Superintendent Joyce March 8, advising him of the selections made and cautioning him about the handling of the two artists involved: "Mr. Weinman and Mr. MacNeil are to visit the Mint for consultation with you and Mr. Barber, and I wish to have placed at their disposal every means of assistance at your command."[24] Despite this pre-emptive effort at avoiding conflict, Woolley had to again write to Joyce on the 29th:

> I beg to enclose a letter to Mr. Barber.
> Confidentially, the sculptors designing the new coins felt that on their last trip Mr. Morgan was much more cordial and cooperative than Mr. Barber was. I realize I am dealing with artistic temperaments at both ends. [25]

As Don Taxay so ably observed in his book, *The U.S. Mint and Coinage,* Morgan was in a much better position to be cordial, as it was not his coin designs that were being replaced. In addition to knowing that his crowning achievements, the matching dime, quarter and half of 1892, were about to be terminated, Barber was further compelled to assist in the adoption of replacement designs by outsiders for the seventh time in less than ten years. This situation was not unique to the United States Mint, as Britain's Royal Mint had recently done away with the position of Chief Engraver, deeming it obsolete. This act of finality did not occur at the U. S. Mint until decades later, but only a few of the new coin designs adopted since 1907 have been created entirely in-house.

"I would therefore request an extension of ten days or two weeks"

For a number of reasons, both technical and personal, the finalized designs for the dime and the other coins were not ready at the anticipated date. Preparing finished models from their initial designs proved more daunting for Weinman and MacNeil than either had imagined. Despite several visits to the Philadelphia Mint from his New York studio during the month of March, Weinman had not devised suitable models which Woolley could share with the Commission of Fine Arts. This is so noted by the Commission in the minutes of its March 31 meeting with Woolley.

The purpose of Weinman's visits to the Mint was to obtain information regarding the technical requirements of his models so that they ultimately could reduced mechanically to suitable master hubs. Chief Engraver Barber proved his usual self, throwing various obstructions in the path of the hapless artist, and therein lay the primary cause of the delays. In one of their first scheduled meetings, Barber was in fact absent, and Weinman entered into a discussion with Assistant Engraver George T. Morgan. It's likely that more useful information was obtained by Weinman in this meeting that in subsequent meetings with Barber, as Morgan had less reason to resent the presence of outsiders at the Mint.

Additional visits to the Mint saw little progress being made, and Weinman was compelled to forestall a meeting with Woolley planned for April 26. In a letter dated the previous day, he tendered his apology:

> I have worked steadily upon the obverse of the Half Dollar and of the Dime but they will not be in shape for your final inspection tomorrow. Though I am pushing the work as rapidly as possible, it becomes quite apparent that the four models for the Half Dollar and the Dime cannot be completed for the date at which I promised them and I would therefore request an extension of ten days or two weeks.[26]

Weinman's delay was due in part to a severe case of tonsillitis which befell him that spring. Although the half dollar would continue to be problematic for some months, it was initially thought that the dime models would be ready for production by the close of the Mint's fiscal year, June 30.

Progress was indeed being made, and Weinman wrote to Charles Barber from Buffalo, New York on June 6. His letter reads in part:

> I am returning by express the remaining three bronze models for the Half Dollar &. the Dime. These should have reached you long before this date, but unfortunately I had been delayed by the founders having trouble with the first cast, which made necessary another set of casts as well as new plaster models.
> I expect to be here for about ten days, but will make a special trip to see the reduction you will make, before my return to New York if you so advise it.[27]

On the 22nd of that month, Weinman wrote Woolley, "Your letter dated May 29, 1916 informing me that the designs submitted by me for the proposed new Half Dollar and Dime have been accepted has just been received."[28]

Weinman goes on to mention that during the previous day's visit to the Mint Barber had shown him two sample half dollars, one having a modeled background and the other a burnished background. This is significant, as sculptors of that era displayed a definite preference for medallic art with modeled or textured fields. The diffused luster exhibited by such pieces allowed for greater study of the design. It's likely that Weinman's original models possessed this feature and that Barber himself initiated the alternative finish, this being more in keeping with his conventional views on coinage. As it turned out, all three of the new coins were initially struck for circulation with textured fields, only to have the fields smoothed out when new hubs were introduced during 1917.

On June 24 the Director wrote to Superintendent Joyce:

> The dime is all right. Please see that working dies for the three mints are made as rapidly as possible, in order that the coinage of the new dimes may be begun quickly. The demand for these coins is exceedingly great.
>
> Everyone to whom the coins have been shown here thinks they are beautiful.
>
> I beg to enjoin you not to pay out any of the new dimes until you have received special instructions from this office...[29]

Woolley was not exaggerating when he wrote of the urgent demand for dimes, as none had been coined since the close of the previous year. In fact, no dies dated 1916 had been created for any of the silver denominations, since it was never imagined that they new designs would still be in the developmental stage so late in the year.

The Director's declaration that the dime was ready for mass production proved premature, as just two days after instructing Superintendent Joyce to begin making working dies for all three mints, he again wrote to him that, "The lettering on the dime appears to be a trifle too indistinct..."[30]

Studying the pattern coins illustrated in Chapter 2, it is almost a certainty that the dime

to which he refers is Judd* variety number 1981, the earliest pattern known for this coin type. It does indeed have very shallow lettering which actually touches the coin's rims. To his credit, Charles Barber would have avoided such a critical error, but for the fine art medallist Adolph A. Weinman, unfamiliar with the demands of high speed coining and mass production, this was an easy mistake to make.

Notwithstanding the fact that the dime models would once again have to be revised, Director Woolley advised Superintendent Joyce on June 28 that, "Mr. Weinman is to receive $4000 for his designs for the half dollar and the dime..."[31]

It appears that these changes took several weeks, during which time the Director waited nervously as evermore reports came in regarding shortages of dimes and quarters in circulation. The halves, it was indicated, had been made in sufficient quantity the year before that stocks were still on hand.

On July 18 Adolph Weinman wrote to Charles Barber addressing the issue of shallow lettering and adding his concern over the smooth fields implemented by Barber without consulting him:

> I am sending you today by parcel post the bronze cast of the reverse of the Dime. I have strengthened the lettering and have slightly simplified the foliage of the olive branch. The obverse for the Dime is now being cast in bronze and should be in your hands within a few days, if the bronze cast turns out satisfactory. I have also made the lettering stronger on this model.
>
> I am troubled about the polished background of the two coins I have here. The reflection from the polished surface is so intense that one cannot get a clear impression of the design at all. W. Woolley agrees with me that the background of these coins should not be polished, and I greatly appreciate an expression of opinion from you in this matter.
>
> Will you also kindly inform me when both dies for the Dime have been completed and a sample coin struck, with the dull surface, and I will come over to see them.[32]

Weinman's sense of diplomacy is quite evi-

---

*USA pattern and trial coins are attributed to the standard reference by Dr. J. Hewitt Judd, now in its eighth edition.

dent in this letter, as he asks Barber for his opinion regarding the sculpted fields, knowing full well what the engraver's view must be. It is obvious, too, from the date of the letter that Woolley's goal of having the models ready by the end of Fiscal Year 1916 had already been necessarily abandoned.

In the mean time, the demand for additional dimes and quarters had built to the point at which the Mint was compelled to begin issuing 1916-dated coins with the old design. Barber must have secretly smiled to himself as his familiar Roman bust of Liberty once again dropped from the presses by the thousands, and then by the millions.

On August 14 Philadelphia Mint Superintendent Adam M. Joyce was summoned to New York "for the purpose of conferring with Mr. A. A. Weinman in regard to the corrections to be made upon the models for the dime of new designs."[33]

This letter was written by Fred H. Chaffin, Examiner of the Bureau of the Mint, in his temporary role as Acting Director. R. W. Woolley had tendered his resignation July 15 to assume his new position as Director of Publicity for the Democratic National Committee, a decision which was likely made easier for him by the frustrating situation with the new coins. Chaffin filled in until the new Director arrived in late August. Though officially no longer the Director, Woolley was still a resident of the Washington, DC area and maintained a keen interest in the new coinage, writing to Superintendent Joyce on August 15 in reference to "an alteration of the designs of the ten cent piece."

Joyce received further instructions that same day from Mary M. O'Reilly, Assistant to the Director. She occasionally alternated with Chaffin as Acting Director after Woolley's departure, an unusual level of responsibility afforded to a woman for that time. O'Reilly's letter to Joyce read:

> Please consider the instructions of the Secretary, to-wit; - "The fault to which he referred in the stamping should be corrected" to cover whatever adjustment of the design is necessary to accomplish the correction necessary.[34]

The exact nature of the problem was not described, as the issue of shallow lettering had already been corrected by Weinman. The problems to which Woolley and O'Reilly alluded, as well as other concerns of a purely mechanical nature, delayed production of the ten-cent piece for some months more. The same was true of Weinman's half dollar, as well as MacNeil's quarter dollar, both of which were even more troublesome than the dime.

"there is no further doubt as to the satisfactory conditions of the respective dies"

Fred Chaffin wrote to Weinman on August 25, authorizing him to come to Washington to confer with the Director about the dime dies. [35] This is the first reference to the new incoming Mint Director, F. J. H. von Engelken, whose Senate confirmation had become effective on the 17th but who would not report for duty officially until the beginning of September. The meeting between Weinman and von Engelken must have been fruitful, as Acting Director Chaffin wrote to Adam Joyce on the 29th with important instructions:

> This letter will be considered authority for you to discontinue the coinage of dimes of the type now in circulation, and to proceed with the execution of dimes from the new designs. Will you please forward to this Bureau the first ten coins issued for the regular stock, which, it is understood you will strike on the 30th instant.[36]

On that same day Chaffin informed Denver Mint Superintendent Thomas Annear that five pairs of dies for the new dime had been shipped, adding, "You will please prepare to operate your mint to capacity, including overtime, on dimes

The Denver Mint, mid-1930s
(Western History/Geneology Department, Denver Public Library)

Denver Mint Employees, 1915
(Western History/Geneology Department, Denver Public Library)

more was required but to let the presses run. Unfortunately, as had happened so many times in that year of 1916, yet another delay ensued. On August 29, the very same day that all the final arrangements had been made to commence mass production of the new dime, Director von Engelken wrote to Adolph Weinman authorizing him to come to the Philadelphia Mint to discuss coin dies with Superintendent Joyce.[40] It seems there was a problem, after all.

A clue to the nature of the problem may be found in a letter from Chaffin to Joyce directing him to send ten of the new dimes for testing purposes to Clarence W. Hobbs, Treasurer of the American Sales Machine Company in Worcester, Massachusetts.[41] His company manufactured coin operated vending machines, so Hobbs naturally took alarm at the suggestion of changes to the existing coinage.

Invoking the name of Mr. Hobbs was enough to send chills down the spine of any Mint officer. Four years earlier his repeated condemnation of the proposed Indian Head/Buffalo Nickel had nearly scuttled the project. No amount of compromise on the part of the Mint or of sculptor James Earle Fraser in modifying the design to Hobbs' requirements seemed to be sufficient. At one point an exasperated Mint Director George E. Roberts had declared with respect to Fraser's magnificent models, "we can better pay him and throw his work away than adopt it if to do so is contrary to sound public policy."[42]

About the same time, Director von Engelken likewise instructed Adam Joyce to send ten examples of the new dime to George K. Thompson of the American Telephone and Telegraph Company in New York City. With its vast network of public telephones, AT&T's need for compatibility between the old dime and the new one is obvious.*

exclusively, beginning the coinage of that denomination on the morning of September 5th, and continuing until further advised."[37] A similar telegram was sent to T. W. H. Shanahan, Superintendent of the San Francisco Mint, advising him of a die shipment that day and instructing him to commence production of the new dimes on the 5th and to continue until further notice.[38]

Yet another letter dated August 29 was sent by Acting Director Chaffin to Adam Joyce at the Philadelphia Mint ordering him to destroy all "experimental coins" [patterns] and to obtain the return of same from the sculptors, "as there is no further doubt as to the satisfactory conditions of the respective dies."[39]

If one were to terminate the correspondence trail at this point, it would seem that nothing

The Complete Guide to Mercury Dimes

Evidently the recipients of these test coins were not pleased with what they saw. On September 5, the very day that the two western mints were to begin mass production of the new Winged Head Liberty Dime, Acting Director Chaffin sent telegrams to Superintendents Annear in Denver and Shanahan in San Francisco instructing, "IF YOU HAVE STARTED USING NEW DIME DIES DISCONTINUE IMMEDIATELY UNTIL FURTHER NOTICE."[43]

Caught with its pants down, the U. S. Mint had no choice but to once again resume coinage of Barber's Liberty Head Dime. "Please forward without delay five pairs of dime dies of the old design to Denver and to SF Mint," was the order from Director von Engelken to Superintendent Joyce in Philadelphia. The Director's embarrassment was compounded by a newspaper article in which Joyce was quoted about the new dime. Von Engelken wrote to him that same day, September 6, instructing that no Mint officers were to talk to the press about any of the three new coins until their problems were overcome.[44] Given that this was his first week on the job, F. J. H. von Engelken must have been having second thoughts about the U. S. Mint as a career move.

Shortly afterward the Director wrote to Denver Mint Superintendent Thomas Annear to advise him of the old type dime dies shipped west on the 6th and instructing him not to use them unless so directed. As we now know, Denver did not coin any dimes of the Barber type in 1916, its production of this denomination being limited to a mere 264,000 "Mercury" Dimes. Just days later, on the 14th, Annear was directed to return the dies of the new type dime, as by now it was evident that further changes were needed. A similar letter was sent to Shanahan in San Francisco.[45]

From the available correspondence it appears that the problem lay in the dime's overall relief. Responding to a request from the Treasury Secretary McAdoo, on September 7 von Engelken reported that it would take six to eight months for Chief Engraver Barber to make duplicate models of his own sculpting replicating those submitted by Weinman in the highest relief possible within Mint requirements. He further reported that, since this time frame was not acceptable, changes had been made by Barber in the width of the rim on Weinman's model to retain the high relief desired. Finally, the Director advised that, if this change were approved by the Secretary, dies could be ready in three weeks that would meet vending machine requirements.[46]

The high relief of Weinman's models was evidently in response to earlier complaints that the design, particularly the lettering, was too shallow (Judd pattern variety 1981). It's likely that the high relief edition the vending machine people found objectionable was J-1984, the rarest of the four known varieties. Nearly identical to the coin as issued, it differs mostly in that the entire design occupies a greater area of the coin's disc. As a consequence the border is narrow, which evidently resulted in a raised wire rim that caused the coin to fail in the tests conducted by Hobbs and AT&T. An unknown quantity of these pieces was mass produced between the onset of coining at the Philadelphia Mint, August 30, and the day on which production was halted there, September 5. As these coins had not yet left the mint, it was a simple enough matter to have them all destroyed, though at least one survives.

While cataloged as a pattern, J-1984 is thus more correctly labeled as an issue intended for circulation but withheld from release. In this respect it is akin to the lone example known of the 1922 silver dollar having a relief higher than that of the common 1922 issue but lower than that of the very rare, high-relief proofs. How exactly the remaining pattern dimes of 1916 (J-1982 and J-1983) fit into the timeline is purely speculative, though they seemingly date between the end of June and the middle of August, 1916.

Another objection to the new dime raised by Hobbs was a familiar one to Philadelphia Mint officials who had been on duty in 1912-13, as the same issue had been brought up with respect to Fraser's nickel. This concerned the distance between the peripheral lettering and the coin's

---

*At that time many home telephones operated by coin, too. Instead of a monthly bill, residential customers would receive periodic visits from telephone company employees who emptied the coin box.

borders. Hobbs had written to Congressman F. L. Fishback in Washington, DC requesting that a gap be provided between all lettering and the borders to facilitate the proper functioning of the detection device within his vending machines. This letter made its

The San Francisco Mint, 1936
(Library of Congress)

sions evidently were limited to a slight, overall reduction of the design's scale, an increase in the space between the lettering and the rims and an attendant broadening of the rims for conformance with the older dimes. Director von Engelken wrote to

way to Director von Engelken, who then forwarded a copy of it to Superintendent Joyce in Philadelphia. That same day, September 8, the Director wrote to Joyce again, instructing him to make the requested changes if possible to do so, as Hobbs' company provided vending machines to the U. S. Post Office, and he didn't want that agency to be troubled by some oversight at his own.[47]

"Treasurer Advises will Order One Hundred Thousand Dollars New Dimes"

The months of September and October were ones of great anxiety within the Bureau of the Mint, as it grappled with both the problems in the new coin designs and an increasingly unacceptable shortage of dimes and quarters in the channels of commerce. Reflective of the confused situation are a pair of letters sent from Acting Director Chaffin to Superintend Joyce. The first, dated September 16, instructs him to send ten pairs of dime dies and four die collars to the San Francisco Mint. Just a few days later, he writes again to clarify that the dies to be sent are those of the old type dime.[48] That it was necessary to make such distinctions underscores the day-to-day uncertainty.

Secretary McAdoo opted to approve the dime models as revised slightly by Barber. These revi-

Superintendent Joyce on October 6th advising him of the Secretary's approval and authorizing him to prepare working dies from the revised hubs. His letter was initialed by McAdoo, as well, so that there would be no doubt as to the order's finality.[49]

A second letter from von Engelken to Joyce was sent that same day requesting of the Superintendent, "Will you please cause to be prepared and forwarded to the Mint at Denver and to the Mint at San Francisco, ten (10) pairs of dime dies of new design." Still another letter instructed Joyce to send ten each of the Philadelphia Mint dimes from the new dies to the American Sales Machine Company and the American Telephone and Telegraph Company for testing purposes. These were to replace the test specimens of earlier dies which had already been returned by them.[50]

Nothing further was heard from Hobbs or AT&T, and so it appeared that all was good to go with the new dime. On October 13 von Engelken wrote to Superintendent Shanahan in San Francisco to advise him that dies of the new type dime had been shipped there that same day. He further instructed him to continue coining dimes of the old type until the current demand was met, after which time San Francisco could commence coinage of the new dimes. These,

The Complete Guide to Mercury Dimes

however, were not to be issued until so authorized by him.[51]

Superintendent Annear at the Denver Mint was likewise advised that ten pairs of dies for the new dime were on their way west, but he was given the unique admonition that, "The dies are not to be used until specific instructions are sent to you." The reason for this was quickly revealed, as von Engelken sent him another letter that same day of the 14th: "Arrange quickly as possible to coin quarter-dollars exclusively until further notified. In this connection please advise me whether you can to advantage, if it becomes necessary, coin quarter dollars and dimes at the same time..."[52]

The urgency of producing more quarter dollars for the region serviced by the Denver Mint did not abate for the remainder of the year, though this situation emerged only slowly amid panicky reports from the United States sub-Treasuries (precursors of the federal reserve banks). In a confusion of instructions, Acting Director Fred H. Chaffin wrote to Superintendent Annear on the 31st ordering him to, "Discontinue coinage of twenty-five cents when you reach $500,000," and telling him to produce only minor coins (cents and nickels) after that until further notice. Less than three weeks later, Chaffin again wrote to Denver informing Annear that the need for quarters has been raised to at least $1,000,000![53]

Here then is an explanation for the very small mintage of dimes at Denver in 1916. Exactly when the 264,000 1916-D dimes were coined is not certain, but this figure could have been achieved in just a single day with multiple presses at work. On October 19 von Engelken instructed Joyce to send the Denver Mint 18 dime collars—twelve for large presses and six for smaller presses.[54] Most of these must have been held over for 1917, given the very small number of dimes struck there in 1916.

That same day the Director authorized Superintendent Joyce to discontinue coining of the old type dime on or after October 30. In a separate letter, San Francisco was instructed to discontinue their production immediately. Von Engelken telegrammed Superintendent Shanahan in San Francisco, "TREASURER ADVISES WILL ORDER ONE HUNDRED THOUSAND DOLLARS NEW DIMES SHIPPED BY YOU TWENTY-FOURTH TO REACH DESTINATION BY THIRTIETH FOR DISTRIBUTION. WILL YOU HAVE THEM."[55] It was particularly urgent that the San Francisco Mint be able to produce sufficient numbers of dimes before the anticipated release date, as Denver would not be able to provide its share. Indeed, in a letter to Thomas Annear informing him of the October 30 release date, von Engelken further advised him that San Francisco would be shipping new dimes to the Denver Mint for distribution in that region of the country![56]

The Director informed Adam Joyce that the Treasurer's office would be asking for at least $150,000 in new dimes to be delivered to the sub-Treasuries on the 28th for distribution two days later.[57] Fred H. Chaffin wrote to von Engelken on the 28th to apprise him of developments:

> The plan as outlined on the new dime has been followed to the letter with two exceptions. San Francisco has been able to furnish $35,000. more than was called for, and Philadelphia $40,000. more than the $150,000 originally promised. Under present conditions, Philadelphia can coin $30,000. per day in dimes, which, of course, is in addition to the heavy minor coinage. San Francisco is producing $10,000. per day in addition to her regular coinage of minor.

The issuance of the new dimes went as planned. Shipments to the sub-Treasuries were made by October 28, and the coins were on hand at the nation's commercial banks for release on the 30th. With but a few exceptions, the Winged Head Liberty Dime was met with great enthusiasm by the press and public. Even a successful coin design, however, will have its detractors among the lunatic fringe, and the new dime was no exception. On November 3 Assistant Treasury Secretary William P. Malburn responded to a letter from a Mr. Henri Gerard of New York City by saying, "The Department is unable to understand your statement that the United States is speculating in coins."[58] Gerard may have found objection with Weinman's prominent monogram, as had happened with Victor D. Brenner's initials on the cent in 1909, or he may have just believed that there was no reason to alter the existing dime.

Although further modifications of a very minor nature were to occur during the next two years, the coin was deemed a success both technically and aesthetically. The changes made to the obverse of the dime during 1917 and 1918 were so slight as to go largely unnoticed even by numismatists (see "Design Modifications" in Chapter 2).

Though he was no longer Mint Director by the time it was published, it was the responsibility of R. W. Woolley to prepare the Mint's annual report to Treasury Secretary McAdoo for Fiscal Year 1916. In it Woolley chose to crow a bit regarding the adoption of new coinage designs:

> By far the most notable achievement of the mint service during the fiscal year 1916 was the selection, with your approval, of new designs for the dime, quarter-dollar, and half-dollar pieces. For the first time in the history of our coinage there are separate designs for each of the three denominations, and their beauty and quality, from a numismatic standpoint, have been highly praised by all having expert knowledge of such matters to whom they have been shown.
> The process of selecting the new designs (authority under sec. 3510 of the U.S. Rev. Stats., approved Sept. 26, 1890) began in January last, when, with your permission, I conferred with the members of the Commission of Fine Arts. Noted sculptors were commissioned to prepare a number of sketch models, and from more than 50 submitted 3 sets were chosen. It is a pleasure to note that the models which you and I selected were also the choice of the members of the Commission of Fine Arts.

The Director's Report for 1916 includes a photo plate illustrating the three new fractional silver coins adopted that year, as well as the McKinley Birthplace Memorial Gold Dollar issued as a commemorative coin. Oddly enough, the illustration for the Winged Head Liberty Dime is actually a photograph of pattern coin J-1982. Whether this oversight was noticed by Woolley or anyone else in the Mint Bureau at the time is not known.

"We have in the new United States dime . . . the handsomest American coin"

In numismatic circles the progress of the new coinage was followed with much anticipation. The Mint's press release of March 3, 1916 had been large on hoopla and a bit shy on facts. As it became apparent that the announced date of introduction for the new designs would not be met, numismatists began speculating and philosophizing as a means of coping with the frustrating delays. Their dislike of the Barber silver coins then in use is apparent in the following statements by Frank G. Duffield, editor of *The Numismatist*:

> We are not betraying a secret when we say that the type adopted in 1892 has not been popular with latter-day collectors...
> In the past 25 years great improvement has been made in the coinage of many foreign countries, and collectors have been patiently waiting for the time limit of our present type to expire, and hoping that the new designs will compare favorably with or even surpass those of some other countries, and will be so beautiful that nothing but necessity will compel us to part with them once they come into our possession...[59]

On May 30 the Mint issued another release announcing the winners of the competition and relating some general features of the designs. About the ten-cent piece is was said, "The design of the dime is simple. Liberty with a winged cap is shown on the obverse and on the reverse is a design of a bundle of rods, and a battle ax, symbolic of unity, 'Wherein Lies the Nation's Strength.'"[60]

The New York Sun observed that, "Not the design on the coins, but the number of them in the pocket, is the matter of gravest concern to all but numismatists..." The newspaper went on to note that, "The Treasury will confer a new series of dimes, quarters and half dollars on us this summer, regardless of the storm that broke over the revisers of the gold pieces."[61] The growing sense of anticipation among the press and general public even led to false sightings:

> Notwithstanding a press dispatch dated Washington, July 1, that the new silver coins had made their appearance in Washington and were in circulation there, it may be stated that none had been issued or even struck up to the middle of July...

During the first two weeks of July operations at the Philadelphia Mint were suspended for the annual stock-taking and settlement. It is possible that the coinage of dimes of the new design may begin with the resumption of operations, and that this denomination may be in circulation by the time this issue of THE NUMISMATIST is printed. The coinage of the quarters and half dollars may not begin until fall.[62]

Further glum reports appeared in the numismatic press in September, as the long watch continued. Editor Duffield related, "It is reported that the model for the new design of the dime, which was not quite satisfactory, has been worked over and important changes and improvements made, and that the dies for these are now being cut."[63]

The picture did not brighten in the fall, as an announcement was made that the new coins had been postponed indefinitely. This delay was attributed to technical difficulties arising from the employment of outside artists.[64] The source of this blow aimed at Weinman and MacNeil was not named, but it may be assumed that Barber was speaking into the ear of anyone who would listen to him.

It was not until December that readers of *The Numismatist* learned of the new dime's release:

> The new silver dime was given to the public during the last days of October, and by the time this issue reaches its readers it will be in general circulation. For five months collectors have been anxiously waiting to get a glimpse of what we were told was to be a beautiful coin, and we have not been disappointed.
>
> The opinion of a single man, whether he be artist, sculptor, numismatist or layman, as to its merits or the beauty of the design, should not weigh heavily, but when a number of men familiar with the coinages of the world from the earliest times all pronounce it a very creditable piece of work and perhaps the most attractive coin this Government has ever put in circulation, its popularity with collectors cannot be a matter of doubt.[65]

In that same issue's monthly message to the readers, Editor Duffield captured the upbeat mood of collectors, who were nearly unanimous in their praise of Weinman's work:

> The girlish Miss Liberty with wings on her cap has already won a place in the numismatist's heart. Of course, dimes are only bits of change in this busy old world, and no one expects to keep them in his pocket for any length of time. They come to us quickly, and go from us even more quickly, without the aid of wings; but this is not an objection to the new coin; those of the old type were equally active in their flights in both directions. The dime has always been a good friend to man, woman and child; it opens many doors to pleasure and amusement. The new one will be fully as good a friend, and a bit of art to admire as well.

The often opinionated but seldom complimentary coin dealer Thomas Elder found favor with the new design, stating, "We have in the new United States dime, designed by Adolph Alexander Weinman, the handsomest American coin."[66]

Adolph Weinman was clearly pleased with the results of his work and had been eager to display his models publicly for some time. He had written to the Treasury Department on August 23, 1916 requesting permission to display them in an upcoming art exhibition. The Acting Treasury Secretary, whose name is not readable in the letter, responded to Weinman informing him that he may not display his models because they are the sole property of the government once they are accepted. One week later Director von Engelken acquiesced to Weinman's request that photographs of his models be published in numismatic journals, but only after the coins had been issued.[67]

Both the Philadelphia and San Francisco Mints coined fairly large quantities of the new dimes during the final months of 1916. Director von Engelken wrote to Superintendent Shanahan in San Francisco November 3 inquiring when the Treasurer's request for new dimes would be delivered, as the demand was quite heavy. Perhaps the delay was due to problems in striking the coins. There was clearly some issue taken with the quality of dimes being struck at San Francisco and, on October 27, Acting Director Chaffin had written to Shanahan requesting 50 new dimes for inspection. These were examined by the Philadelphia Mint's staff, and a report was prepared evaluating the 'S' Mint dimes. This report was sent to Shanahan on November 15, along with samples of a 1916(P) dime and a milled planchet.[68]

Though this report has evidently not survived, some idea as to its content may be gleaned by examining 1916-S "Mercury" Dimes. Typically, these coins are weakly struck in the lower diagonal band of the fasces, as well as displaying the weakness at the center horizontal bands common to many dimes of this type. It's likely that the purpose of enclosing a milled planchet was to show the coiners at San Francisco how a press-ready planchet for this coin type should look. A milled planchet is one that has been run through the upsetting mill, a machine which forms a raised rim on the blank so that it will strike up better during coining. The demonstration must have been an instructive one, since the 'S' Mint dimes of 1917 and later years no longer have the weakness in the lower diagonal band so often seen on 1916-S pieces.

In 1917, and for the next several years, many millions of the new Winged Head Liberty Dimes were struck for circulation. Within its first decade the new type had largely supplanted the Liberty Head design of Charles Barber in general circulation, though the older coins continued to circulate in ever smaller numbers as late as the 1950s. For much of that time, Barber's dime was known to collectors as the "Morgan" Dime, due to its superficial resemblance to George T. Morgan's silver dollar of 1878-1921. Barber himself did not live to witness this indignity, as he died suddenly on February 18, 1917.* This erroneous nomenclature was ultimately corrected, but not before Barber's Liberty Head had vanished from circulation.

In an ironic twist, Weinman's Winged Head Liberty had by then become known almost exclusively as the "Mercury" Dime. This misattribution appeared almost immediately in the popular press, as writers imagined that the obviously female Liberty was actually a representation of Mercury, messenger to the Roman gods of mythology and quite certainly a male. It is popularly known as the Mercury Dime even today, despite noble but ill-fated attempts by some publications to reverse this error. All efforts to restore its original title have met with little success, collectors evidently favoring the misattribution for purely sentimental reasons.

Behind the enormous output of dimes and other fractional silver coins during the years 1916-20 lay largely hidden a serious threat to the nation's economy. The international price of silver bullion was rising steadily during this period and had driven silver coins from circulation in most of the world by 1918. The Great War, as World War I was then known, was largely responsible for this speculation in silver, though other pressures were likewise put to bear. The insatiable demand for silver in the Asian market had already prompted Congress to order the melting of hundreds of millions of silver dollars for transport to India as silver bullion. This was the infamous Pittman Act of 1918, an attempt to control the ruinous speculation that was occurring there and endangering the stability of our British ally's most important colony. It proved to have precious little effect, and the price of silver continued to rise, peaking in the early months of 1920 at a level well above the point at which it was profitable to ship silver dollars overseas as mere commodity items. Writing to *The Numismatist*, San Francisco correspondent Farran Zerbe related this alarming development:

> The San Francisco Mint has paid as high as $1.36 per ounce for silver in recent days, the highest Government purchase price record, and local sales for commercial purposes are reported as high as $1.40.
>
> When it became more profitable to use silver dollars than to purchase bullion, silver dollars, so long as obtainable, left San Francisco by the million during the late weeks of 1919 (for export across the Pacific) with an expected average price, delivered, of $1.07 per dollar and the promised profit of $55,000 per million pieces after the payment of transportation and insurance.
>
> Except on demand in exchange for Silver Certificates, no silver dollars are now obtainable at the Treasury, and Silver Certificates have been withdrawn from circulation."[69]

---

*In *The Annual Report of the Director of the Mint* for Fiscal Year 1917 the month is given as January, but the February date is believed to be correct.

Since United States dimes, quarters and halves were subsidiary coins, containing less silver than in an equivalent face value in silver dollars, the threat to the fractional pieces was not as immediate. While the loss of silver dollars was not a serious matter to everyday commerce, given that they circulated only in the western states, the potential loss of the many millions of fractional silver coins then in circulation posed the ominous specter of economic paralysis. Their place would have to be taken by base-metal replacements or, even worse, fractional paper currency. This is just what had happened amid the last such crisis during the dark days of America's Civil War.

Legislation was introduced early in 1920 for the reduction of the silver content in both the dollar and its fractions, a step about to be effected by Britain and Canada and one already completed by Mexico. Before any such bill was passed, however, the price of silver began to recede, ending the crisis. Amazingly, the average American took little note of this threatening episode, and there were no documented incidents of fractional silver coins being hoarded or melted.

The coinage of dimes was greatly curtailed during 1921 and suspended altogether during 1922, as the worldwide economy hit a postwar slump. The Mint took advantage of this brief but severe economic recession to direct its efforts toward recoining the silver dollars destroyed under the Pittman Act. Having achieved most of this recoinage by the middle of 1923, the Mint resumed its production of fractional silver pieces. With only a few exceptions, mintage figures for the dime remained fairly substantial throughout the 1920s. Coinage slowed in 1930 and 1931 and was suspended completely during 1932-33, as the effects of the worldwide Great Depression reduced the demand for fresh coins. Much of the mintage from this period was released only after a delay of several years. This accounts for the greater than expected availability of dates such as 1930-S and 1931-D in Uncirculated condition, despite their being scarce in lower grades. Many pieces were saved in rolls by eager collectors and speculators.

When prosperity began to return in 1934, the demand for additional coinage was renewed. Mintage figures are high for this and all subsequent years through 1945, the final date of the Winged Head Liberty type.

The death of popular President Franklin D. Roosevelt in April of 1945 led to a call for a circulating commemorative with his portrait. As the late president had been a major proponent of the March of Dimes Campaign to combat polio, selection of the dime as the coin to bear his likeness was assured. This news was disappointing to a small group of individuals who had for some years been promoting the coinage of a Benjamin Franklin Dime. In fact, preliminary models for such a coin had already been prepared by the U. S. Mint's Chief Engraver, John R. Sinnock. The work was temporarily shelved, until being revived for adoption on the half dollar. Sinnock's death in 1947 was only a brief setback, as his successor, Gilroy Roberts, prepared the final models for the Franklin Half Dollar. This coin was introduced the following year.

The Roosevelt Dime was released to circulation on January 30, 1946, the 64th anniversary of the late president's birth. Mint Director Nellie Tayloe Ross gave the following eulogy for the Mercury Dime:

> The winged Liberty Head dimes now outstanding will continue to circulate, but no more will be minted. The first ten-cent coins bearing the pattern created thirty years ago by Adolph A. Weinman, were struck in 1916. As of late December 1945, when the last of the Liberty dimes passed through the presses, the Mint had put out a total of 2,677,232,488 of these coins.[70]

Mercury Dimes remained a familiar sight through the mid-1960s. Only the introduction of copper-nickel-clad coins in 1965 and the subsequent hoarding of all silver coins by the general public led to their complete disappearance from circulation. The author recalls them fondly, having begun his collecting experience around that same time. The high mintage issues from 1940 through 1945 could then still be found in circulation, but older pieces had already vanished into collections. As these collections and hoards are dispersed, the coins await discovery by successive generations of coin enthusiasts for whom the finding of a Mercury Dime in pocket change is merely a romantic dream.

Notes to Chapter 1, History

[1] Ganz, David L., editor. *Coinage Laws of The United States 1792-1894.*
[2] "Movement to Change United States Coin Designs." *The Numismatist*, January 1915.
[3] National Archives & Records Administration, Record Group 104, Bureau of the Mint, Letters Received, Box 303.
[4] ibid.
[5] NARA, RG-104, Letters Sent, Volume 412.
[6] ibid, Volume 409.
[7] ibid, Volume 411.
[8] ibid, Volume 412.
[9] ibid, Volume 409.
[10] Gibbs, William T. "Poet's Wife Becomes Weinman's Model." *Coin World*, June 28, 1991.
[11] Giedroyc, Richard. "1916 design competition between three artists." *Coin World*, December 28, 1998.
[12] NARA, RG-104, Letters Sent, Volume 411.
[13] Taft, Lorado. *The History of American Sculpture.*
[14] NARA, RG-104, Letters Sent, Volume 411.
[15] ibid.
[16] ibid, Volume 412.
[17] ibid, Volume 411.
[18] ibid.
[19] ibid, Volume 417.
[20] ibid.

[21] NARA, RG-104, Letters Sent, Volume 417.
[22] *The Numismatist,* April 1916.
[23] NARA, RG-104, Letters Sent, Volume 417.
[24] ibid, Volume 414.
[25] ibid.
[26] Taxay, Don. *The U.S. Mint and Coinage.*
[27] Carlson, Carl W. A. "Letters Show Designer's Thoughts on 1916 Dime." *Coin World,* July 24, 1991.
[28] ibid.
[29] NARA, RG-104, Letters Sent, Volume 414.
[30] ibid.
[31] ibid.
[32] Carlson.
[33] NARA, RG-104, Letters Sent, Volume 415.
[34] ibid, Volume 414.
[35] ibid, Volume 415.
[36] ibid, Volume 414.
[37] ibid, Volume 416.
[38] ibid, Volume 414.
[39] ibid.
[40] ibid, Volume 415.
[41] ibid, Volume 414.
[42] ibid, File 305310.
[43] NARA, RG-104, Letters Sent, Volumes 414 & 416.
[44] ibid, Volume 414.
[45] ibid, Volumes 414 & 416.
[46] ibid, Volume 415.

[47] ibid, Volume 414.
[48] ibid.
[49] ibid, Volume 415.
[50] ibid, Volume 414.
[51] ibid.
[52] ibid, Volume 416.
[53] ibid.
[54] ibid, Volume 414.
[55] ibid.
[56] ibid, Volume 416.
[57] ibid, Volume 414.
[58] ibid, Volume 415.
[59] *The Numismatist,* July 1916.
[60] ibid.
[61] ibid.
[62] *The Numismatist,* August 1916.
[63] ibid, September 1916.
[64] ibid, October 1916.
[65] ibid, December 1916.
[66] Gibbs, William T. "Winged Liberty Head 1916-1945." *Coin World,* June 19,1991.
[67] NARA, RG-104, Letters Sent, Volume 417.
[68] ibid, Volume 414.
[69] "Will the United States Substitute White Metal for Silver Coins? *The Numismatist,* March 1920.
[70] ibid, February 1946.

Design Changes

The Winged Head Liberty Dime of 1916 features a very busy pictorial for such a small coin. Nevertheless, all of the elements are arranged attractively and make for a pleasing whole.

The obverse of Adolph A. Weinman's dime is dominated by the left-facing profile bust of a young woman whom we know to be the goddess Liberty. She has thickly curled hair framing her face, and these curls are held in check by the close fitting cap she wears. Her cap is somewhat suggestive of a cloche hat, fashionable for women circa 1924-30. Still, the folded top to the cap reveals that it is not so tight fitting as this. Her head is further adorned with a pair of wings, only one of which is visible. Arranged in a peripheral arc is the legend LIBERTY. To the left of Liberty's neck is the motto IN GOD WE TRUST, while to the right appear the designer's monogrammed initials, a W superimposed over an A. Below the truncation of Liberty's bust is the date of coining. Surrounding the whole is a plain, raised border.

The coin's reverse features a fasces, the symbol of power and authority carried by Roman magistrates in ancient times. The fasces was a wooden handled ax encased within a bundle of wood or iron rods. The rods were held securely against the handle by a leather thong wound around them both horizontally and diagonally. Above the rods protruded the ax head.

Balancing the theme of strength with one of peace, the fasces is intertwined with an olive branch. Arranged peripherally in large letters are the legend UNITED STATES OF AMERICA above and the denomination ONE DIME below. Serving as stops to these inscriptions are a pair of five-pointed stars at the four o'clock and eight o'clock positions, respectively. The individual words that proclaim the nation's identity are distinguished through the placement of tiny dots. To the right of the fasces appears the Latin legend E PLURIBUS UNUM. A plain, raised border encloses all.

The Winged Head Liberty Dime of 1916-45 conforms to the standard specifications in effect for this denomination from 1873 through 1964.

Its gross weight is 2.50 grams of .900 fine silver, the balance of the alloy being copper. It has a diameter of 17.9 millimeters and, like all United States dimes before or since, it bears a reeded edge.

....

As the first of the three new silver coins to appear in circulation, the dime drew the lion's share of attention from the numismatic community. Upon its release, Frank G. Duffield, editor of *The Numismatist*, wrote to Adolph A. Weinman seeking the artist's own interpretation of his work. Weinman replied thusly:

> In response to your letter of November 14, requesting a word of explanation as to my reasons for selecting a winged female head for the design of the obverse, and the fasces for the reverse of the new dime, permit me to say that the law on the coinage of the United States stipulates that on all subsidiary coins there shall appear upon the obverse a figure or representation of Liberty. Hence the head of Liberty, the coin being obviously too small in size to make the representation of a full-length figure of Liberty advisable.
>
> The wings crowning her cap are intended to symbolize liberty of thought.
>
> As to the reverse of the dime, the law does not stipulate what is to appear upon this side of the coin, while it does specifically state that upon the reverse of the quarter dollar and the half dollar shall appear the figure of an eagle.
>
> I have selected the motive of the fasces and olive branch to symbolize the strength which lies in unity, while the battle-ax stands for preparedness to defend the Union. The branch of olive is symbolical of our love of peace.[1]

The Numismatist, in its December 1916 issue, published letters from several prominent figures, relating their views of the new coin. Some were simple and straight to the point, such as the evaluation by tireless numismatic promoter Farran Zerbe, "I am delighted with the new dime." Henry Chapman, the elder statesman of Philadelphia dealers, proclaimed, "I think the new dime a very creditable production, and am glad to see such an artistic coin come out from this country." Fellow dealer J. W. Scott provided perhaps the grandest pronouncement when he declared, "The new dime is the best piece of work that the United States mint has turned out in a century."

Others qualified their praise, such as numismatic researcher Edgar H. Adams: "The new dime, in my opinion, is one of the handsomest coins of the denomination that has been issued for regular circulation in this country. There are a few minor features which may be criticized [sic], but the general effect is very commendable." Dealer and publisher Wayte Raymond of New York City likewise had some doubts: "I think very favorably of the new dimes. The head of Liberty has considerable resemblance to some coins of the Roman Republic, and is very artistic. The only criticism I have to make is the fact that the words 'In God We Trust' and the date seem to be placed on the die as an afterthought, as there is really no place for them on the obverse."

Raymond's comments seem a little unfair to the artist, given the statutory requirements for United States coins under which all designers must labor. The intrusive nature of all these inscriptions was a subject touched upon by classical numismatist Howland Wood:

> The new dime by Adolph A. Weinman is without a doubt the finest example of our new coinage which was begun in 1907 with the advent of the $20 and $10 gold pieces. Before commenting on any of the new pieces it is but fair to consider the limitations and difficulties that beset the designer. Artistic rendering and a super-abundance of lettering do not go hand in hand towards the best results. Our artists at the start are handicapped by having to place on the coin "United States of America," "E Pluribus Unum," "Liberty," "In God We Trust," the date and the denomination. In other words, six separate mottoes or legends. Consequently, the artist cannot strive for simplicity, and, despite his best endeavors, one or both sides of the coin are bound to be chopped up with a lot of discordant elements.

In keeping with his commercial nature, B. Max Mehl's review of the new dime was supplemented with an appraisal of the marketing advantages to be realized:

> To my mind it did not require very artistic efforts to excel the old issue. The new issue is indeed a welcome addition to our coinage, and one which I think will meet with the approval of thinking numismatists. From a business stand-

point I think any new issue is a good thing for the numismatic profession, as it seems to stimulate interest not only among collectors, but among non-collectors, and is the means of bringing out a considerable number of new collectors.

Perhaps the most interesting comments were those of David Proskey, one of the more highly respected numismatic authorities of that time. In his letter to Editor Duffield, Proskey lets slip a most revealing reference:

> The new dime is far more beautiful than any since the 1807 issue – but not nearly so beautiful in execution nor so appropriate in design as any of the issues from 1796 to 1807. The profile of "Liberty" is strongly masculine as to chin. The Phrygian cap, typical of Liberty, is adorned with a wing similar to that we are accustomed to see on the cap of Mercury...[2]

Herein lies the earliest association of the Winged Head Liberty Dime with the male god Mercury. While Proskey's remarks are not likely to have led directly to Weinman's design becoming known as the Mercury Dime, this appellation has achieved the status of conventional wisdom among the general press and public. No attempt at correction by the numismatic community has ever been able to dislodge such false notions, and the misnomer Mercury Dime has been in general usage almost since the coin's inception.

Persons knowledgeable as to the exact outfitting of the Roman god Mercury would realize that the similarities are only superficial. Mercury, or Hermes as he was known to the Greeks, was the god of commerce, property and wealth. Furthermore, he served as messenger to the gods. To move with the speed desired of a messenger, Mercury wore winged sandals and, in some depictions, a winged helmet. This hat was in no way similar to the cap depicted on Weinman's Liberty, but the concept was enough to make a ready association between the two figures. Mercury's hat is typical of that worn by messengers in ancient times. Known as a *petasus*, it displayed a flat, shallow crown and broad brim. This is quite unlike the cap of Liberty, which covers nearly her entire head with enough material remaining to fold over in a loose bun. Hers is more typical of the Phrygian cap, a fact noted by

Proskey. Here is yet another symbol which survives from the ancient Greeks. This cap, also known as a *pileus,* was worn by freed slaves in proclamation of their new status. It is a recurring feature on the coinage of the United States, as it denotes liberty. Clearly, this was Weinman's intent in using it.

Although few objections were made to the youthful portrait of Liberty, the same could not be said for the reverse of the Winged Head Liberty Dime. Its lack of simplicity as compared to earlier types drew some unfavorable comments from within the numismatic community, but the principal objections seemed to be with the design's political implications. Despite being subdued somewhat by the presence of an olive branch symbolizing peace, the aggressive implications of a coin bearing a fasces were deemed a bad omen by many observers. Indeed, within six months of the dime's introduction America was at war with Germany and the Central Powers.

After the end of World War I, yet another problem arose. This centered around the use of the fasces as a rallying symbol by the "blackshirts" of Italy's Benito Mussolini. This development led to the coining of a new word, "fascism." Proponents of fascism espoused a philosophy which was the very antithesis of American liberty, and this proved a source of consternation to some. Typical of many letters to the editors of newspapers and to government officials is the following. It differs from most only in that the writer does not reveal an ignorance of our coinage so typical of the non-numismatic public. The letter was written by J. Milton Strauss and addressed to Andrew L. Somers, chairman of the House Committee on Coinage, Weights and Measures:

> The fasces, which is the emblem of Fascism, the present form of government in Italy, strangely enough appears on the reverse of our dime. Although it appears on this coinage as early as 1916, and although it was not officially adopted by Mussolini and his followers until 1919, future world historians delving into the past through numismatics, as is often their custom, are liable to draw the conclusion that the United States and not Italy was the birthplace of Fascism.

> Let us somehow immediately correct any such possibility, and at least remove this design, as the fasces is now most un-American and might some day cast a reflection on our constitutional form of government.[3]

A more organized movement to displace Weinman's design was staged in 1939, when a resolution was introduced in Congress to have the delicate portrait of Liberty replaced with a bust of Benjamin Franklin. According to *The New York Times,* "A resolution adopted by the Sons of the American Revolution asking that the likeness of Benjamin Franklin be placed on the dime will appeal to those Americans who believed that there are never too many ways in which to pay honor to one of the greatest of Americans. The present dime, with its fasces, olive branch and feminized Mercury, might have come from a European mint..."[4]

No action was taken at that time, since the Winged Liberty Dime had not yet reached its statutory minimum life of 25 years. When this time finally came in 1940, no alterations were undertaken, despite the ongoing movement to replace Liberty with a portrait of Ben Franklin. The onset of World War II had revitalized American industry, and the increased demand for coins evidently kept the U. S. Mint fully occupied. A change in existing designs would certainly result in decreased production of the affected denomination, if only for a few months. In 1941 Mint Director Nellie Tayloe Ross responded to a letter from American Numismatic Association President L. W. Hoffecker with respect to the proposed Franklin Dime:

> No change in the design of the current dime is at present contemplated. Should a change, however, be determined upon, you may be sure that consideration will be given to the advocacy of the American Numismatic Association that the portrait of Benjamin Franklin be used, who was outstanding among the early patriots for his brilliance, versatility and usefulness. [5]

Even when Italy declared war on the United States, protests over the fascist dime were insufficient to bring about any but the most essential changes in our coinage for the duration. Such changes were limited to replacing critical metals needed for the war effort with more readily available materials. As silver was abundant in the United States, the dime was not affected by any wartime measures. Only the death of President Franklin D. Roosevelt and the call for a circulating commemorative with his portrait ultimately led to the replacement of the Mercury Dime after 1945. The honoring of Benjamin Franklin was postponed until 1948, when his bust was placed on the half dollar following the retirement of Weinman's other design.

Notes to Chapter 1, The Design

1 *The Numismatist,* December 1916.

2 ibid, January 1917.

3 ibid, October 1936.

4 *The Numismatic Scrapbook Magazine,* August 1939.

5 *The Numismatist,* May 1941.

Adolph Alexander Weinman

The future creator of the Winged Head Liberty Dime and the Walking Liberty Half Dollar was born December 11, 1870 to Gustave Weingaertner, a shoemaker, and his wife Katharina.[1] He left his native Karlsruhe, Germany in 1880 at the age of ten to live in America with a relative in the grocery trade. Some time after his arrival in the United States, he simplified his name to Weinman, a practice continued by his descendants.

A precocious talent for drawing and modeling in clay led the 15-year-old Weinman to an apprenticeship with Frederick Kaldenberg. This indenture was for five years, during which time he carved utilitarian objects such as mirror frames and smoking pipes out of wood and ivory. Although he no doubt sought the life of an artist rather than an artisan, young Weinman dutifully fulfilled his obligation to Kaldenberg. One year into his training, however, he enrolled in New York City's legendary Cooper Union for the Advancement of Science and Art. There, and at the Art Students League, he studied drawing. Upon leaving Kaldenberg's workshop at age 20, he joined the studio of medallist Philip Martiny.[2] With this initial exposure to the medallic art, Weinman was inspired to make this his life's work.

His reputation under Martiny was evidently enough to secure for him the position of assistant director in the studio of Olin H. Warner. The year was 1895, and the sculptor was then just 25. Warner's premature death less than a year later prompted another move to the studio of Augustus Saint-Gaudens. The Dublin-born Saint-Gaudens was just then achieving the status of America's pre-eminent sculptor, and this step in Weinman's career was a prestigious one. It too was cut short, however, with the elder artist's decision to remove himself to Paris in 1898. Returning just a few years later, Saint-Gaudens would ultimately design the United States eagle and double eagle of 1907. Sadly, he would not live to see his work coined, nor would he bear witness to his disciple's rendering of the dime and half dollar in 1916.

Following Saint-Gaudens' departure for France, Weinman joined the studio of Charles H. Neihaus for five years. Neihaus was likewise an accomplished medallist, though not of the stature of Saint-Gaudens.

Having paid his dues as student and assistant to others, Adolph A. Weinman went into partnership with Daniel Chester French, another sculptor of renown. French would later go on to have several connections to United States coinage, most of them indirect. In addition to serving on the Commission of Fine Arts, which oversaw the selection of coin designs, adaptations of his work appear on two USA coins. His seated figure of Abraham Lincoln for Washington's Lincoln Memorial appears in extreme miniature on the reverse of the cents coined since 1959. The half dollar commemorating the sesquicentennial of the battles of Lexington and Concord features his portrayal of the Continental Minuteman. Both coins were executed by other sculptors.

Weinman's partnership with French came to an end after some two years, at which time he resolved to open his own studio. Among his first commissions was the award medal for participants in the Louisiana Purchase Exposition held at St. Louis in 1904. The many examples of this medal were coined at the Philadelphia Mint, and the reverse of his design is somewhat suggestive of his later reverse for the half dollar. It's not known whether Weinman's efforts ran afoul of the Mint's defensive Chief Engraver, Charles E. Barber, but he was no doubt treading on safer ground in the field of medals rather than coins.

Adolph Weinman's only other connection to the Mint before 1916 was in his 1905 collaboration with Saint-Gaudens on the inaugural medal for President Theodore Roosevelt. Roosevelt was a great admirer of the elder sculptor, and high hopes were placed on this private commission. The frail Saint-Gaudens, his mind still alive with ideas, drew on his former assistant Weinman to do the actual modeling.[3] In opting to portray the president in the style of the great Renaissance medallists, Saint-Gaudens achieved an effect far bolder than that of Barber and George T. Morgan

in their officially sanctioned medal for the same occasion. The partnership of Saint-Gaudens' grand vision and Weinman's talented hands made for an artistic triumph.

....

At the suggestion of the Commission of Fine Arts, Adolph A. Weinman was one of three sculptors invited to submit designs for a new dime, quarter dollar and half dollar in 1916. His entries were selected for the smallest and largest coins, while those of Hermon A. MacNeil were to appear on the quarter. The obverse figures for both of Weinman's coins were derived in part from the bust of Elsie Kachel Stevens that he executed around 1913. Her features appear in close-up on the dime and in miniature as part of a full figure on the half dollar. After many trials and tribulations, the finished coins entered circulation in October 1916 and January 1917, respectively. Despite their popularity with collectors, both coins would succumb within two years of one another to a changing taste in art and to the exigencies of politics. The dime was discontinued after 1945, the half dollar after 1947. The obverse of Weinman's half dollar was revived in 1986 for the United States Mint's silver one-ounce bullion coin and thus remains current.

....

Other notable works by A. A. Weinman include monuments to Abraham Lincoln at Hodgenville, Kentucky and Madison, Wisconsin.[4] His "Fountains of the Tritons" decorates the grounds of the state capitol at Jefferson, Missouri, while a statue of Major General Alexander Macomb stands in Detroit. The Museum of the City of New York was graced with his statues of Alexander Hamilton and DeWitt Clinton. Weinman created two allegorical scenes for the 1915 Panama-Pacific International Exposition titled "The Rising Sun" and "The Descending Night."[5] Numerous other works of monumental sculpture bear his signature, as well.

In addition to his two coin commissions, Weinman was highly sought as a medallist. In speaking of his work in this medium, Cornelius Vermeule could not conceal his admiration:

"Weinman's medals leave no room for doubt that he was an exceptionally talented sculptor. His feeling for subtleties of relief on a small scale, in the framework of a medallic tondo, was most perceptive."[6]

Further medallic works include a World War I commemorative for the staff of New York's Mt. Sinai Hospital and the J. Sanford Saltus Award for Medallic Art, a tribute bestowed by the American Numismatic Society. Fittingly, Weinman himself received this award in 1920. Other recipients whose names will be familiar to students of United States coinage include Victor D. Brenner, James Earle Fraser, John Flanagan and Hermon A. MacNeil.[7] Among Weinman's most widely disseminated works is the Victory Button, presented to all veterans of World War 1.

Adolph A. Weinman died on August 7, 1952, five years after the last of his coins had been superseded by more modernistic designs. Able to look back over a lifetime of remarkable achievements in the art of sculpture, it's doubtful that he experienced much regret at the passing of his coins from production. In any event, both pieces remained abundantly familiar in circulation for some years following his death. Today, they enrich the cabinets of numismatists worldwide.

Elsie Kachel Stevens

Weinman selected as his model for the dime of 1916 one of his tenants. Elsie Stevens and her husband, the celebrated poet Wallace Stevens, rented rooms in a building which the sculptor owned and in which he maintained his studio. This house, at 441 W. 21st Street in New York City, was home to the couple from shortly after the time of their marriage in 1909 until they relocated to Hartford, Connecticut, seven years later.[8] Around 1913 Weinman asked the young Mrs. Stevens to sit for a portrait bust. In it he captured the 27-year-old woman's attractive features, including her long blond curls which would appear so distinctively on the dime. It was from this bust, rather than from life, that the artist transformed Mrs. Stevens' profile into a portrait of the youthful Winged Liberty.

The future model for one of America's most beautiful coins was born on June 5, 1886 to Howard Irving Kachel* and Ida Bright Smith at

The lost bust of Elsie Stevens reveals the similarity of her profile to that on the dime
(Courtesy of Random House)

Reading, Pennsylvania. The following year, young Elsie Viola's father died, and Ida Kachel remarried when her daughter was about eight years old. Although Lehman Wilkes Moll never legally adopted his stepdaughter, Elsie was encouraged by her mother to assume his surname. Thus, it was as Elsie Viola Moll that she was introduced to a young attorney named Wallace Stevens in the summer of 1904. Following a five-year courtship, in which the two came to know one another primarily through mutual correspondence, Wallace and Elsie were married on September 21, 1909.[9]

Although his career had begun with a succession of disappointments, Wallace Stevens found his niche as an attorney in the insurance industry. In 1908 he joined the New York office of the American Bonding Company of Baltimore, Maryland.[10] The couple's relocation to Hartford in 1916 was precipitated by his new employment with the Hartford Accident and Indemnity Company. There he rose to prominence, ulti-

---

*Some branches of the family spell the name "Kochel."

Elsie Stevens with daughter Holly, 1924
(Random House)

mately becoming a vice-president of the firm by the 1930s.[11]

The letters written by Wallace Stevens in childhood reveal a precocious talent with words. It's therefore not surprising that he developed this interest into a series of poems, written either for his love of Elsie or for his own self-realization. This curious mix of successful businessman by day and dreamy-eyed poet by night made him a popular figure in New York literary circles, although national and worldwide recognition of his work would not come until much later. He ultimately received the Pulitzer Prize for literature in the final year of his life, 1955.

Wallace Stevens and Elsie Moll had come from widely divergent socio-economic backgrounds. This fact, as well as other differences, evidently caused some distance between them. The poet in Stevens may have created an image of his beloved that proved more idealized than real. In addition, Elsie was disturbed by the subsequent publication of his poems to her, not being disposed to see them in their larger literary context.[12] Nevertheless, the marriage lasted nearly 46

years until Wallace's death. It also produced a daughter, Holly, born in 1924.

Elsie Stevens clearly knew of her indirect involvement in the creation of the Winged Liberty Dime, and she remained fond of the bust which was given to her by the artist. Following her husband's death, Elsie relocated to a smaller home, and she offered the bust to her daughter at that time.

Holly Stevens Stephenson, in recalling the occasion said, "I declined the gift, because while mother never talked about it, I knew she had a great attachment to it."[13]

Eight years after the death of Wallace Stevens, his widow fell ill and was tended to by Mrs. Stephenson. By that time the bust had somehow disappeared, and it remains missing to this day. Elsie Stevens died shortly afterward, still unable to recall what became of her portrait. Whether or not the Weinman bust still survives is unknown. If it does yet exist, the present holder may know nothing of its connection with the dime of 1916. In looking at the photograph of this bust, however, numismatists will always be able to envision the youthful goddess Liberty.

Notes to Chapter 1, Adolph Weinman & Elsie Stevens

[1] *The Numismatist,* November 1952.
[2] Gibbs, William T. "Poet's Wife Becomes Weinman's Model." *Coin World,* June 26, 1991.
[3] Vermeule, Cornelius. *Numismatic Art in America.*
[4] *The Numismatist,* November 1952.
[5] Vermeule.
[6] Ibid.
[7] Ibid.
[8] Stevens, Holly. *Letters of Wallace Stevens.*
[9] Stevens.
[10] Ibid.
[11] Risser, John. "Wallace Stevens." *Susquehana Magazine,* April 1990.
[12] ibid.
[13] Gibbs.

CHAPTER 2

Pattern Coins

✳

Design Modifications

Pattern Coins

J-1981, Early Die State showing the textured fields of Weinman's models.
(Smithsonian Institution, Tom Mulvaney photographs)

J-1981, Late Die State with the dies lapped to provide the brilliant
finish desired by the Mint. Note the loss of low-relief design elements.
(Smithsonian Institution, Tom Mulvaney photographs)

As with any new coin design, Adolph Weinman's Winged Liberty Dime required a certain amount of trial and error before master hubs suitable for the production of dies were obtained. The story of how Weinman was compelled to repeatedly revise his models is told in Chapter 1. It's the results of these experiments which are of interest here, as the patterns taken from each evolutionary step are of the greatest rarity and desirability.[1]

Unlike many earlier United States pattern coins, the dimes, quarters and halves of 1916 were struck in very small numbers. In keeping with official policy, these pieces were not made available to collectors and were not supposed to leave the Philadelphia Mint, except as needed for examination by the artists, the Director of the Mint and the Commission of Fine Arts. All coins so loaned were to be returned and destroyed as soon as they had served their intended purpose. That, at least, was the official policy, as outlined in a letter from Acting Mint Director Fred H. Chaffin to Philadelphia Mint Superintendent Adam M. Joyce, dated August 29, 1916. Chaffin instructs Joyce to destroy all "experimental coins" and have any such pieces in the hands of Weinman and his fellow sculptors returned to the Mint for that same purpose, "as there is no further doubt as to the satisfactory conditions of the respective dies."[2]

As related in Chapter 1, examples of the new dime as it progressed through the trial stage were sent to the American Sales Machine Company and the American Telephone and Telegraph Company. Ten each were sent to these companies for testing in their coin operated devices around September 1, 1916.[3] The coins failed to operate the machines properly, evidently as a result of their narrow borders and wire rims. Ten additional dimes were sent to each company around October 6, after the defective pieces had been returned.[4] The author could not locate any documentation that these revised coins were returned by their recipients, but then the fact that they proved satisfactory in all respects establishes that no further changes were made. Thus, the test coins would have been indistinguishable from the balance of the 1916 circulating issue. It seems that all recorded coins of preliminary designs had been sent back to the Philadelphia Mint for destruction.

In actual fact, a number of pieces went for a walk, as evidenced by their existence today in the hands of collectors and dealers. Several of these are worn from circulation and, in some instances, damaged. This is not too surprising, given their similarity to the adopted designs. It's easy to imagine their being mistaken for ordinary coins and spent by unknowing individuals. In fact, this appears to have been the case. Some years ago, in his "Numismatic Depth Study" column, Q. David Bowers quoted a letter from Rogers Fred of Virginia revealing the story of how several of these 1916 patterns came to be worn:

J-1983
(Courtesy of Auctions by Bowers & Merena)

J-1984
(Tom Mulvaney photos)

> Living in Leesburg at the present time are Mr. and Mrs. Charles Robb who are good friends of mine. Their son, Chuck, married Lynda Johnson, daughter of President Lyndon Johnson. Frances Robb (Mrs. Charles Robb Sr.) is the daughter of Mr. Wooley [sic], who was Director of the Mint in 1916... Mr. Wooley is dead now, but I knew him myself when we both lived in Washington in the 1930s and 1940s. I have talked to Frances Robb many times about her father and coins and she told me that in the 1920s her father's home was robbed. Among the things taken was a box containing coins. The thieves were not really interested in the coins as such,

but since the robbery was of a general nature they took anything that had value and could be disposed of easily.

> Mrs. Robb has said that her father had patterns of the 1916 coinage in that box... the 1916 patterns are very similar in design to the regular issue and it is reasonable to assume that the thieves thought that the coins were just regular issues and simply spent them. This would explain how the coins got out of the Mint in the first place, and how they got into worn condition in the second place.[5]

The fact that a few of the known pattern dimes of 1916 are not worn suggests that they were obtained by individuals other than Woolley and were thus not among the coins taken in the robbery of his home. Likely recipients include Treasury Secretary William G. McAdoo, Chief

Engraver Charles E. Barber, members of the Commission of Fine Arts and, of course, Adolph Weinman. It's possible, too, that influential numismatists such as Philadelphia coin dealer Henry Chapman may have been favored with a specimen or two. All of this is of course purely speculative, as no documentation exists to link the known pattern dimes with their original owners. The sole exception to this rule is the Smithsonian Institution's National Museum of American History, which acquired its two specimens when the U. S. Mint Collection was transmitted to the Smithsonian in 1923.

There should actually be four examples in the National Numismatic Collection, according to surviving correspondence. On June 16, 1917 Mint Director Raymond T. Baker informed Philadelphia Mint Superintendent Adam M. Joyce, "You are hereby authorized and directed to place in the Numismatic Collection of the Mint at Philadelphia, the following experimental coins from dies for the subsidiary silver coins: Three Half Dollars; four quarter-Dollars and four Dimes. The balance of the experimental pieces on hand are to be destroyed."[6] What became of the other two examples, and whether these represent varieties presently unknown to numismatics, are questions that may never be answered.

Pattern Mercury Dimes, as stated earlier, are quite similar to the adopted type in their overall arrangement. It is therefore in the details alone that they are readily distinguishable from ordinary coins, at least to a numismatist. The relative sizes and positions of the date and lettering account for the most common variations. Another tip-off may be the absence of the designer's monogram which appears so prominently on the production coins.

These patterns are cataloged by Judd numbers, a reference to the standard work on USA pattern and trial coins originally published by J. Hewitt Judd, MD in 1959 and now in its eighth edition. These patterns are listed in their supposed order of emission, and the author agrees entirely with this sequence, as each successive pattern reveals changes alluded to in the surviving correspondence. J-1982 and J-1983 are nearly indistinguishable, the only apparent difference being that J-1983 is lacking the sprig of leaves to the right of letter E in ONE. Of the four known varieties, J-1984 is the most deceptive, as it is nearly identical to the coin as issued for circulation, excepting in its unusually high relief. It also bears Weinman's monogram of a letter W surmounting an A, something not seen on any of the other Judd varieties.

Several Mercury Dime patterns were allegedly retrieved from circulation at various times from the 1930s onward. Specific instances have proved difficult to verify, although two examples were reportedly found circa 1955 and 1961, respectively. The latter was said to have been change from a vending machine.[7]

Notes to Chapter 2, Pattern Coins

[1] Most of the information appearing in this section is taken from two standard references on pattern coins: *United States Patterns and Related Issues*, by Andrew W. Pollock III; and *United States Pattern Coins, Experimental & Trial Pieces*, by J. Hewitt Judd, MD, Eighth Edition, edited by Q. David Bowers.

[2] National Archives and Records Administration, Records Group 104, Bureau of the Mint, Letters Sent, Volume 414.

[3] ibid.

[4] ibid.

[5] *Coin World*, October 9, 1974.

[6] NARA, RG-104, Volume 414.

[7] Pollock. Both pieces were originally published in *Coin World* and *The Numismatic Scrapbook Magazine*.

Design Modifications

Whenever new coin designs are anticipated there is always a certain eagerness to get the coins into circulation quickly. Persons who are not skilled in the techniques of preparing coin models and hubs are rarely sympathetic to the seemingly endless minor adjustments called for by the Mint's Engraving Department. Oftentimes it's the coin's designer who fails to comprehend the technical delays in seeing his vision realized. In other instances the numismatic community has played a role in hastening the preparation of working dies for coinage; but particularly subject to such fits of impatience are politicians, who may see the introduction of new coin designs and denominations as being complimentary to their administrative prowess. This sense of urgency usually results in the coining of an issue which is later viewed as being somehow flawed or incomplete. Such was the case with the Winged Head Liberty, or "Mercury," Dime.

The issuance of new dimes, quarter dollars and half dollars was originally announced by Mint Director R. W. Woolley for July 1, 1916. When this date came and went with all three coins still undergoing die trials, a groan of disappointment could be heard within the numismatic community. Director Woolley, his service with the Mint about to come to an end, was even more frustrated. The need by banks and businesses for additional dimes and quarters was urgent by that time, and the Mint had no choice but to prepare dies of the old Liberty Head type dated 1916. As the old style silver pieces fell from the presses, Woolley must have wondered whether any of the new coins would appear before year's end.

By late summer it was determined that the dime models had progressed to a point where suitable working dies could be prepared. Coinage began in September, and the first examples were released to circulation on October 30, 1916. While viewed by most numismatists and the general public as entirely satisfactory, there were those who detected some undesirable features in the Mercury Dimes of 1916. On January 17, Woolley's successor as Mint Director, F. J. H. von

Engelken, wrote to Superintendent Adam M. Joyce of the Philadelphia Mint. In his letter he noted that the new quarters and dimes had been criticized for "having a fin and being coined with a dirty die."[1] He further added that his own examination with a glass had confirmed these accusations.

In numismatic terminology, von Engelken's "fin" was a wire rim, a protruding flange around the coin's border. This was probably caused by one or both dies being misaligned within the collar and was not directly attributable to a flaw in the design. The "dirty die" to which he alluded is characteristic of the dimes, quarters and halves of 1916 and early 1917. In vogue at that time was a style of modeling which gave coins and medals a rough hewn or textured field. It was believed by sculptors (and correctly so) that such a treatment of the fields produced a more diffused luster which permitted the viewer to study the design in greater detail. The blinding luster typical of earlier United States silver coins was specifically disliked by Adolph Weinman, who made his view known to the Mint's Chief Engraver, Charles E. Barber.

Despite the obvious aesthetic advantages enjoyed by coins having sculpted or textured fields, von Engelken's letter and the engraving staff's resistance to new ideas conspired to bring about some modifications to all three of the new coins. Early in 1917, revised master hubs were prepared which differed slightly from those of the original issue. As a number of working dies bearing the date 1917 had already been prepared during the closing months of the previous year, dimes dated 1917 reflected the use of working dies taken from either old or new hubs. This was true for all three mints, albeit in differing ratios.

In addition to the aforementioned textured fields, the original Mercury Dime master hubs possess several distinctive features. Notable among these is the overall higher relief of the obverse. This would become more obvious as the coins wore down, following a wear pattern somewhat unlike that of later dates, but it's evident in Mint State coins as well. The most distinctive feature of the old obverse hub is the very high relief of the curls framing Liberty's face. This is particularly true of the one curl which projects forward and is directly across from Liberty's nose. It's quite noticeably bolder on the old hub, which the author has elected to call the Type of 1916. On the new hub introduced in 1917, described hereafter as the Type of 1917, this curl is shallow even on well struck coins. Also bolder on the Type of 1916 is the motto IN GOD WE TRUST.

The leading edge of Liberty's wing is likewise in higher relief on the Type of 1916 than on the Type of 1917, although the remainder of the wing is rather shallow and indistinct. With the new hub, the feathers are more deeply incised and thus stand out distinctively against Liberty's head, particularly along their trailing edges. The textured fields of the Type of 1916 are absent in the Type of 1917. Also missing are the slightly broader borders which characterized the old hubs. In fact, these last two features are the only distinctions between the old and new reverse hubs, all other details being the same.

The obverse Type of 1917 was used only in that year. A noticeably upgraded version of it appeared beginning with the coinage of 1918, and this is called the Type of 1918. It was used thereafter through the remainder of the series. Thus, Mercury Dimes dated 1918 and later are a composite product of the obverse Type of 1918 and the reverse Type of 1917.

The new obverse hub of 1918 varies from the one introduced in 1917 only in the details of Liberty's hair and in the contour and detailing of her wing. The arrangement of her curls is ever so slightly different from one hub to the other, as is evident in the photographs. Liberty's wing follows the contour of her head on both the Type of 1916 and the Type of 1917, curving away from the viewer and toward the coin's field. On the Type of 1918, the wing projects straight backward and remains within a single plane. This may be a bit difficult to see in a two-dimensional photograph, but it's plainly evident when examining actual coins. Further distinguishing the Type of 1918, the tip of each long feather is clearly highlighted by a raised outline not seen on the earlier hubs. As a final improvement, the gaps between

each of the smaller feathers have been increased to make the feathers more easily distinguished.

These subtypes within the Mercury Dime obverse hub were first published by Frank S. Robinson in 1970.[2] They were detailed more fully in the first edition of this book, yet the hobby has as yet taken little notice of them. With proper promotion, a market could be created for the two subtypes and six date/mint combinations of 1917, but for now collectors may quietly cherrypick them at no premium whatsoever.

No further changes were made to the master hubs for the Mercury Dime. The only noteworthy variations after 1918 are found within the size, shape and placement of mintmarks. Being that they were applied with hand held puncheons, mintmarks naturally varied in their exact location from one working die to another. Therefore, such positional irregularities are not considered significant unless severe. A few examples of wildly placed mintmarks may be found within the date and mint analysis in Chapter 6.

This leaves the size and shape of mintmarks as the only other variables which can be placed under the heading of design modifications. When Mercury Dimes were first coined in 1916, the 'D' and 'S' mintmark puncheons employed for them were already in existence, having been created for the Lincoln Cent some years earlier. New puncheons were introduced for both mints in 1917, and their debut coincides with the introduction of the Type of 1917 hubs and dies.

No new mintmark styles appeared on the dime until 1928, when a tall and slightly bloated 'S' puncheon was used for a portion of the cents, dimes, quarter dollars and half dollars coined with that date. This was an anomalous issue, and the puncheon did not reappear after 1928. The usual Small S of 1917 was also used in 1928 and for some years thereafter through 1941.

A new, Large D puncheon debuted on the cents of 1933, and it was used interchangeably with the Small D mintmark for the dimes of 1934. It's likely that the Small D dies were leftover from 1931 or earlier, as these would have been put in storage until needed. From 1935 onward this new puncheon was used for all Denver Mint dimes through the end of the series in 1945.

The next appearance of a new mintmark style was on the San Francisco Mint dimes of 1941. Most dimes of this date and mint bear the Small S used since 1917, however, two reverse dies have been identified with a new and larger mintmark. It has been dubbed the "Trumpet Tail S," due to its large, bell shaped lower serif. This style was used again in 1942, alongside another new puncheon known simply as the "Large S." It is quite symmetrical and attractive, with prominent serifs similar to those of the unique Large S of 1928. This mintmark style comprises a majority of the 'S' Mint dimes coined during 1943. Most 1944-S dimes likewise feature the Large S, but a minority of them displays a new mintmark style known as the "Knob Tail S." This is the most commonly seen mintmark punch for 1945-S dimes, which feature no fewer than three styles altogether.

More common for 1945-S than the Trumpet Tail S, but more rare than the Knob Tail S, is the "Micro S." The smallest mintmark used for the Mercury Dime series, it was created in 1907 for the Philippine Islands coinage struck at San Francisco until 1920, and it was resurrected only this once in 1945.

Notes to Chapter 2, Design Modifications

[1] Taxay, Don. *The U.S. Mint and Coinage.*
[2] Robinson, Frank S. "Mercury Dime Questions Unresolved". *The Numismatic Scrapbook Magazine,* August 1970.

D Mintmark 1916-17, 1929	D Mintmark 1917-34	D Mintmark 1934-35	S Mintmark 1916-17	S Mintmark 1917-41

S Mintmark 1928	S Mintmark 1941-43, 45	S Mintmark 1942-44	S Mintmark 1944-45	S Mintmark 1945

Type of 1916 — Obverse

Type of 1916 — Reverse

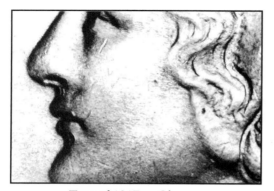

Type of 1917 — Obverse

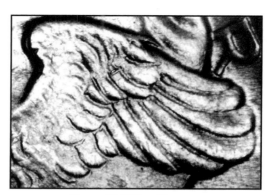

Type of 1917 — Reverse

Type of 1918 — Obverse

Type of 1918 — Reverse

CHAPTER 3

Collecting
Mercury Dimes

Though countless Americans saved one or more pieces of the Mercury Dime upon its release in 1916, as evidenced by the large number of Mint State and About Uncirculated survivors, there doesn't appear to have been widespread interest in collecting the entire series by date and mint. There were, of course, those established collectors who purchased one or two examples of every issue, buying them annually from the individual mints at just face value plus postage, but this series did not gain a devoted following until the mid-1930s.

One of the few individuals publishing observations about current United States coins was Robert H. Lloyd of North Tonawanda, New York. In 1927 he borrowed a popular expression of the time in titling his article, "Making the Cheese Snappier." In it, Lloyd observed that, "The post-war coinage of the United States has shown a tendency to be irregular. That is, certain pieces have not been struck every year, or pieces of a denomination have been entirely of one mint mark." With respect to dimes, he noted that, "1922 marks the first break in the dime series in more than one hundred years. Since 1923 dime coinage has been normal, except for a low coinage of 1926 S dimes."

While there was then only limited collector interest in what are now the highly desirable issues dated 1916-31, two events occurred almost simultaneously that together served to create a broad mar-

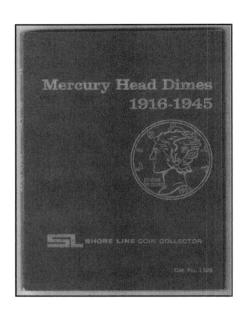

ket for these coins. The first was the creation of several low-mintage issues in 1930-31. Though there had been a number of low-mintage dates before, such as 1916-D, 1921(P), 1921-D and 1926-S, these had been quietly released into circulation without much notice from the hobby, making Uncirculated pieces quite scarce in later years. This rarity actually had the short-term effect of discouraging collecting. The scarce dimes dated 1930-S, 1931-D and 1931-S, however, were a different story. The Depression-racked economy of those years did not demand any additional coinage of dimes, and most of these coins went into storage. By this time, hobby publications such as *The Numismatist* had begun to publish monthly and annual coinage figures, and the small mintage of 1930-31 dimes drew some notice. Not having been distributed to commercial banks, these coins remained mostly unavailable, as were the 1931-S cents and 1931-S nickels for the same reason. This artificial scarcity created a speculative market in what appeared to be rare issues.

When finally released in 1934-35 many of these dimes were immediately hoarded by speculators, though most of this activity centered on the more popular cents and nickels. The low-mintage dimes of 1930-31 nevertheless found ready buyers, while they remained fairly rare in circulation. The 1931-D dimes, in particular, seemed to have been saved in very large numbers and were among the most often advertised Mercury Dimes for the next decade or so. The timing of this development couldn't have been better, as the demand for modern issues was growing rapidly.

This brings us to the second key development in the popularity of collecting Mercury Dimes. The very first coin albums appeared late in 1928 when Martin Luther Beistle introduced this new product. M. L. Beistle was a manufacturer of paper novelty items in Shippensburg, Pennsylvania, and the coin album was a natural blending of his business and his coin collecting hobby. Beistle's concept was one that's become very familiar today. He devised cardboard pages pierced with holes into which coins could be placed. The coins were then secured within their holes by celluloid slides that were inserted into the end of each page. Finally, the pages were punched with holes in their margins for mounting within a ring binder built to suit.

Though Beistle's product was somewhat crude by current standards, it was the concept that sold it. Previously, collectors had kept their coins in expensive, wooden cabinets with felt-lined drawers or had simply placed them in paper envelopes of an appropriate size. Beistle's album design was promising enough that prominent New York City dealer Wayte Raymond bought the rights to it around 1931 and began marketing these albums under the National Brand, selling them through the Scott Stamp and Coin Company.

National albums were still a bit expensive, and their target market was the established coin collector who was already well versed in the hobby. Though many albums were sold to collectors of Mercury Dimes, the real popularity of this series began when simpler and less expensive coin holders became available. This became a reality in 1934 with the introduction of the first coin board. Consisting of simply a paper-backed sheet of 11" x 14" cardboard pierced with holes of the appropriate size and lettered to suit, the coin board was the invention of J. K. Post in Neenah, Wisconsin. Post contracted with Whitman Publishing Company in nearby Racine to manufacture the boards. A manufacturer of games, jigsaw puzzles and children's books, Whitman was well suited to mass-producing inexpensive paper products for hobbyists. The first boards were made for collecting Indian Head or Lincoln Cents, but titles for Liberty Head and Buffalo Nickels were introduced in 1935 and proved to be an immediate success. These were followed very shortly by boards for "Morgan [Barber] Dimes" and Mercury Dimes.

So successful, in fact, were the boards that Post was overwhelmed by the demand and found himself unable to market the boards effectively on a part-time basis. Whitman Publishing bought the rights from him in 1936, reportedly in settlement of his debt to the company. Whitman employee Dick Yeo, later to achieve fame as "Red Book" author R. S. Yeoman, was given the uncertain assignment of making this potential white elephant profitable. He not only did so, but he greatly expanded the list of titles and developed new product lines, as well. From that point onward Whitman was at the forefront of the coin collecting supply business, and it remains one of the key players to this day.

Though most of the popular coin series fit quite neatly onto a single board, the ongoing Lincoln Cent and Mercury Dime series soon outgrew this format. By the early 1940s, the large boards had been replaced by the three-panel folders so familiar to later generations of collectors.

Providing some idea of what it was like to collect Mercury Dimes from circulation during the 1930s is a survey published in *The*

Numismatic Scrapbook Magazine.[1] Dr. J. Robert Schneider examined some 5000 dimes that came his way between December of 1937 and September of 1938 in the area of Rock Island, Illinois. In addition to finding nearly a complete set of Barber Dimes, with numerous duplicates, Dr. Schneider turned up the following quantities of Mercury Dimes:

1916	64	1919-S	28	1925	155	1928-S	25	1935	363
1916-D	1	1920	225	1925-D	34	1929	112	1935-D	99
1916-S	42	1920-D	75	1925-S	22	1929-D	45	1935-S	28
1917	198	1920-S	59	1926	144	1929-S	12	1936	567
1917-D	37	1921	9	1926-D	43	1930	10	1936-D	101
1917-S	77	1921-D	3	1926-S	6	1930-S	3	1936-S	12
1918	98	1923	236	1927	143	1931	15	1937	261
1918-D	52	1923-S	25	1927-D	26	1931-D	7	1937-D	26
1918-S	70	1924	117	1927-S	23	1931-S	8	1937-S	5
1919	131	1924-D	33	1928	104	1934	89	Unclear	36
1919-D	39	1924-S	26	1928-D	24	1934-D	54		

Clearly, the 1916-D dime was already a rarity within 20 years of its release. Not surprisingly, dimes dated 1921(P), 1921-D, 1926-S 1930-S, 1931-D and 1931-S were also quite scarce in circulation. The small quantities reported for 1936-S and 1937-S simply reflected the fact that these coins had not made their way across the country yet, since neither issue would prove to be rare a few years later. It's interesting to note too that so many Mercury Dimes were already worn to the point that Schneider described them as "poor date" pieces. These were coins whose dates he could not make out clearly. In contrast, only seven of the Barber Dimes he observed had unreadable dates.

While the appearance of the coin board in 1934 did indeed revolutionize the coin hobby, making it affordable to most Americans and creating a previously unimagined demand for circulated coins, it was really Beistle's albums that first put the Mercury Dime series in the spotlight. Until the late 1920s it was quite rare to find ads offering modern coins by date and mint. While there were a few people quietly collecting these pieces, the premiums attached to them evidently didn't merit the placing of ads in *The Numismatist*. It was in 1928 that the first offerings of current series appeared. These began

with Indian Head and Lincoln Cents but were later extended to include Buffalo Nickels and Mercury Dimes. The Beistle/Raymond albums provided a means by which to collect these coins, and the premiums attached to Uncirculated pieces grew steadily during the 1930s.

The primary suppliers of modern coins by date and mint were F. C. C. Boyd in New York City, A. C. Gies in Pittsburgh and William Pukall in Union City, New Jersey. All were in businesses that gave them access to large quantities of coins, and they financed their own collecting in part by placing these modern pieces with mail-order collectors. In order to promote sales of his albums, Wayte Raymond ultimately bought out these individual hoarders, and he remained a primary source of both common and scarce issues until his death in 1956. His estate included large quantities of these pieces, and they were wholesaled to various dealers for the next several years.

The hoards have long since been dispersed, and roll quantities of any coins before the 1930s have become something of a rarity.

It's ironic that during the Great Depression of the 1930s, a time when the prices of truly rare

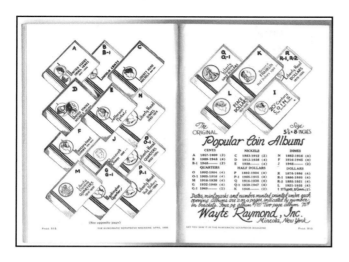

coins were temporarily in decline, there were startling advances in prices for what were essentially common coins. These included the many commemorative issues of the period, as well as what were then current series such as Buffalo Nickels and Lincoln Cents. This contradiction reflected a demographic shift in the coin collecting hobby, as many newcomers began checking their pocket change for dates needed to fill their boards. This became a popular family hobby, though it was still essentially a male activity. As these new collectors grew in sophistication, they began to seek Uncirculated pieces to replace their "hole fillers," and the prices for Mint State Mercury Dimes and other current or recent series rose accordingly.

A 1940 advertisement placed by John R. Stewart

of Milwaukee is fairly typical of that time and gives a good idea of what collectors were paying for Uncirculated Mercury Dimes:

1916-P	$.85	1916-D	$9.50	1916-S	$.60
1917-P	.85	1917-D	2.00	1917-S	.75
1918-P	2.00	1918-D	2.00	1918-S	1.20
1919-P	2.00	1919-D	1.60	1919-S	1.60
1920-P	2.00	1920-D	1.60	1920-S	1.60
1921-P	4.50	1921-D	2.00		
1923-P	1.65	1923-S	1.75		
1924-P	1.65	1924-D	2.00	1924-S	1.75
1925-P	1.20	1925-D	2.00	1925-S	1.60
1926-P	1.20	1926-D	2.00	1926-S	3.00
1927-P	1.20	1927-D	2.75	1927-S	1.20
1928-P	1.20	1928-D	1.50	1928-S	.85
1929-P	.50	1929-D	1.00	1929-S	.85
1930-P	.75	1930-S	.85		
1931-P	.50	1931-D	.75	1931-S	.60
1934-P	.25	1934-D	.35		
1935-P	.25	1935-D	.35	1935-S	.25
1936-P	.20	1936-D	.25	1936-S	.25
1937-P	.20	1937-D	.20	1937-S	.20
1938-P	.20	1938-D	.20	1938-S	.20

It's interesting to note some of the trends evident from this ad. The 1916-D, 1921(P), 1926-S and 1927-D dimes had already emerged as keys, yet 1921-D was still considered a fairly routine entry in the series at that time. Note also that the several of the early 'D' Mint and 'S' Mint dimes, now considered so scarce in Uncirculated condition, were then priced less than Philadelphia Mint issues of the same years. The low mintage dimes of 1931 from all three mints were quite reasonably priced in 1940, reflecting the fact that these issues had been widely hoarded. These concentrated hoards have long since been dispersed, and current prices are much more in line with overall availability.

In 1942 famed Texas coin dealer B. Max Mehl offered a complete set of Mercury Dimes from 1916 through 1941, in which the 1936-41 'P' Mint pieces were proofs, for a total of $125 in Uncirculated condition.[3] This level of pricing was not to last, however. The 1940s saw a tremendous growth in the coin collecting hobby, due to the unique nature of the wartime economy. Those remaining on the home front earned unprecedented wages, often working multiple shifts or extensive overtime. At the same time, the production of most consumer goods was either restricted or completely curtailed in favor of items essential to the war effort. Unable to buy many of the things they desired, but with pockets bulging, most Americans spent their money on entertainment. This was one of the few pleasures that remained in abundant supply. Sales of movie tickets reached a climax during this period, and hobbies of every kind experienced unprecedented growth. The collecting of both stamps and coins soared in popularity, though the rationing of paper supplies occasionally interfered with the production of albums and guide books.

New records were set at nearly every coin auction during the years 1943-48, and it was only toward the end of the decade that the coin market entered a slump. Recovering by 1952, the growth that followed actually dwarfed the expansion of the 1940s, as there were now no restrictions whatsoever on the supply of hobby products. New albums and holders made of plastic rivaled the cardboard types as early as 1945, though paper-based albums predominated through the 1950s. Joining Whitman in the manufacture and sale of coin albums and folders were the Daniel Stamp Company (DANSCO), Harris (of stamp collecting fame), Meghrig, Library of Coins,

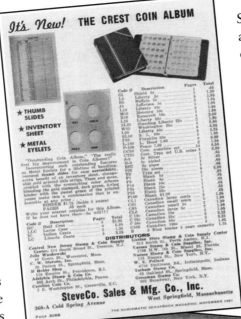

Shoreline (one of the many Whitman look-alikes), Harold Cohn (HARCO) and dozens of regional and local brands completely forgotten today. The peak production of albums coincided with the apex of popular coin collecting in the years 1958-64, when the coin hobby was frequently the subject of media attention.

Throughout this period the Mercury Dime series remained a perennial favorite. Continual circulation, however, took its toll on the number of pieces having readable dates or otherwise considered to be in collectable condition. Persons not old enough to remember silver coins in general circulation cannot imagine how rapidly they wore down as compared to our current copper-nickel-clad issues. Popular numismatic writer Jack W. Ogilvie sheds some light on the subject in an article from 1949. Reporting that a company in his area had placed national advertisements in which dimes were solicited in some sort of promotion, Ogilvie took this opportunity to sort through the several thousand coins received and make some observations on their makeup.[4]

He noted that 80% of the Mercury Dimes were dated between 1935 and 1945–not surprising given the much greater mintages of these years as compared with most earlier dates. Some 15% comprised coins dated 1923-34, while the remaining 5% were of earlier dates. Ogilvie managed to locate one 1916-D dime and two 1921(P) dimes, the latter being considered the second scarcest date in the series at that time. "What was really astounding," Ogilvie stated, "was the scarcity of some of the other dates. The 1916-S was noticeable by its absence, as well as the 1921-D, 1926-S, 1927-D—really a surprise—1930-S and the 1931 all mints. In the more recent dates, the 1938 and the 1938-D seemed the more evasive."

Also a revelation to Ogilvie was that over half of the dimes dated between 1916 and 1921 were worn to a point where the final digit of the date was just barely discernible or entirely gone. The mintmarks, if any, were likewise rendered unreadable. "Junk!," he declared, adding that, "It would take three of them to buy what was once a ten-cent cigar!" The majority of the remaining Mercury Dimes dated before 1923 graded only Poor to Fair in his estimation. Within the 1923-26 issues he found that just 40% graded as high as Good to Very Good, while a mere 5% achieved the grade of Fine, the remaining pieces being severely worn. Most of the 1927-34 dimes were reportedly Very Good to Fine, while Ogilvie stated of the 1935-45 pieces, "to save anything other than Uncirculated is almost sacrilegious."

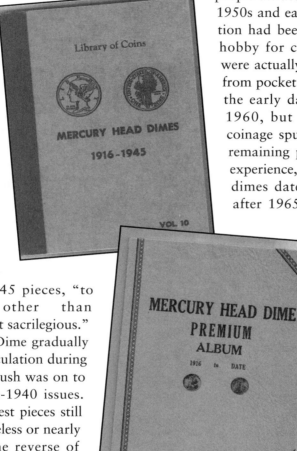

As the Mercury Dime gradually disappeared from circulation during the early 1960s, the rush was on to secure all of the pre-1940 issues. By this time the earliest pieces still to be found were dateless or nearly so from wear. As the reverse of this coin type wore more rapidly than the obverse, the mintmark area was often completely obscured. There's no telling how many hours have been lost by collectors and dealers who struggled in vain to make out a small 'D' on the reverses of 1916 dimes.

The coin hobby entered a period of decline beginning in the mid-1960s, due to a variety of causes. The speculative market that developed in rolls and even bags of recent coins collapsed in the latter months of 1964, leaving many of the fair-weather collectors strapped for cash and quite disillusioned. Beginning in the fall of 1965,

coins formerly made of silver were quickly replaced by ones of copper-nickel, and all remaining silver pieces were driven from circulation within two to three years. Sales of proof sets were suspended from 1965 through 1967, and in their place were offered overpriced Special Mint Sets of mediocre quality.

These factors drove away many of the people attracted to coin collecting during the 1950s and early '60s whose primary motivation had been greed, but it also ruined the hobby for countless kids and adults who were actually having fun filling their folders from pocket change. As for Mercury Dimes, the early dates were already scarce after 1960, but the discontinuance of silver coinage spurred efforts to remove the last remaining pieces. Speaking from personal experience, the author can relate that only dimes dated 1940-45 were to be found after 1965, and silver coins of any date had all but disappeared by the end of 1968.

Serious collectors who had already committed themselves to buying quality coins at premium prices were largely unaffected by the exodus of casual hobbyists, and they may have even viewed the lower prices as a welcome opportunity. Even so, this bursting of the coin bubble was a blow from which the greater hobby never fully recovered, though there are signs of hope. The onset of the 50-State Quarters program in 1999 drew a lot of new blood into the hobby, and this launched a general revival in the production and marketing of coin albums for all popular series. As this is written at the beginning of 2005, the coin market is in a boom cycle, with the values for key-date coins such as the 1916-D dime advancing rapidly.

One of the interesting by-products of the coin collecting mania of the late 1950s and early '60s was the great fluctuation of prices for certain issues within the Mercury Dime series. In the first edition of this book, published in 1993, it was noted that many of the semi-key dates such as 1927-S had peaked in value in the lower grades during the early 1960s. The values of these coins in grades Good through Fine either declined or remained stagnant after that time and had still not recovered thirty years later. Little hope was offered for upward price movement, as it seemed these coins were not wanted by anyone at that time.

When the popularity of collecting coins was widespread, these pieces commanded relatively large premiums. The subsequent decline in values suffered by these issues can be traced to a major change in the nature of the coin collecting hobby. The inclination of collectors during the 1950s and early 1960s was to hunt for needed dates by examining pocket change and by searching rolls obtained from a nearby bank. With most collectors living in the East or the Midwest, S-Mint dimes seemed particularly elusive and acquired a peculiar mystique. All that was necessary to dispel this illusion was to speak with dealers in the West, most of whom possessed these dates in abundance. Such coins had been widely hoarded in low grades during the 1940s and '50s and were therefore more common than was generally believed.

As the 1960s passed, a new generation of collectors who had never known the thrill of assembling a Mercury Dime collection from circulation entered the market. While previous generations had been content to purchase the semi-key dates in low grades, as these coins matched the ones already acquired from circulation, the new collectors quickly learned to seek only higher grade pieces. There was a particular emphasis on Mint State coins, as the stellar gains they'd made since the 1940s became part of the new investment climate. At the same time that the "pocket change" generation was being driven away from coin collecting, the "deep pocket" generation was pushing up the prices of coins grading XF and higher. The knowledge that low-grade, semi-key coins were overrated, combined with a dwindling market for such grades, had the inevitable effect of depressing the prices for several dates.

In 1993 it seemed that this trend was irreversible. In fact, most Mercury Dimes in the grades of Good through Fine have made modest gains during the intervening years. While forty years of inflation has proved these coins to have been a bad investment overall, there are signs that the collecting of even well worn Mercury Dimes is on the ascendancy.

The collecting of Mercury Dimes entered a new period of sophistication during the 1970s, along with the coin market in general. New entrants into the coin hobby were often lured by the prospect of profiting from an investment in rare coins, and most dealers shifted their sales pitches in this direction. Prices rose rapidly during the latter part of the decade, as coins were increasingly viewed as a hedge against double-digit inflation. The coin market eventually overheated, and this led to a sharp decline in the value of Mint State and Proof coins during the early 1980s. While some collectors and investors dropped out, often hastily selling their coins at a loss, there remained a greater number of people active in the coin hobby/business than there had been a decade earlier.

Along with the Walking Liberty Half Dollar series, Mercury Dimes were at the forefront of this speculative activity during the onset of the cycle in 1978. Prices for Mint State dimes, particularly those having Full Bands, rose sharply at that time. For many years these two series were considered bellwethers of the investment coin market, though the onset of grading and encapsulation services in the 1980s, with their published population reports, soon dispelled the notion that Mercury Dimes and Walking Liberty Halves of the 1940s were rare. Prices for these more common issues declined, while those of the scarce, early dates continued to rise.

One of the less desirable developments to come from a general increase in values from the 1950s onward was the appearance of numerous counterfeit and altered coins. Before the 1970s, most such pieces were crude and did not pose a threat to knowledgeable buyers. The science of counterfeit detection was in its infancy, however, and it was not long before more sophisticated fakes were devised. This led to the creation of the American Numismatic Association Certification Service in the 1970s. Its initial role was merely to authenticate coins and attribute varieties, but the ever-increasing values led to disputes over grading. Published grading guides existed for circulated coins, but most of the abuses and complaints centered around Mint State and Proof pieces, for which there were no published standards.

In 1979 ANACS expanded its services to include grading. It began issuing grading certificates for coins, and these included photographs of the piece in question. The intent of this service was simply to arbitrate disputes over specific pieces on an as-needed basis, but coin dealers quickly realized that these grading certificates could be used as marketing tools. Soon, it became almost essential to have valuable coins certified by ANACS, and this service was the primary source of the American Numismatic Association's revenue throughout much of the 1980s.

The success of ANACS led to the next logical development in the marketing of coins. Though each certificate was accompanied by photos of the subject coin, there always existed the risk that the coin depicted was not the one being offered for sale. Two untoned and Uncirculated coins of the same date and mint could appear quite similar in a photograph, and substitutions were sometimes made at the expense of the buyer. This weakness was addressed with the creation in 1986 of the Professional Coin Grading Service, a commercial venture that placed both the certificate and the coin inside a sealed holder. Neither

could be swapped without it being evident from examination of the holder. PCGS was followed just a year later by Numismatic Guaranty Corporation (NGC), and several other commercial grading services now compete with these two major players. ANACS was sold by the ANA to Amos Press, publisher of *Coin World*, in 1990 and continues to operate successfully. In its place the ANA established the American Numismatic Association Authentication Bureau (ANAAB). While it provided valuable expertise for a number of years thereafter, without the revenue from its former grading operation it could not endure, and the ANAAB ceased operations early in the new century.

The impact of these developments on the collecting of Mercury Dimes has been profound. While there are still many who place circulated pieces inside traditional paper-based albums or plastic display frames, most serious collectors now prefer their coins to be certified and encapsulated. These encapsulations are stored upright within plastic boxes made specifically to fit them. Publication of the grading services' certified populations by date, mint and grade has lessened the perceived rarity of some issues while revealing other dates to be important condition rarities. It is now known with some certainty which Mercury Dimes are truly rare in the higher grades, as is their relative rarity with full bands.

The traditional avenues of acquiring coins for one's collection, such as neighborhood coin shops and local or regional coin shows, are now but a small part of the overall coin market. In fact, many collectors never buy coins in person, preferring to shop by mail order from published advertisements or online via their home computers. This has had a profound effect on the way in which rarity is interpreted. When the first edition of this book was published, it included a rarity rating for each date and mint combination in the series, including proofs. This rating was determined by each entry's frequency of appearances at coin shows, information that is becoming increasing irrelevant to most collectors. For that reason, the old rarity ratings and rankings have been deleted from this edition, as the certified population data provides a more meaningful guide to expected availability. These data are, of course, supplemented by the author's own observations regarding rarity.

The latest development in certified grading is the online collection registry, in which collectors can have their sets compared and ranked against those submitted by other individuals. This activity is greatly facilitated by the widespread growth and acceptance of the Internet and the prevalence of home computers having Internet access. Easy scanning of coin images and posting of these images at registry websites add to the collecting experience. Both NGC and PCGS maintain extensive registry websites. While NGC's registry may include coins certified by either of these major grading services, the PCGS registry is limited to its own product.

The prevalence of certified coins, with their guaranteed authenticity, has all but driven out counterfeit and altered pieces. These are still a menace at small coin shows, country auctions and the like, but both dealers and collectors are careful to have valuable coins certified. Counterfeit and altered coins still turn up with some regularity when collections assembled between about 1950 and 1980 are brought to market, so caution is urged when purchasing uncertified, key-date coins.

While much of the fun of assembling collections within albums has been lost to the present generation of collectors, the coins themselves enjoy far greater protection from the environment. Even the best made albums leave coins somewhat vulnerable to mechanical damage from the albums' moving slides, and the less expensive ones subject coins to chemical reactions with both the cardboard and the atmosphere. Some of the newer album lines introduced since 2000 specifically address the issue of chemical reaction by including only inert materials in their construction and/or by featuring a sacrificial lining that draws atmospheric contaminants toward itself, thus sparing the coins. Collectors of circulated coins needn't worry about these issues, so long as the coins are not in contact with degradable plastics. The last such line of coin albums went out of production a few years ago, so the matter seems settled. A final caution is that coin folders, in which the coins are simply pushed into the hole and rest against a paper backing, should be used only for beginning collections of inexpensive coins. They afford no protection from the materials used nor from the atmosphere.

As this is written in 2005, the collecting of Mercury Dimes has never been more popular. This is by far the best educated generation of coin collectors in terms of both historical and technical knowledge, though the rapid influx of newcomers to the hobby since 1999 presents an educational challenge for us all.

One area of growth for the Mercury Dime series is in the field of variety collecting. While the number of varieties known for this series continues to be frustratingly limited, there are some good ones to be found. These are, of course, in addition to the well known overdates of 1942. A perusal of the Bibliography offered in Appendix C will reveal titles of a specialized or general nature pertaining to Mercury Dimes.

Old collections of Mercury Dimes still come back onto the market with some frequency. Of course, most of these are incomplete sets of wellworn pieces acquired 40-50 years ago from circulation or purchased inexpensively from mailorder dealers or local coin shops. In fact, go into any coin shop and you are likely to find stacks of such incomplete sets lying on the floor or on a bookshelf, because the dealer's time is simply too valuable to be spent removing coins that, for the most part, have only their silver value. Like it or not, most Mercury Dimes in heavily worn condition are very common coins whose numbers exceed the population of potential buyers.

The offering of a high-grade collection, complete with the rare issues, is an important event and seldom occurs outside of major auction houses. There have been several such significant collections of high-grade Mercury Dimes during just the past five years, the popularity of online registries being an important factor in getting these collections properly highlighted within auction catalogs. More often than not, new price records are set with each such offering.

Notes to Chapter 3

[1] *The Numismatic Scrapbook Magazine,* November 1938.
[2] *The Numismatist,* January 1940.
[3] ibid, May 1942.
[4] Ogilvie, Jack W. "The Mercury Dime." *The Numismatic Scrapbook Magazine,* January 1949.

CHAPTER 4

Gallery of Errors

✳

Counterfeit & Altered Coins

Gallery of Errors

The most often seen errors within the Mercury Dime series are laminated planchets, broadstrikes and off-centered coins. These are not especially difficult to find, but all other error types are quite scarce. Exotic pieces such as double-struck and wrong planchet errors are very rare.

The following collection of errors was assembled from a variety of sources, as noted. The photographs are arranged in chronological order. The author would like to take this opportunity to extend a special thanks to those who shared with him these instructive and amusing examples of the minting process gone awry.

1917-S T17 — This error is known as a broadstrike. The retaining collar which encloses the two dies at the moment of striking was not in place, probably as the result of having jammed around the lower die when it retracted. Such errors are not rare by type, but being a high grade example of an early date makes this one special. *(Courtesy of Jim Checkovich)*

1917-S T17 — Among the most seldom seen errors, particularly for the Mercury Dime, is the flipover double strike. This example was struck once, adhered to the upper or reverse die momentarily, fell back onto the obverse die and collar in an inverted position and was then struck a second time, off-centered. *(Photo by Bob Everett, courtesy of Kenneth R. Hill)*

1919(P) — Struck about 15-20% off-centered, this error is another nice, early date example. *(Courtesy of David Woloch)*

1920 (mint unknown) — Mercury Dimes struck this far off-centered (45-50%) are scarce. *(Courtesy of Michael L. Chambers)*

1924-D — This boldly struck and beautifully toned example of a scarce date was struck on an incomplete planchet, also known as a "clip." Two clips are evident, as is the rim depression opposite the larger of the two. This feature often distinguishes genuine clips from ones which have been contrived. *(Courtesy of Pete Bishal)*

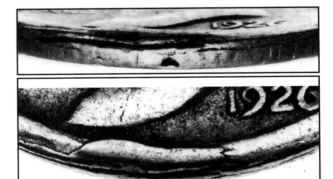

1926-D — This error began as a laminated planchet which split before striking. Some of the detached metal then folded over at the moment of striking. *(Courtesy of Ralph Huntzinger)*

1934? (mint unknown) — This dual-error coin has been identified as 1934 solely by the style of 4, this final digit being the only identifiable element of the obverse. Struck 90-95% off-centered, the planchet was punched out from the edge of the rolled metal strip and displays a straight clip. *(Courtesy of Mark W. Clark)*

1935(P) — 30% off-centered. *(Courtesy of Bill Fivaz)*

1941(P)- 25% off-centered. *(Fivaz)*

1937(P) This incomplete planchet error, or clip, circulated for some years. *(Fivaz)*

1935-S — Another example of an oftseen error is this sharply detailed broadstrike. *(Courtesy of Eugene Bruder)*

1941(P) — Like the 1934 dime above, this coin has a straight clip. It is also broadstruck. *(Chambers)*

1941(P) — This dime had not passed through the upsetting mill before being delivered to the press. Thus, it was struck on a Type 1 blank lacking a raised rim. This may have led to its becoming a nicely centered broadstrike, as its diameter would have been too great to fit within the restraining collar. It may be seen where the reeded collar made contact with the planchet's obverse periphery. This highlights the fact that the obverse die was in the lower position for Mercury Dimes, with the reverse as the upper or hammer die. *(Checkovich)*

1941(P) — This is a good example of a laminated planchet error. Due to either improper mixing of the alloy or the presence of trapped gas within the metal, the planchet began to split and flake prior to striking. *(Courtesy of Vic Rollo)*

1942(P) — Another incomplete or clipped planchet, this one shows how the pressure of striking has diminished the radius of the missing portion's arc. Before coining, this would have possessed the same curvature as the struck coin. *(Fivaz)*

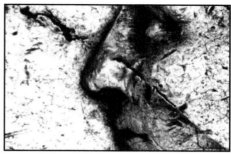

1942(P) — Seemingly an ordinary dime, this was in fact struck on a brass planchet of .800 copper and .200 zinc. Its weight is 30.2 grains, revealing that the planchet was intended for the five-centavos coin of Ecuador, an issue then being coined at Philadelphia. *(Woloch)*

1943(P) — Lamination errors seem to have been particularly common during the war years. *(Rollo)*

1944(P) — This broadstrike is similar to the 1941(P) example above in that it was coined on a Type 1 or unmilled blank. In this instance, however, the collar made no contact with the planchet. *(Woloch)*

1944(P) — Well centered broadstrikes are scarcer than off-centered ones. This specimen could easily escape the notice of non-specialists. Only its slightly larger than normal diameter and the absence of reeding reveal the error. *(Checkovich)*

1944(P) — This date is noted for poor quality control and frequent errors. The reverse of this dime was struck through a thick layer of grease. This coating may have been intended to protect the die from corrosion during storage and was not completely removed, or it may have simply oozed out from the press. *(Fivaz)*

1944(P) — Double-struck Mercury Dimes are exceedingly rare. This one rotated about 90 degrees between strikes, suggesting that it may have momentarily adhered to the upper die before falling back onto the lower die. Evidently, both strikes occurred within the collar. *(Courtesy of Fred Weinberg)*

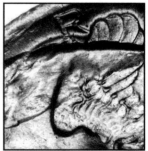

1944(P) — Another pre-strike lamination, this one left too little metal to fill the die. *(Huntzinger)*

1944-D — Some foreign matter came between the planchet and the die, causing a partial obscuring of the design. *(Bishal)*

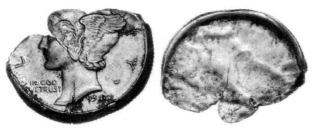

1944 (mint unknown) — In this multiple error, the coin was originally struck on a piece of scrap metal from the planchet punching process. It then adhered to the obverse die while incoming planchets landed on top of it. Repeated strikings led to a bold obverse, while the reverse was obliterated by successive blank planchets. This effect is called a brockage and is rare for Mercury Dimes. (Weinberg)

1945(P) — Like the 1942(P) above, this dime was struck on a planchet intended for the coinage of another country. In this case the composition is .835 silver, .165 copper and the weight is 19.2 grains, corresponding to the 1/4 bolivar coin of Venezuela. Now that the United States Mints are no longer producing coins for other countries, this type of error has become obsolete. (Woloch)

1945(P) — This centered broadstrike was on an unmilled or Type 1 blank, and it's evident that the obverse made some contact with the reeded collar. Note also that the coin displays full bands, something rarely seen on normal 1945(P) dimes. This added feature was made possible by the redirected metal displacement common to such errors. (Fivaz)

1945(P) — Another off-centered broadstrike, this is possibly the most common type of Mercury Dime error. (Checkovich)

1945(P) — Full bands appear on this off-centered broadstrike, as well. The lines on the obverse are merely scratches obtained from circulation. (Rollo)

1945-S — One of the more common errors is an incomplete or clipped planchet. This one is only about 5% clipped and carries a modest premium. (Rollo)

1945-D — A fragment of copper, possibly dislodged from a cent planchet or some foreign planchet, was struck through on this dime. It has been outlined in the photo for clarity. (Fivaz)

1945(P) — This dime was struck through some foreign matter lying atop the obverse die. The extra compression of metal caused by such material being within the die cavity has given the coin nearly full bands, a feature rarely seen on ordinary strikes of this date and mint. (Fivaz)

192 (date uncertain, mint unknown) — From the nearly closed style of 9 one can tell that this dime was coined in 1926 or 1927. It's about 40% off-centered. *(Weinberg)*

(date unknown, Philadelphia Mint) — Another 40% off-centered dime, this one clearly displays its upset or milled planchet in the unstruck portion. *(Woloch)*

(date unknown, Denver Mint) — With its small D mintmark, this 30% off-centered dime dates from before 1935. *(Woloch)*

(date unknown, Denver Mint) — Another Small D variety, 1934 or earlier, this dime's planchet exhibits some occluded or trapped gas. This flaw may have been rendered invisible in a normal strike, or it may have caused a lamination. Its presence in the unstruck portion makes for an interesting and instructional specimen. *(Woloch)*

Counterfeit & Altered Coins

Any coin of sufficient value is subject to being counterfeited. During the years in which Mercury Dimes were minted, those counterfeits seen were apt to be circulating fakes, intended to pass only at face value. Such pieces were crudely cast from sand or plaster molds, rather than being die-struck like genuine coins, and the metal of choice was lead. The resulting coins were scarcely good enough to pass as the real thing, even when painted silver, as many were. Relatively few cast counterfeits of the Mercury Dime have surfaced, though cast pieces of other denominations from this period are common. Why Mercury Dime casts are so elusive is not known, and one could not be located for illustration.

More troubling to the collector of Mercury Dimes are the many alterations of otherwise genuine coins. The most often targeted date is 1916-D. The tremendous disparity in value between Philadelphia and San Francisco Mint dimes of this date on the one hand, and those struck at Denver on the other, has led to countless examples of the more common 'P' and 'S' Mint pieces being rendered into crude approximations of their more valuable cousin from the Mile-High City.

The most common technique is to remove a D mintmark from a common date coin and apply it to a 1916 Philadelphia Mint dime which, of course, has no mintmark. Either epoxy or solder is used to affix the tiny letter, which may seem to float atop the surface of the coin rather than blending into it. Realizing this, many fakers will then use a finepoint tool to work the mintmark's sides into the coin's field. The skill with which this is done varies from one person to another, but the work is always detectable with proper magnification. A stereo microscope is ideal, but a hand held glass of 10X or so is usually enough to spot such alterations. Any signs of discoloration or tooling marks in the area of the mintmark are reason enough to be suspicious.

Another variation on the same theme is to remove the 'S' mintmark from a 1916-S dime and replace it with a 'D.' Also fairly common is the reshaping of the existing 'S' mintmark into a 'D.' Inversion of the second numeral 9 on a genuine 1919-D is less often attempted, since this coin is valuable in itself in higher grades. All of these techniques are crude, and their effectiveness depends entirely on a lack of numismatic learning on the part of the potential buyer. Most such alterations date from the late 1950s through the late 1960s. This period corresponds to the years in which coin collecting enjoyed its most widespread popularity. A vast number of unknowledgeable persons, including many children, were discovering the hobby for the first time, and they were easy prey for the unscrupulous. Along with 1914-D Lincoln Cents, 1913-S Type 2 Buffalo Nickels and 1932-D and 1932-S quarters, the 1916-D Mercury Dime was high on the list of most frequently altered coins.

Other common subjects of falsification have been dimes dated 1921(P), 1921-D and 1942/41(P). The first two are most often simulated by removing the numeral 4 from genuine dimes dated 1941(P) and 1941-D, respectively, and replacing it with the 2 from one dated 1942. To the knowledgeable, however, there are several ways to detect this ruse. First of all, the 9 on a genuine 1921 dime is open, rather than being closed as on a 1941 dime. In addition, the numerals 1 on a 1921 are of a unique style used only in that year. Finally, the mintmark on a 1921-D dime is of the small size used 1917-34, while the 1941-D has a much larger 'D' of the type used 1934-45. A comparison of the genuine 1916-D, 1921(P), 1921-D and 1942/41(P) dimes shown in Chapter 6 with the altered coins illustrated here will reveal these various distinctions. The characteristics of the genuine coins are likewise shown in enlarged photographs within Chapter 6.

Beginning in the 1970s a concerted effort was undertaken to drive such fakes from the marketplace. Working with reputable coin dealers, the American Numismatic Association did much to educate collectors with respect to the characteristics of genuine key date coins. A further advance was the introduction by the ANA and the International Numismatic Society of authentication services staffed by skilled counterfeit detectors. These services have largely been supplanted in recent years by commercial grading companies. Implicit in the grading and encapsulation of any piece submitted is the graders' conclusion that the subject coin is genuine, and the major grading services carry authentication guarantees. All of these developments have been effective in making altered and counterfeit coins at least as rare at coin shows as their genuine counterparts. Fakes are still known to make the rounds at country auctions and flea markets, but then these have never been good places to buy rare coins. Making coin purchases through Internet auctions should likewise be approached with considerable caution, as few sellers carry reliable guarantees. Ideally, collectors should buy only from legitimate numismatic dealers and auctioneers who sell previously authenticated coins or are prepared to refund the purchase of any piece which subsequently proves to be counterfeit or altered.

Although die-struck counterfeits of numismatic quality are fairly rare within the Mercury Dime series, both 1916-D and 1942/41(P) dimes have been the subject of skillfully crafted fakes. These were manufactured during the early 1970s and may still be lurking within the marketplace. They were apparently struck from transfer dies which had been generated from authentic coins. In the case of the 1916-D counterfeits, although sharply detailed, they lack the textured fields and slightly diffused luster characteristic of this date, having the more brilliant surfaces typically seen in later coins. Still, both of these fakes are good enough to deceive collectors and dealers who possess average numismatic knowledge, and one's best bet is to have coins of these dates authenticated.

Although it's technically illegal to possess a counterfeit United States coin, the cruder examples are considered sufficiently non-threatening that they've become collectable. These pieces are always traded with the clear understanding that they're bogus, and many hobbyists like to own a few for purposes of education and amusement.

Within the Mercury Dime series, two pieces stand out as perhaps the most interesting counterfeits to have surfaced. These are the so-called "Soviet" counterfeits dated 1923-D and 1930-D, two date/mint combinations never coined by the United States Mint. Therein lies their mystery and charm.

Like many coin collectors growing up during the 1960s, the author scanned each day's pocket change carefully for Mercury Dimes needed to fill his Whitman folder. In between discoveries, much time was spent in going through the Red Book,[1] memorizing mintage figures and daydreaming of the wonderful early date dimes which never seemed to materialize. Among the more puzzling entries was a footnote informing the reader that dimes dated 1923-D and 1930-D were counterfeit. No further information was given, and one was left wondering when and where such coins had been found. As with most dates before 1940, these too eluded the author in his search for Mercury Dimes.

The story of these mystery coins actually begins during the 1930s, but this account will start with the first knowledge of them by American collectors. A small notice was published in The Numismatist in June of 1940, the earliest reference to these strange coins: "D. F. Townsend, of Fort Dodge, Iowa, reports that a friend of his has a 1930-D dime in his collection in very fine condition. The mint reports show no coinage for the dimes at the Denver Mint in 1930. Can any readers give some information on this issue?" Obviously no one could, as nothing further appeared in the literature at that time, and the matter was quickly forgotten for the next few years.

A 1949 letter to Editor Lee F. Hewitt of The Numismatic Scrapbook Magazine began with a reference to a previously published letter in which another reader reported finding a 1933-D dime, a piece which no doubt was altered from 1938-D or some such thing. (Collectors of that time possessed little knowledge of how coins were made, and people were always reporting fanciful items of no real merit). What makes this follow-up letter interesting is that it contains the first published reference to a coin which would become the source of more than a little controversy over the next fifteen years:

> ...I have a 1923-D dime and it certainly appears to be genuine. I had it to a couple dealers and they weighed it and said if it is counterfeit it is a wonderful job.

> I wrote to the Denver Mint and asked them if there were possibly some minted for that year and they said that none had been minted. However the date and the D seem so perfect that I wonder.

> I found it while going thru some coins about two years ago. After seeing that item in your magazine I thot [sic] this little bit of information might interest you.

> E. B. Hurley, Phoenix, Ariz.[2]

Like many items published in Hewitt's monthly journal, this letter was printed without comment or investigation and was soon forgotten by most readers. It was not until two years later that a second dime of similar character was reported by A. H. Leatherman of Doylestown, Pennsylvania:

> A local Mercury dime collector complained to me that the dime board she had did not provide spaces for all the dimes. I told her if she had a dime for which no space was provided I wanted to see the dime, — not the board. Sure enough, she did have such a dime. It was a 1930 Denver Mint, out of circulation, of course. The Mint record says none were coined and I never saw any before. I gave it a searching examination and can find nothing wrong with it except the motto on the obverse is distinctly double struck. I showed it to several of my dealer friends in New York and Phila. and they are equally mystified by such a monstrosity. I am convinced it must be a phony of some kind but none of us can detect what is wrong with it. I wonder, has anyone else seen anything like that at any time? [3]

The answer to Mr. Leatherman's inquiry was, of course, yes. It had been just two years since the reporting of an almost perfect 1923-D dime and eleven years since the first announcement of a 1930-D. Evidently, no connection was made at the time. These two accounts are eerily similar in

that both persons suspected their dimes were counterfeit, while the local experts were unable to decide just what was wrong with the coins.

Amid the oftseen and quickly forgotten reports of unusual and hitherto unknown coins, claims which were so common to the hobby at that time, the dimes dated 1923-D and 1930-D stood out. In fact, these became the imaginary coins which would not go away. Rumors of their existence continued throughout the 1950s, as specimens turned up in limited numbers nationwide. As of 1959, some 47 examples of the 1923-D dime had been counted.[4] All seemed to be quite worn; in fact, nearly all specimens were identically worn. In most instances the degree of wear was also not consistent with other dimes of similar vintage then still in circulation.

By 1963 the subject of these mystery coins could no longer be avoided in print. Responding to an inquiry from a collector in Florida who owned a 1923-D dime, the weekly newspaper *Coin World* launched an investigation which sought to settle the matter once and for all. As with other owners of 1923-D and 1930-D dimes, the individual who provided his specimen for examination reported that the dealers to whom he'd shown it could not reach a consensus, being about equally divided as to whether it was genuine or counterfeit. Using this example as a test case, *Coin World* enlisted the services of several recognized authorities in United States coins. The first to render an opinion was Q. David Bowers, well known today as a prominent dealer and the author of countless books and articles on USA coins. In 1963 he was in partnership with James F. Ruddy as Empire Coin Company. His observations were published as follows:

> This coin is one of the most famous American counterfeits, a coin which appears several times a year in various places to plague collectors, and usually disappoints its owner after he spends time and effort only to learn that it is a counterfeit.

> This piece is not a cast or an electrotype, but is struck from dies. The lettering is thinner and not as well formed as on the originals.

This coin falls into the interesting category of counterfeits in which the counterfeiters were not numismatists, and created coins which had no official counterparts ...[5]

Two of the most prominent figures in the study of United States coins at that time were Don Taxay and Walter Breen. At the time of the *Coin World* study, they staffed the Institute of Numismatic Authenticators, a now forgotten commercial venture which was the pioneer in this field. Under the banner of the INA, Breen and Taxay prepared the following joint determination:

The 1923-D dime is nothing more or less than a struck counterfeit, made from skillfully hand-cut dies at some unknown time and place, but thought to have been possibly of Soviet Russia origin like numerous other modern silver struck counterfeits.

The variations found in the 1923-D dime which enable it to be positively identified as not from dies produced from Philadelphia Mint hubs follow...[6]

The two experts went on to detail the characteristics of a genuine Mercury Dime and specified how the corresponding features of the counterfeit 1923-D differed. They then amplified their comments:

After 1916, dime dies were fully hubbed, any differences (other than placement and possible size of Mint marks) being microscopic or nearly so, and originating in clashing, minor shifting, or (as in the case of the overdate) unintentional use of two different hubs on the same working die.

Differences in letter placement or shape can be excluded by knowledge of the minting processes then in use, and their presence on a suspected coin is confirmatory of its non-Mint origin.

When this situation is combined with the presence on the coin of a date-mint mark combination not known to exist on genuine dimes, as in 1923-D and 1930-D, evidence of non-Mint (counterfeit) origin, already conclusive, becomes blatant.

In their summation, Breen and Taxay addressed the background of these counterfeits:

The 1923-D dimes have only been reported since World War II, and all are similarly worn... an extremely suspicious circumstance even for coins reported from circulation, as they have more than the normal amount of wear for dimes of the 1920's. [Author's comments: In fact, they were less worn than most genuine dimes of those years. They were also known as early as 1940, but this fact had been forgotten by 1963.]

In conclusion, the combination of excellent die work and an egregious blunder (of a non-existent date-mint mark combination) points to a foreign origin, very likely the Soviet Union, which has a known record of counterfeiting U. S. silver coins during World War II.

This last remark lies at the heart of what makes these counterfeit dimes so interesting and collectable. The mystery which began for American coin collectors during the late 1940s actually originated in the Stalinist Russia of the 1930s. Although rumors of a Soviet connection had passed in some circles, the collecting fraternity was not apprised of this fact until 1957.

At that time New Netherlands Coin Company in New York City was one of the prestige firms of the hobby, and its house organ *Numisma* was eagerly awaited by advanced collectors seeking knowledge of United States coins. John J Ford, Jr. was the editor of *Numisma*, and it was he who penned the following account. His wartime service in the army saw him posted to the American headquarters for the European Theater of Operations, a position in which he would have been privy to the gossip concerning Russian/American relations. His remarks reveal much of the curious history behind the dimes dated 1923-D and 1930-D:

To the best of our knowledge, these are counterfeits made of good silver and struck from excellent false dies — evidencing better technical facilities than those available to American crime rings. They were made, along with many worn-appearing (dateless) Liberty Standing quarters, prior to and during World War II — and probably to the present day — in the Soviet Union. Evidence of this practice turned up during the war, but nothing was done because of the probability of antagonizing our "gallant Soviet ally!" The Soviet technical experts evidentially perfected some process of transferring genuine designs from coins to plaster and from plaster to steel dies, the latter presumably by some machine similar to the Contamin portrait-lathe used in Philadelphia and Tower Hill (English) mints for over a century. They also have good silver, heavy presses and collars — equipment available to no American counterfeiter. The purpose has nothing to do with numismatics. So far as we know these coins were intended (like those made by the Chinese and Italian imitators of American gold coins) to pass as a circulating medium. Silver, or gold, in the form of coins seemingly backed by a stable government, can be spent at a far better rate (i.e. has a higher purchasing power) than its bullion price as ingots. The Soviet imitations have evidently succeeded, as to date all specimens seen are considerably worn. The differences between them and the genuine are microscopic. It is highly likely that other dates have been manufactured and passed unnoticed. Fortunately for us, the quantities passed in this country have apparently been too small to disturb the economy.[7]

To the opinions of the above-quoted authorities, the author has only a few comments to add. The first of these is that much of the wear evident in these counterfeit dimes seems to have originated with the host coins from which the transfer dies were evidently made. In other words, two different coins (hence the mismatched date/mintmark combination), both moderately worn, were employed in the generating of counterfeit dies. The author does not agree with Breen and Taxay that the dies were hand cut. The similarity of these coins to genuine pieces is simply too great to allow for this possibility.

The weight of the 1923-D dime illustrated is 2.41 grams, less than a tenth of a gram under normal. This observation, when combined with the fact that the dime was obviously coined of fine silver, establishes that it was not the work of conventional counterfeiters. The net profit would simply have been too small for a circulating counterfeit, and there was little chance of establishing this coin as a numismatic rarity. There remains no reason to doubt that the Soviet connection was a valid one, and this makes for a very interesting and collectable tie-in for a set of Mercury Dimes.

Dimes dated 1930-D are far more scarce than examples of 1923-D, and a specimen could not be located for inclusion in this book. It's assumed that its characteristics are similar to those of the more abundant 1923-D. Curiously, more than 40 years after they were widely publicized in *Coin World*, these infamous counterfeits are largely unknown to the current generation of hobbyists. They still appear in the Red Book as a footnote, but specimens of either date are now rarely seen in the marketplace or in the numismatic press. It's likely that their fame fell victim to the passing of Mercury Dimes from circulation.

Although not intended to deceive numismatists, another category of altered Mercury Dimes exists which may cause some misunderstanding when first encountered. Within this category fall love tokens, magician's coins and elongated dimes.

A love token is any coin on which one or both sides have been partly or wholly effaced to receive an engraved message or sentiment. Most commonly seen on dimes, these personalized tokens were presented to loved ones as a remembrance of the giver or as a souvenir of some special occasion or anniversary. The practice of manufacturing love tokens reached a climax during the years 1880 to 1900, and this accounts for the fact that most were fabricated from Seated Liberty and Barber Dimes, very few from Mercury Dimes. A rare example of the latter is illustrated here, along with one piece which was engraved without any particular message. It seems to have been simply the result of a few moments idleness in which the engraver revised the outlines of Liberty's hair and wing.

A numismatic curiosity of a more commercial nature is the traditional magician's coin. This is made by halving lengthwise a dime and a cent and then bonding the two together. This makes for a coin which is a dime on one side and a cent on the other. Through sleight of hand, the magician can make the coin appear to change from cent to dime, or vice versa.

Since the cent is larger in diameter, its edge must first be turned down in a lathe or simply filed to the appropriate size. The accompanying photos show how the coins are mated. Two magician's coins may be produced from each such operation. Another, simpler trick is to cut two dimes and bond the halves such that one two-headed dime is produced, along with one having two tails. Although many such coins have actually been used by magicians, most were made to sell as novelty items. Quite a few have no doubt guaranteed the outcome of a coin toss.

A popular area of collecting is the field of rolled-out, or elongated, coins. These are ordinary coins which have been compressed between two rollers, one being blank and the other having a souvenir or commemorative design. This special design is thus imparted to the host coin, while the coin's other side retains a faint image of its original design. These novelty coins first appeared during the World's Columbian Exposition at Chicago in 1893. Although outlawed briefly around the time of World War II, their manufacture has been a thriving business in recent years. The author has encountered no examples of rolled-out Mercury Dimes but it's reasonably safe to assume that some must exist, and more can be made from new elongate dies at any time.

A rolled-out souvenir of another sort was created in 1923 by legendary numismatist Farran Zerbe, who was then president of the Pacific Coast Numismatic Society. He forwarded it to a friend in San Francisco, along with a typewritten note:

> A 1923 U.S. dime over which passed the funeral train (Penna.R.R., two locomotives and twelve pullmans) of President Harding at Tyrone, Penna., at 1:07 a.m., Thursday, August 9, 1923. All that could from the surrounding country and the town assembled in silent sad tribute. No train could have moved less noiselessly; no people could have been more reverent.
>
> Placed on the rails by me particularly for my pal Charles B. Turrill of San Francisco. *(signed)* Farran Zerbe.[8]

President of the United States Warren G. Harding had died suddenly while in San Francisco, and his funeral train made a slow and dramatic journey across the continent enroute to Washington, D.C. Zerbe created this souvenir while in his hometown of Tyrone, Pennsylvania. Charles B. Turrill succeeded him as president of the PCNS in 1924 and served in that capacity until his death three years later. In the settlement of his estate, this commemorative piece was presented to the society, where it remained until the recent dispersal of the society's various collections.

Finally, in the realm of the ridiculous are dimes which have simply been damaged or chemically corroded. An example of the latter is illustrated. Surprisingly, such coins still make their way to the columnists in weekly coin newspapers who must tactfully explain to the submitters that their prizes are nothing more than worthless junk. It seems that every new collector is puzzled by these mystery coins at one time or another. It's therefore all the more important to study the genuine error coins shown previously in this chapter so that an understanding of the minting process may be gained.

---

[1] Yeoman, Richard S. *A Guide Book of United States Coins.*
[2] *The Numismatic Scrapbook Magazine,* July 1949.
[3] ibid, June 1951.
[4] ibid, August 1959.
[5] "Noted Numismatists Offer Comment on Controversial 1923-D Mercury." *Coin World,* October 18, 1963.
[6] ibid.
[7] *Numisma,* July-August 1957.
[8] Archives of the Pacific Coast Numismatic Society.

1916-D with added D of the style of 1916-17. *(Courtesy of the American Numismatic Association Museum)*

This love token bears ornate letters "GB," likely being the initials of either the giver or receiver *(Courtesy of Ken Barr)*

1916-D with added D of the style of 1934-45. *(ANA)*

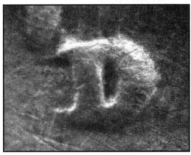

This false mintmark appears to have been created by chasing the coin's field. *(ANA)*

The obverse of this 1916-S dime has been enhanced through some amateur engraving. In this respect, it's akin to the engraved "hobo nickels" which are still being made by those having an abundance of free time. *(Barr)*

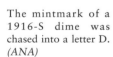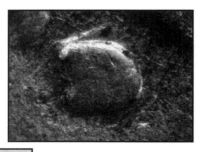

The mintmark of a 1916-S dime was chased into a letter D. *(ANA)*

1921(P) devised by removal of the 4 from a 1941 dime and the addition of the 2 from a 1942 dime *(ANA)*

A genuine 1916 dime obverse was attached to a genuine "D" mint reverse of another date. *(ANA)*

1942/41 devised by the addition of the 2 from a 1942 dime to an ordinary 1941(P) dime. Note that the upright of the 4 has also been altered to simulate the genuine overdate and the entire coin abrasively cleaned to conceal the work. *(ANA)*

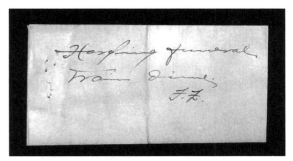

A 1923 dime flattened by President Harding's funeral train. The fasces is just barely visible on the reverse of this coin, though it's difficult to see in the photo.
(Courtesy of the Pacific Coast Numismatic Society)

The envelope in which Zerbe presented the funeral train commemorative bears his notation.
(PCNS)

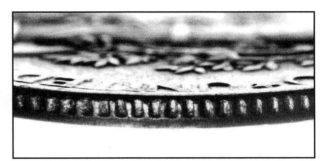

Dual denomination "magician's coin".
(Courtesy of Peter F. Hamilton)

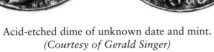

Acid-etched dime of unknown date and mint.
(Courtesy of Gerald Singer)

The infamous 1923-D Soviet dime.
(Courtesy of Vic Rollo)

CHAPTER 5

Grading

✳

Estimating Rarity

Grading

In comparison with many other United States coins the Mercury Dime is one of the easier types to grade. Aside from some irregularities in strike, particularly among the coins from 1917 through 1928, the established criteria (as modified somewhat in this guide) may be applied to any date in the series.

There are some general guidelines that apply and which should be taken into consideration when grading. The first of these is that no Mercury Dime struck from 1925 through 1945 will be as finely detailed as well struck specimens of earlier dates. The reason for this is that the master hubs from which new master dies were drawn became worn with repeated use. This is particularly true of the obverse master hub, as a new obverse master die had to be sunk for each date in the series. The reverse master die could be used as long as it remained serviceable, and thus its master hub did not deteriorate as quickly.

Such loss of detail is most evident in the hair curls framing Liberty's face. The finest lines were obliterated by 1925, and further erosion occurred as the series progressed. Evidence of this is found in examining the proof dimes of 1936-42. One would expect these to be the finest examples available to represent the Mercury Dime type. While their high relief detail is superior to that of the typical production coin from the same period, they fall short of the standards set by the best circulation strikes of 1916 through 1924. These deficiencies are noteworthy only for

grades Very Fine through About Uncirculated, as lower grade coins lack the details in question.

Another point which bears mentioning is that most dimes coined at the Denver and San Francisco Mints from 1917 through 1928 will exhibit some areas of weakness. This is commonly seen in the centers of their obverse and reverse or around their peripheries. In particularly bad instances, deficiencies will be found in both locations. The 1925-D Mercury Dime illustrated here is a textbook example of this most extreme case. Liberty's curls are almost entirely flat, the lower diagonal band and all horizontal bands are flat and the peripheral legends are "topless." Both the date and mintmark are indistinct, the latter being particularly so. From its luster and its absence of wear this dime technically grades About Uncirculated, but how is a value determined for such a coin?

Experience will enable one to distinguish between weakness of strike and legitimate wear. The matter of how to price weakly struck coins remains an ongoing concern for both dealers and collectors, with no obvious solution in sight. In practice, coins which meet most of the criteria for the assignment of a particular grade will usually receive that grade and may be valued in accordance with current price guides. This is particularly true of dates which are highly in demand but which are often found inadequately struck. Well struck specimens of the same dates will usually command a premium.

For the most part the grading criteria presented here are in agreement with the standards established by the American Numismatic Association in its book, *Official Grading Standards for United States Coins,* Fifth Edition. There is one minor exception, however. In careful examination of a great many circulated coins, it was the author's conclusion that the reverse of the Mercury Dime wore more rapidly than most grading standards suggest. This was probably due to the slightly shallower rims of the reverse offering less protection. When graded by conventional

standards, most circulated coins will have a split grade such as Fine on the obverse and Very Good to Fine on the reverse. In numismatic shorthand this is expressed as F/VG-F. While the conventional standards for all series of U. S. coins dictate that a coin grading Good will have complete rims on both sides, this is rarely true of the Mercury Dime, as its reverse rim will have worn into the lettering by the time its obverse has been reduced to the grade of Good.

In selecting coins for the following grading guide, the author has compensated for such bias by including pieces which show the actual relationship between obverse and reverse at the various grade levels. It's believed that the reader will find the standards presented here to be truly reflective of coins encountered in the market-place. **These standards, however, do not exactly reflect those published by the American Numismatic Association.**

AG-2 (ABOUT GOOD)

OBVERSE: Liberty's head is entirely outlined but with no details visible. All digits of the date can be identified, although heavily worn. The rim has worn away the top of each letter in the legend.

REVERSE: The fasces is entirely flat. The rim has worn halfway through the legend and touches the bottom of the fasces.

G-4 (GOOD)

OBVERSE: The curls of Liberty's hair, although flat, are outlined clearly against her cap. The date is entirely distinguishable, although the final digit may be weak. The rim is worn to the tops of the letters.

REVERSE: The fasces is flat but separated from the rim, which has worn one-third of the way through the legend.

VG-8 (VERY GOOD)

OBVERSE: The rim is complete and entirely separated from the legend. Some details are evident in Liberty's wing.

REVERSE: A few lines are visible in the fasces. The rim is entirely separated from the legend.

F-12 (FINE)

OBVERSE: Liberty's curls are partly distinguishable against her face. Her wing feathers are evident, although heavily worn. The rim is bold and the date entirely separated from it.

REVERSE: The vertical lines are about half visible though a portion of all of them will show. The horizontal and diagonal bands are visible only at their extremities. The rim is distinct, though shallow.

VF-20 (VERY FINE)

OBVERSE: Libertys curls are distinct against her face. The wing is complete, though moderately worn.

REVERSE: The vertical lines are entirely visible but shallow. The horizontal and diagonal bands are complete but flat at their centers. The rim is bold.

XF-40 (EXTREMELY FINE)

OBVERSE: All details are distinct though lightly worn. Some mint luster may be evident within protected parts of the design such as the legend and the date.

REVERSE: The vertical lines are sharp. All bands are distinct but may be lightly worn at their centers. The diagonal bands are three-dimensional. Some mint luster may be evident within protected parts of the design such as the legend, the olive branch and the denomination.

AU-50 (ABOUT UNCIRCULATED)

OBVERSE: All details are bold. Only slight wear is evident on the highest points of Liberty's face, hair and wing and in the exposed parts of the field. One-third to one-half of the mint luster remains.

REVERSE: The bands are bold. Light wear is evident on the bands and in the exposed parts of the field. One-third to one-half of the mint luster remains.

AU-55, AU-53 & AU-58
(ABOUT UNCIRCULATED)

These grades are similar to AU-50 in that they represent nearly unworn coins. The distinction is made in their relative surface quality and in the amount of luster evident.

The AU-53 grade was created by commercial certification companies and is not recognized by the ANA. It is so seldom used by these companies that it typically carries no premium over AU-50, except in the case of very valuable coins. It may be described as a "nice" AU-50.

AU-55 is applied to a coin which displays about two thirds of the original luster and no serious marks.

AU-58 describes a coin which is essentially uncirculated but may have been mishandled. Coins of this grade may have been chemically dipped as a means of cleaning, but this should not be obvious to the casual observer. Nearly full luster must be present. Specimens grading AU-58 are sometimes called "sliders," because when sold uncertified they are often labeled by the seller as Uncirculated.

MS-60 (MINT STATE)

This is the lowest numerical grade at which a coin may qualify as being Mint State, or Uncirculated. Such coins must show no sign of wear and have no breaks in their luster, yet nearly any other detraction is permissible. This includes numerous or heavy abrasions, nicks and scratches, spotting or unattractive toning. It may also be that a particular coin is simply deficient in luster or strike, as made.

MS-63 (MINT STATE)

A coin having several noticeable contact marks but which is lustrous and reasonably well struck will merit this grade. Some fine hairlines may also downgrade an otherwise gem coin to the MS-63 level. It's perhaps the most popular grade with collectors of Mint State coins because it offers the best compromise between beauty and economy. In this book's date/mint analysis, coins grading MS-63 are often referred to simply as "choice" specimens.

MS-64 (MINT STATE)

Essentially, MS-64 describes a coin which is better than MS-63 and not quite as good as MS-65. The distinction between the three grades lies primarily in overall surface quality and in the placement and severity of contact marks. A mark on Liberty's cheek or in the exposed fields may render a coin MS-63, while the same mark hidden within the wing or the olive branch can elevate that specimen to MS-64. A less severe mark likewise hidden within these finely detailed elements can result in an MS-65 grade. The term "choice" is sometimes used within the date/mint analysis of this book to describe dimes grading MS-64.

MS-65 (MINT STATE)

The grade favored by investors, MS-65 is the coin market's designation for a "gem," by which term these coins may also be referred to in the date/mint analysis. It describes a specimen which is fully lustrous, well struck though not necessarily fully struck, and free of any but the most minor contact marks. It is likewise free of hairlines.

MS-67 (MINT STATE)

The book Official A.N.A. Grading Standards for United States Coins defines this grade rather vaguely as, "Virtually flawless but with very minor imperfections." Therein lies the problem in attempting to describe grades above MS-65: It is simply impossible to do so effectively in words or photographs. Collectors will have to learn these subtle distinctions for themselves by examining coins certified by the major grading services. Another valuable tool is the hands-on grading seminars conducted by the ANA in connection with major coin shows or during its two-week annual Summer Seminar at the ANA's headquarters in Colorado Springs. Both are highly recommended for persons desiring to own Mercury Dimes in these higher grades.

A NOTE ABOUT THE REMAINING GRADES: In addition to the grades listed above, it is no secret that additional grade levels are recognized within the marketplace. For example, a dime grading G-VG may also be abbreviated as G-6. Other grades within the circulated span include VG-10, F-15, VF-25, VF-35 and XF-45. Whether or not a particular Mercury Dime merits an intermediate grade is a matter of opinion, though these grades are recognized and used by the major grading services

Additional grades for Uncirculated coins include MS-61, MS-62, MS-66 and MS-68 through MS-70. The first two are little used with respect to this series, as only a handful of dates in the Mercury Dime series advance enough in price from MS-60 to MS-63 to warrant submitting them to the certification services. Still, such grades are occasionally assigned by the commercial grading services, particularly for pre-1928 issues. The grades of MS-66 and MS-67 are widely used for later issues in the Mercury Dime series, as these coins often survive in such splendid condition. The MS-68 and MS-69 grades are very difficult to achieve, the latter presently being limited to just a few dates within the certified population reports.

MS-70 was, for many years, merely a reference point, as it identifies a theoretically perfect coin. With the growing popularity of modern (1965 and later) coins, however, this grade has been employed for pieces that are flawless to the naked eye. Since this describes no Mercury Dime yet seen by this author, it's doubtful that any coin in this series, whether Mint State or Proof, will achieve this grade.

A NOTE ABOUT FULL BANDS: Mercury Dimes are among the few series of United States coins in which otherwise equal coins may be of dramatically different value as the result of a minor feature. Being directly opposite the highest relief point of the obverse design the central horizontal bands of the fasces are often struck incompletely. The displacement of metal at the moment of striking is not sufficient to entirely fill the die cavity, and this particular element usually bears the loss.

Although the large premiums attached to full band coins did not appear until the 1970s, collectors have long sought to complete their sets of Uncirculated Mercury Dimes with all of the date/mint combinations having fully struck bands. This is a near impossibility, as certain dates are almost unknown in such condition. The most glaring example of this is 1945(P), an otherwise common entry in the series which is extremely rare with full bands. Other dates for which full band specimens are rare include 1917-D, 1918-D, 1918-S, 1919-D, 1919-S, 1931-S, 1935-D and 1939-S. In reviewing the date/mint analysis that follows, it will be seen that these and many other dates carry noticeable premiums when found with full bands.

The photographs present three examples having different degrees of separation and fullness in their central bands. On the first of these, the bands are entirely flat. The second dime has central bands which are separated but are lacking in relief. Although purists may consider this to be an example of simply "split bands," the marketplace generally accepts this degree of separation as representing "full bands." The third photo is of a coin with fully separated and rounded bands which entirely filled the die. Notice the degree of relief in comparison with the split bands coin. While this example is the ideal of "full bands," many coins so designated in the marketplace will not be quite this bold. A certain license is granted for dates which are rare with full bands, and this fact is accepted by most parties.

This dime grades About Uncirculated but is so weakly struck
that it is barely identifiable as a 1925-D.
(Courtesy of David & Ginger Pike)

  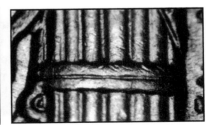

Flat bands
(Courtesy of Bill Fivaz)

Split bands
(Fivaz)

Full bands

Estimating Rarity

Determining the rarity of the various date and mint combinations within the Mercury Dime series in circulated grades is largely a matter of experience, as most issues are not valuable enough to merit submission to the grading services. While individuals will each have their own particular issues which they consider to be underrated "sleepers," a general concensus has evolved over the years as to the availability of each coin in the various grades. This is the basis of the price structure that's in effect at any given time. In assembling a collection of this series, one will come to learn firsthand whether or not the current price structure is valid.

Acquiring a working knowledge of the rarity of this series in Mint State or Uncirculated grades has been made easier in recent years with the advent of grading services. These companies issue population reports which include a running total of the grades assigned by them to the coins submitted for certification. These reports appear in hardcopy editions either monthly or quarterly, but more frequent updates appear at the companies' websites. Over time, a pattern emerges to indicate which coins exist in various levels of preservation. Although circulated pieces are not excluded from these reports, only a few issues have sufficient value to justify their submission. Thus, with the exception of these key dates, the population reports are essentially limited to Mint State and Proof coins.

Although a useful tool, these population reports are not entirely accurate. Even if one assumes that the grades assigned are agreeable to the majority of collectors and dealers, the nature of the grading business is such that misleading figures may appear. The most obvious problem is that there is no way to prevent the same coin from being submitted again and again in an effort to achieve a higher grade. If the coin is first removed from its certified encapsulation, it will be recorded as an additional coin in the population report rather than as a resubmission. Recognizing this flaw, the grading services encourage submitters to return certification labels

for removal from the published population. While it's hoped that this will cut down on the number of blind resubmissions, there is no way to enforce this policy on an unwilling submitter. Likewise, there is no way to prevent the removal of a certified coin from its holder and its subsequent submission to another service. In a booming market for rare coins, a single specimen may be resubmitted to the same service or to another one upwards of a dozen times, since the profit differential between one grade and the next highest grade is sometimes enough to justify the additional overhead.

These irregularities in the population reports are not sufficient reason to discard this information altogether. On the contrary, the certified population of a particular coin has become a valuable reference figure, not to mention a useful marketing tool in the case of rare pieces. This brings up an important point: A low certified population for an expensive coin is more meaningful than a low figure for an inexpensive coin. Obviously, the value of a particular specimen has to justify the expense of having it certified, which generally includes payment of registered mail fees in addition to the cost of the service itself. A low population report may simply mean that a particular issue is simply too valueless to warrant certification. Many dates after 1935 do not warrant the price of certification in today's market unless they are expected to achieve a high grade.

This brings up another cautionary note about certified populations. Most inexpensive Mercury Dimes are submitted under bulk submission programs offered exclusively to dealer customers. When large quantities are submitted, the coins may be graded and encapsulated at fees lower than those published for the public, which is the only way to make the certification of common dates cost effective. The reason this affects the certified population in a misleading manner is that the submitter will always specify a minimum grade below which the coins are not to be encapsulated. Thus, while 300 common date Mercury Dimes may be submitted for grading, perhaps only half that number will achieve the specified minimum grade, the remainder being returned in raw form. This tends to exaggerate the relative percentage of high grade coins for the common dates, implying that gems are the norm for these issues.

As for circulated coins, the population reports are meaningful mostly with respect to the following dates: 1916-D, 1921, 1921-D, 1942/1 and 1942/1-D. These coins are the ones most likely to be submitted in circulated grades, because there are concerns about authenticity and value across the entire grade spectrum. Semi-key dates such as the mintmarked coins from 1917 through 1926 are also candidates for certification in grades Very Fine and higher. It is rare for any other dates to be submitted for certification in less than Mint State condition (though many of the AU listings are likely for coins that the submitter believed to be Uncirculated). There are, however, unique exceptions to this logic. As a longtime employee of NGC, the author has seen numerous instances in which collectors, for reasons known to themselves alone, opted to submit common date, heavily worn Mercury Dimes for grading and encapsulation. These are coins that carry only their bullion value in the coin market, but they must have possessed some sentimental value to their submitters.

In the current coin market very few collectors still seek to complete the Mercury Dime series in grades below Fine, only the key dates being desirable in such condition. This is a reflection of the changing pattern of coin collecting in general. Until the 1960s a person could begin assembling a partial set from circulation. While the key dates were always difficult to locate, the greater part of the series could be obtained with diligence, even as late as 1960. Building on this foundation, collectors seeking to complete their sets by purchasing the dates still needed were apt to be satisfied with low grade examples, as these matched the coins they'd taken from pocket change. It was only when Mercury Dimes disappeared entirely from circulation that this notion of simply filling the various holes with the first available example came to an end. Subsequent generations of collectors have been required to purchase even the

most common dates at a premium. This has led to a greater emphasis on quality, with the result that there now exists little demand for low grade examples of any but the scarcest dates.

In its most extreme form, this shifting emphasis toward quality has resulted in gem examples of certain dates bringing many times the value of average Uncirculated pieces. In the mainstream of collecting, however, the greatest interest in this series lies in the grades of Fine through Mint State 64. Particularly popular with budget minded collectors are Mercury Dimes grading Extremely Fine and About Uncirculated, as these grades offer a wealth of detail and a certain degree of luster, while being priced well below the Mint State levels. Sadly for collectors and dealers alike, it's in these very grades that so many dates are least often found. This is particularly true of mintmarked dimes from 1917 through 1931, which are in some instances more available in Mint State than in grades XF and AU. When found in the higher circulated grades, such coins are very often damaged and/or badly cleaned. Ironically, though often scarcer and in more demand than the low-end Mint State grades, the values of these XF-AU coins are held in check by the depressed prices for the MS-60 through MS-62 grades, in which most Mercury Dimes are difficult to sell.

All of this has had the effect of discouraging the dispersal of collections. No one is likely to offer better date XF and AU Mercury Dimes for sale when their prices have advanced so little in recent decades. It's therefore difficult to assess just how many coins are in existence in these grades. Much the same may be said of pre-1934 issues grading Fine and Very Fine, as the values of these coins have likewise been subdued by limited movement within the lower Mint State grades. As this is written in early 2005, the coin market is experiencing a wave of rising prices that has seen the value of coins such as the 1916-D dime nearly double in just a couple of years. If this trend continues to affect the entire Mercury Dime series, then conditions will be right to draw out some of these scarce coins that presumably have been sitting idle for decades.

CHAPTER 6

Date & Mint Analysis

GUIDE TO USING THIS ANALYSIS:

1. "Ranking" refers to the placement of that particular date/mint combination's mintage within the overall series from lowest mintage to highest. In other words, the date/mint with the lowest mintage is ranked 1/77, while the issue with the highest mintage is 77/77.
2. "DDO, DDR, RPM, and OMM" designations are taken from CONECA's master index.
3. "Combined NGC & PCGS Population" refers to the total number of coins certified by Numismatic Guaranty Corporation and Professional Coin Grading Service in the respective grades listed. The grades included are the ones most sought by collectors of Mercury Dimes. These figures are taken from the October 2004 editions of the *NGC Census Report* and the *PCGS Population Report*.
4. Values listed for 1945 are taken from the *The Standard Catalogue of United States Coins 1945 Edition*, Wayte Raymond, Editor. Values listed for 1955, 1965, 1975, 1985, 1995 and 2005 are from the 8th, 18th, 28th, 38th, 48th and 58th editions of *A Guide Book of United States Coins* by R. S. Yeoman, more recently edited by Kenneth Bressett. The earlier editions did not use numerical grading, but it may be assumed that entries described simply as "UNC" described what we now call MS-60. Therefore, the values taken from these editions have thus been assigned the MS-60 grade for continuity with later entries. The values for higher grades are more volatile, being subject to changes in the certified population. Readers are referred to *The Coin Dealer Newsletter, The Certified Coin Dealer Newsletter* and *Numismedia* for current valuations.
5. The term "choice" in reference to grading describes a coin whose numerical grade would be MS-63 or MS-64. The term "gem" refers to a coin grading MS-65. The term "superb gem" refers to a coin grading MS-66 or higher.

1916

Mintage:
22,180,080
(Ranking 42/77)

Popular Varieties: None are reported.

The Mercury Dime series is not especially rich in varieties. Despite the earnest efforts of many variety specialists searching through many thousands of Mercury Dimes, precious few collectable varieties have surfaced.

Rarity: As the first year of issue, thousands of 1916 Mercury Dimes were set aside. Since the majority of coin collectors, as well as the population in general, then lived in the Eastern states, most saved were from the Philadelphia Mint. These coins survive today as Uncirculated or nearly so. Gem specimens having full bands (designated FB by the grading services) are plentiful, as are low grade coins ranging from Poor to Very Good. Sliders, or dimes grading About Uncirculated, are usually available. Grades Fine through Extremely Fine are somewhat less available, and this remains true of most issues through the 1920s.

A fair number of examples have been certified in grades higher than those listed below, a fact which is rarely true of other issues before the mid-1930s. Nearly 150 have graded MS-67 FB, while almost twenty have achieved the remarkable grade of MS-68 FB.

COMBINED NGC & PCGS POPULATION										
AU58	MS62	MS62FB	MS63	MS63FB	MS64	MS64FB	MS65	MS65FB	MS66	MS66FB
80	19	134	30	531	114	1327	89	1053	38	545

Values:

	1945	1955	1965	1975	1985	1995	2005
G	——	.15	.35	.60	1.75	1.50	3.00
F	——	.25	.75	1.25	3.50	4.00	6.00
XF	——	——	1.50	5.00	8.00	9.00	10.00
MS60	1.50	1.25	6.50	20.00	——	——	——
MS63	——	——	——	——	37.50	50.00	45.00
MS65	——	——	——	——	——	——	100.00

Comments: The first dimes of this type were not released until October 28, 1916, following a months-long build-up in the press. As the first of the three new coin types to enter circulation, the Winged Liberty Dime (as it was officially designated by the Mint) was eagerly hoarded by the general public. Of the 1,800,000 pieces included in the initial release, it's likely that a good percentage were set aside as keepsakes.

Unlike most new American coins, which are traditionally met with criticism and suspicion, the new dime was received favorably by all elements of society. Numismatists in particular were relieved to be done with Barber's old Liberty Head type, a coin considered an embarrassment to the aesthetically attuned. Both the general press and the public erroneously identified the bust of Liberty as a representation of Mercury, an appellation which survives to the present day.

The widespread availability of 1916 Mercury Dimes from the Philadelphia Mint has always been acknowledged within the hobby, so the price appreciation for this issue has followed a steady and uneventful track. The higher than expected 1985 value for examples grading Good simply reflects the residual effects of a speculative market in precious metals during the years 1979-80. From this point onward, the catalog values for Mercury Dimes in grades Good and Fine are pretty much in lock step for all common dates, and they are based more on the price of silver bullion than true numismatic values. This means that the slight differences in rarity within these dates, something plainly evident in the catalog values provided in earlier guide books, is no longer apparent.

1916-D

Mintage:
264,000
(Ranking 1/77)

Popular Varieties: Two of the four reverse dies known for this rare coin feature repunched mintmarks, but this issue is seldom collected by varieties, due to its high value. All four reverses are illustrated below primarily as a deterrent against counterfeit and altered pieces.

Rarity: As a natural consequence of its very low mintage for a 20th Century United States coin, this issue has long been celebrated as a rarity. In fact, only in grades Fine and higher is it really scarce. Nevertheless, the popularity of 1916-D dimes among date and mint collectors keeps the supply of low grade examples about even with the demand. Mint State coins are scarce, not rare, and are usually available to the well-heeled. So too are nearly Mint State, or AU, coins. The greatest shortfall is within the more widely sought grades of Fine through Extremely Fine. These are forever on dealers' want lists.

The *PCGS Population Report* does not break out the individual totals for grades VG, F and VF, so it is not possible to list these highly desirable grades separately. At the top end of the spectrum, a mere eight examples have been certified higher than MS-66. This is in stark contrast to the relatively large number of Philadelphia Mint examples in higher grades.

COMBINED NGC & PCGS POPULATION						
VG-VF	XF40	XF45	AU50	AU53	AU55	AU58
750	59	65	44	41	85	80

COMBINED NGC & PCGS POPULATION									
MS62	MS62FB	MS63	MS63FB	MS64	MS64FB	MS65	MS65FB	MS66	MS66FB
24	46	26	83	11	178	10	51	3	21

Values:

	1945	1955	1965	1975	1985	1995	2005
G	——	6.00	82.50	95.00	375.00	375.00	750.00
F	——	35.00	175.00	200.00	750.00	950.00	1800.00
XF	——	——	325.00	350.00	1400.00	2400.00	3750.00
MS60	40.00	135.00	625.00	900.00	——	——	——
MS63	——	——	——	——	2800.00	4500.00	7000.00
MS65	——	——	——	——	——	——	18500.00

Comments: 1916-D dimes are nearly always well struck, with many Mint State examples qualifying for full bands status. Their luster is typically quite good, and the textured fields which are characteristic of the 1916 hub are seen on all coins of this date and mint. As many of the Uncirculated survivors are coins which were set aside as keepsakes by the non-numismatic public and were not well protected, most won't grade higher than MS-64. Still, gems are available if within one's budget.

This entire issue was released in the month of November, 1916.[1] Coinage of dimes was then halted at Denver so that the presses could be redirected to meeting a sudden and urgent demand for quarter dollars. Before dime coinage could resume, the 1917 dies were on hand and a new year had begun.

The decision to halt dime coinage at the Denver Mint was made at a meeting called by Mint Director F.J.H. von Engelken on November 24, 1916. With him in Washington were the three mint superintendents: Adam M. Joyce of Philadelphia, T.W.H. Shanahan of San Francisco and Thomas W. Annear of the Denver Mint. Also present were New York Assay Office Superintendent Verne M. Bovie and E.D. Hawkins (chief coiner?) of the San Francisco Mint.[2] At this meeting it was revealed that the Treasury Department had placed orders with the Mint for some four million quarter dollars. Superintendent Annear was directed to suspend the coinage of all denominations save the quarter dollar and to strike these pieces to the limit of the Denver Mint's capability.

As the first year of issue, more of these coins were saved in Mint State than would have been the case with an existing design. Thus, the 1916-D Mercury Dime was spared from the otherwise certain fate of being uncollectably rare in this condition. Still, the relatively small number of true coin collectors in the Midwest at that time kept the population of Mint State survivors low.

The key to the Mercury Dime series, the 1916-D has been in demand by collectors in all grades since the mid-1930s. This early awareness of its rarity resulted largely from the introduction of inexpensive coin boards in 1934. These novel collecting tools are described fully in the chapter on collecting Mercury Dimes.

Previously, only established numismatists sought these coins, and their preference was for Mint State examples. The assembling of collections from circulation created a demand even for worn specimens of 1916-D, 1921 and 1921-D. By the end of the 1930s, these three dates typically brought from 50 cents to a dollar in low grades. Mint State examples of the 1916-D were rarely offered, then as now. In what is to the author's knowledge the earliest comprehensive offering of Uncirculated Mercury Dimes, dealer John R. Stewart of Milwaukee placed an advertisement in the January 1940 issue of *The Numismatist* selling Uncirculated 1916-D dimes at $9.50. This was in sharp contrast to his price of 85 cents for 1916-P and a mere 60 cents for 1916-S.

The substantial premiums attached to this date have in the past proved too much for the unscrupulous to resist. While outright counterfeits are seldom encountered, perhaps thousands of alterations have been devised by adding a 'D' mintmark to genuine but less valuable 1916 dimes of the Philadelphia Mint. Another popular (though less often successful) activity has been the reshaping of the mintmark 'S' on San Francisco Mint dimes to resemble the letter 'D.' These forgeries are covered in some detail in Chapter 3, while the characteristics of genuine 1916-D dimes are described and illustrated below. Such is the prevalence of altered and counterfeit examples that even those which meet the established criteria for genuineness should be authenticated by a reputable certification service. Uncertified specimens may prove very difficult to sell.

Characteristics of genuine 1916-D dimes

Note date style of genuine 1916-D date
(ANAAB)

Die 1
*(Courtesy of American Numismatic
Association Authentication Bureau)*

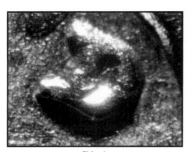

Die 1
(ANAAB)

Die 2, RPM-1
(ANAAB)

Die 3, RPM-2
(ANAAB)

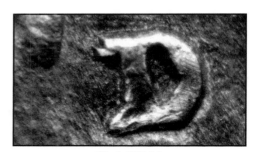

Die 3, RPM-2
(ANAAB)

Die 4
(ANAAB)

Die 4
(ANAAB)

1916-S

Mintage:
10,450,000
(Ranking 30/77)

Popular

Varieties: There are no significant varieties for this issue, but a few minor die-state features have been observed. A die crack may be found through the lower left portion of the wreath.

The mintmark is often very highly placed relative to later dates (photo). This is true also for 1917-S dimes coined with reverse dies leftover from the 1916 delivery. While not a true variety, mechanical or strike doubling is known (photo).

Rarity: Most that are seen grade About Good through Very Good, or else grade About Uncirculated. The former were in circulation as long as forty-five years, while the latter are mishandled coins set aside by the general public at the time of issue. Coins grading Fine through Extremely Fine are moderately scarce, as are ones in true Mint State. Fully struck gems are elusive. Just about two dozen 1916-S dimes have been certified above MS-66.

COMBINED NGC & PCGS POPULATION											
AU58	MS62	MS62FB	MS63	MS63FB	MS64	MS64FB	MS65	MS65FB	MS66	MS66FB
64	39	39	141	135	263	335	164	178	77	64

Values:

		1945	1955	1965	1975	1985	1995	2005
	G	——	.25	.65	1.60	1.50	3.00	4.00
	F	——	.50	1.40	4.00	6.00	6.00	9.00
	XF	——	——	5.00	9.00	14.00	15.00	18.00
	MS60	2.00	2.00	11.50	27.00	——	——	——
	MS63	——	——	——	——	65.00	65.00	65.00
	MS65	——	——	——	——	——	——	200.00

Comments: An overall weakness of strike in the central portions of both obverse and reverse characterizes this issue. Particularly affected by such weakness is the upper half of the lower diagonal band. This band is directly opposite the highest point of relief on the obverse, and the resulting displacement of metal during striking is the cause of this specific pattern of weakness, which is seen for many dimes, particularly those coined at the San Francisco Mint.

Textured fields with pleasing luster are the norm for 1916-S, as is a very small mintmark tucked up close between the olive branch and its lowermost leaf *(photo)*. Within the Mercury Dime series, this style of mintmark is exclusive to the 1916-S mintage and a portion of the 1917-S dimes.

A bit of reading through old hobby publications reveals that until the mid-1940s this date was valued at less in Uncirculated condition than its Philadelphia Mint counterpart. Since it is clearly scarcer today, the reason for this transposed pricing must lie in small hoards of the Philadelphia Mint issue that had been held back from the market until that time.

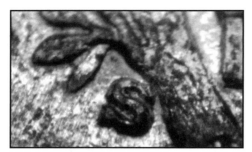

Highly placed S

Strike doubling is evident
on the wreath and mintmark
(Courtesy of Vic Rollo)

1917

Mintage:
55,230,000
(Ranking 62/77)

Type of 1916

Type of 1917

Popular Varieties: Two distinct and transitional hub pairings are known. While better described as subtypes than varieties, they are nonetheless quite collectable. This date is known to exhibit dramatic strike doubling, a curiosity common to many dates in this series *(photos)*. A clashed obverse die is also noted.

Rarity: This issue is common in all grades through MS-65, though slightly scarcer in gem than the 1916(P) dimes. Many Mint State pieces have full bands. Both luster and strike are excellent with this issue.

COMBINED NGC & PCGS POPULATION											
AU58	MS62	MS62FB	MS63	MS63FB	MS64	MS64FB	MS65	MS65FB	MS66	MS66FB
86	14	70	24	219	64	379	38	214	9	62

Values:

		1945	1955	1965	1975	1985	1995	2005
	G	——	.25	.35	——	1.25	1.25	2.00
	F	——	.50	.75	.75	2.00	2.00	3.00
	XF	——	——	1.75	3.50	4.25	6.00	8.00
	MS60	1.25	2.25	7.25	18.00	——	——	——
	MS63	——	——	——	——	29.00	50.00	60.00
	MS65	——	——	——	——	——	——	150.00

Comments: Only a relatively small number, about one dime in eight, were coined from dies of the old hubs used in 1916. New obverse and reverse hubs were introduced early in 1917, and dies sunk from these hubs were employed in coining the majority of the dimes produced at the Philadelphia Mint. Dies from both old and new hubs were used for branch mint coins, as well.[3] The new obverse hub is lower in overall relief, most noticeably in the curls framing Liberty's face and along the leading edge of her wing. More subtle is the narrowing of the obverse border and the shallower relief of the motto IN GOD WE TRUST. Gone are the textured fields of the original model.

For purposes of identification, the author has chosen to describe these subtypes as the Type of 1916 (T16) and the Type of 1917 (T17). These designations apply principally to the obverse hub types, as the only distinction evident between the old and new reverse hubs is the presence or absence, respectively, of a textured field. In all other features, the reverse types are indistinguishable.

The overall higher relief in Liberty's portrait which helps to distinguish the Type of 1916 is evident in even the lowest grades. In such coins, the tips of Liberty's wing feathers remain visible when all other details have been obliterated. For this reason, dimes of the Type of 1916 can be slightly puzzling to grade below Very Good when using conventional standards. A bit of experience and observation will enable one to overcome this difficulty.

The lowering of relief on the obverse deprived viewers of much of the design's boldness, and numismatics was certainly the loser in this action. The winner was clearly the Mint's coining and engraving departments, which may have benefited from the extended die life for which purpose these changes were likely made. Further modifications to the obverse hub appeared in the following year. Both the Type of 1916 and the Type of 1917 are illustrated above. For close-up photos of the distinguishing features, see Chapter 2.

The mintage of dimes at the Philadelphia Mint in 1917 was remarkably high for that era. Acting Mint Director Mary M. O'Reilly wrote to Philadelphia Mint Superintendent Adam M. Joyce on June 28 with an urgent plea: "Will you please arrange as early as possible to coin dimes exclusively for the present. The Treasurer reports that he has a supply of quarters and halves in the sub-treasuries at present, but needs all you can give him of dimes."[4]

The need for an increase in productivity was brought about by the tremendous upsurge in demand for fractional coins during 1917. This resulted from America's growing industrial output as the major provisionary and banker for Britain and France during World War I. This nation's entry into the war in April of that year further increased the demand for newly coined silver. Around the clock operation of three shifts per day soon became routine at all United States Mints. An increase in both personnel and security necessitated the closure of the Philadelphia Mint to visitors on February 3.[5] This policy remained in effect until one month before the war's end and was soon extended to the other mints, as well.

Strike doubling

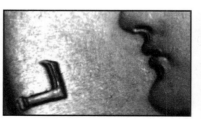

Strike doubling

Strike doubling

1917-D

Type of 1916

Mintage:
9,402,000
(Ranking 27/77)

Type of 1917

Popular Varieties: A prominent die chip in the date is known *(photo)*. Additional patterns of die cracking are reported.

1917-D T16 dimes have the very small D mintmark used for dimes only in 1916 and 1917. 1917-D T17 dimes have the equally small but somewhat differently shaped mintmark used 1917-34.

Rarity: Only slightly scarce in the lower grades, 1917-D becomes more challenging in grades Fine and higher. Both choice and gem pieces are rare, with just a single example having been certified above MS-66. About half of the certified coins have full bands.

COMBINED NGC & PCGS POPULATION											
AU58	MS62	MS62FB	MS63	MS63FB	MS64	MS64FB	MS65	MS65FB	MS66	MS66FB
74	60	52	106	104	118	142	21	39	7	8

Values:

		1945	1955	1965	1975	1985	1995	2005
	G	——	.35	1.25	1.50	2.75	3.50	4.50
	F	——	2.50	4.25	5.00	7.00	8.00	11.00
	XF	——	——	16.50	22.00	30.00	38.00	45.00
	MS60	3.50	17.50	55.00	75.00	——	——	——
	MS63	——	——	——	——	190.00	325.00	350.00
	MS65	——	——	——	——	——	——	1200.00

Comments: Exists as both Type of 1916 and Type of 1917 in a ratio of approximately five to one. Mint State coins usually exhibit weak strikes, particularly those having the T17 obverse. In addition to their lack of textured fields, T17 dimes are characteristically well defined at their centers, while being weak around their peripheries. Although displaying this peripheral weakness, 1917-D T17 dimes are more likely to possess full bands. Conversely, 1917-D T16 dimes are better struck overall, but they are more often seen with flat bands. Since this pattern is evident in all dimes dated 1917, it suggests that a subtle change in the curvature of the fields was part of the modifications made in the Type of 1917. Such a change might easily channel a greater flow of metal toward the coins' centers.

The fact that T17 dimes do not strike up well around their peripheries indicates that the Mint's presumed goal of improving striking quality and extending the life was not achieved with the introduction of the new hubs. This notion is supported by the appearance of yet another obverse hub in 1918.

The placement of the mintmark 'D' is also distinctive from the old dies to the new. On the former, the normal position is up high, as in 1916. Dies from the new hub typically have the mintmark well centered between the olive branch and the border, a location favored ever afterward through 1945. This suggests that the 1917-D T16 reverse dies were from the original shipment of 1916. So few dimes were coined at Denver in 1916 that most of these dies would have remained on hand at the beginning of 1917.

Die chip in 7
*(Photo by Alan Herbert,
courtesy of Krause Publications)*

The Complete Guide to Mercury Dimes

1917-S

Type of 1916

Mintage:
27,330,000
(Ranking 51/77)

Type of 1917

Popular

Varieties: Two styles of 'S' mintmark may be found for this issue. T16 dimes seem to all have the very compact 'S' used in 1916, while the T17 dimes observed have all featured the small but more open mintmark style used 1917-41.

Rarity: Fairly common in all grades through MS-64, only gem examples can be considered rare. Coins certified with full bands were once in the minority, but slightly relaxed standards by the grading services have resulted in a greater balance.

COMBINED NGC & PCGS POPULATION										
AU58	MS62	MS62FB	MS63	MS63FB	MS64	MS64FB	MS65	MS65FB	MS66	MS66FB
89	43	33	73	106	154	212	81	108	33	67

Values:		1945	1955	1965	1975	1985	1995	2005
	G	——	.35	.60	——	1.25	2.00	2.00
	F	——	.50	1.50	1.50	4.00	4.00	5.00
	XF	——	——	5.50	7.00	8.00	10.00	12.00
	MS60	2.00	4.50	18.50	30.00	——	——	——
	MS63	——	——	——	——	75.00	160.00	175.00
	MS65	——	——	——	——	——	——	500.00

Comments: Like all dimes of this date, 1917-S exists both as Type of 1916 and Type of 1917. The latter is much scarcer, representing only about one dime in ten. Most 1917-S dimes of either type exhibit some weakness of striking. T17 examples are subject to being weakly struck around their peripheries, less so in their centers. It's likely that most of the coins certified with full bands are from this later emission.

All things considered, the introduction of new hubs detracted materially from the design's attractiveness. Although the lower relief may have extended die life, presumably the Mint's goal at this time, the price paid brings into question the wisdom of such a change.

This issue typically has excellent luster. On 1917-S T16 dimes the effect is one of shimmering, due to the textured fields. Those struck from dies made from the new hubs are usually quite brilliant and may even be semi-prooflike. This mirror surface appears more frequently on 'S' Mint dimes of later years, particularly during the late 1930s and early 1940s.

As with the 1917-D dimes, a new mintmark was introduced for this issue. While the old mintmark is very short and squat, the new one is noticeably taller and more open within its curves. This new letter 'S' appears on all subsequent dates until it was replaced in 1941 with a much larger mintmark. The sole exception is the 1928-S issue, in which an experimental, Large S was used, as well. Placement of the mintmark seems to have changed along with its style. The mintmark of 1916-17 always appears quite close to the olive branch, while the new mintmark puncheon used 1917-41 typically is well centered between the branch and the border.

The reverse of the illustrated 1917-S T16 dime displays evidence of severe die polishing, probably done in an attempt to remove clash marks. Although no polishing lines are visible, the tremendous loss of low relief detail in the olive branch is plainly seen.

The large mintages of 1917 necessitated that a far greater than usual number of coins be set aside for assaying purposes. The Trial of the Pyx, or Annual Assay, as it's more commonly known in this country, was a traditional event mandated by Congress. (Until being abolished by President Carter's administration in 1977, the Assay Commission included distinguished members of the public, among them prominent numismatists.) From each periodic delivery of coins during 1917, a certain number (approximately 5 per 10,000) was set aside and then forwarded to the United States Treasury in Washington, D.C. Thus, the greater the total coinage, the greater was the number of reserved coins.

When the Assay Commission met, early in 1918, it was presented with the following quantities of dimes for testing purposes: Philadelphia Mint, 27,615; Denver Mint, 4,701; San Francisco Mint, 13,665.[6] It may be seen that the number of coins reserved was directly proportional to the total coinage produced. Only a small percentage of the reserved coins were actually melted and assayed, as it was assumed that all coins of a given periodic delivery were representative of the whole.

1918

Mintage:
26,680,000
(Ranking 50/77)

Popular

Varieties: A die crack appears from wingtip to rim, and similar cracks are known for nearly every date in the series. The location of a major design element such as Liberty's wing so close to the coin's border created a pressure point at which die failure was likely to occur.

Rumors of an overdate are simply wishful thinking (see "Comments" for 1918-D).

Rarity: This issue is common in low grades, slightly scarcer in grades VF-AU. Mint State coins are generally available, though most are weakly struck around their peripheries. Very rare in the higher grades, just four 1918(P) dimes have been certified as MS-67 and none higher.

Coins having full bands are scarce. The high percentage of certified full bands coins likely represents a greater tendency to submit full bands coins for grading.

COMBINED NGC & PCGS POPULATION										
AU58	MS62	MS62FB	MS63	MS63FB	MS64	MS64FB	MS65	MS65FB	MS66	MS66FB
39	13	41	20	99	41	206	22	131	5	37

Values:

		1945	1955	1965	1975	1985	1995	2005
	G	——	.25	.60	.65	1.25	2.00	2.50
	F	——	.50	1.50	2.00	4.00	5.00	6.00
	XF	——	——	6.50	15.00	20.00	22.00	24.00
	MS60	2.50	11.00	25.00	38.00	——	——	——
	MS63	——	——	——	——	95.00	125.00	135.00
	MS65	——	——	——	——	——	——	435.00

Comments: Yet another obverse hub was introduced this year. Essentially a modification of the Type of 1917, the Type of 1918 (T18) is characterized primarily by its different contour on the trailing edge of Liberty's wing. Previously, this edge followed the shape of Liberty's head, curving away from the viewer and toward the coin's field. On the revised hub, the wing remains in a single plane, thrust straight backward and highlighted by a single outline accenting each feather. For close-up photos distinguishing the Type of 1917 from the Type of 1918, see Chapter 2. This change of obverse hubs was not transitional; there are no 1918-dated dimes displaying the Type of 1917, nor are there any 1917-dated dimes with the T18 obverse.

Although this change represented a marked improvement in the appearance of the wing, no corrective action was taken regarding the tendency of these coins to be weakly struck around their peripheries. Note that the illustrated coin displays the characteristic peripheral weakness, particularly in the reverse border and lettering. This flaw is characteristic of both T17 and T18 dimes. The T18 obverse was used without change through the remainder of the series, and such weakness may be observed for every date/mint combination.

The Mint Director's Report reveals that some 423 obverse dies and 307 reverse dies were employed in the coining of 1918(P) dimes. The average number of coins obtained was thus 63,996 per obverse die and 88,178 per reverse die. These figures are rather low, which suggests that a number of the dies either failed or simply were not used. Typical die life should have been around 200,000 to 300,000 coins. A total of 55 dime dies for this year's coinage were never delivered, and the report also contains an unexplained entry for two "trial dies."[7]

Given the large mintages of the time, it's not difficult to see why so many dies were required. It's also easy to imagine that not all were prepared with the utmost skill. Some of the deficiencies noted in the coinage of 1918 may be attributable to improper hardening of the dies or to the use of poor die steel from the outset. Such dies would wear quickly and lose their fine details. Another explanation for the decline in quality might be the use of temporary, inadequately skilled workers during wartime.

1918-D

Mintage:
22,674,800
(Ranking 44/77)

Popular Varieties: No significant varieties are reported, although severe die polishing resulted in at least one instance of the motto IN GOD WE TRUST being reduced to skeletal letters. This was a recurring phenomenon for nearly all dates, and such die-state phenomena draw little interest from collectors.

Several die cracks may be found *(photos)*. Rumors of a 1918/7 overdate are unfounded (see "Comments").

Rarity: 1918-D is common in grades below Very Fine. Higher circulated grades and Mint State coins are plagued by peripheral weakness. This is accompanied by indistinct center bands on all but a few of the Uncirculated population. Fully struck gems are genuinely rare. Just three pieces have been certified as MS-67 and none finer.

COMBINED NGC & PCGS POPULATION											
AU58	MS62	MS62FB	MS63	MS63FB	MS64	MS64FB	MS65	MS65FB	MS66	MS66FB
51	62	21	124	35	233	89	85	23	11	3

Values:

	1945	1955	1965	1975	1985	1995	2005
G	——	.35	.65	.65	1.25	2.00	3.00
F	——	1.50	2.50	3.00	4.00	4.50	5.00
XF	——	——	10.00	15.00	19.00	25.00	23.00
MS60	4.00	15.00	36.00	50.00	——	——	——
MS63	——	——	——	——	125.00	225.00	250.00
MS65	——	——	——	——	——	——	600.00

Comments: In addition to being perhaps the rarest Denver Mint dime with full center bands (FB), 1918-D frequently exhibits weakness in the lower diagonal band. Despite its high wartime mintage, this date offers relatively few coins which will satisfy collectors.

Claims have occasionally been made of a possible overdate for 1918 dimes of this mint and for the other two, as well. It's likely that these allegations are prompted by the known overdates of this year for the nickel and the quarter dollar. Such reports have all been made with respect to well worn coins for which verification was extremely difficult, if not impossible. The author has examined several such pieces from all three mints and remains unconvinced.

The Denver Mint received a total of 152 obverse dies and 118 reverse dies for coining 1918-D dimes. This resulted in an average number of strikes per die of 150,682 for the obverse and 194,099 for the reverse.[8] However, if one does some simple division of the total mintage by the number of dies, the actual figures achieved are slightly higher. It seems likely that the Director's Report subtracts those dies not actually used from the total shipped to Denver.

Die crack through motto.

The same coin displays a crack from wingtip to rim, a position noted for nearly all dates.

1918-S

Mintage:
19,300,000
(Ranking 38/77)

Popular Varieties: The often seen die crack from wingtip to rim is the only variety reported, aside from periodic claims of a non-existent 1918/7 overdate.

Rarity: All circulated grades are fairly common, with the possible exception of VF, XF and AU. Mint State coins are far more elusive. Fully struck gems with complete bands are at least as rare as for 1918-D. Only five examples have been certified as MS-67 and none higher.

Cud die break
(Courtesy of Ken Hill)

COMBINED NGC & PCGS POPULATION										
AU58	MS62	MS62FB	MS63	MS63FB	MS64	MS64FB	MS65	MS65FB	MS66	MS66FB
44	46	9	103	37	169	82	58	28	19	21

Values:

	1945	1955	1965	1975	1985	1995	2005
G	——	.35	.65	.65	1.25	2.00	3.00
F	——	1.50	2.25	2.50	3.50	4.00	5.00
XF	——	——	9.00	15.00	13.00	14.00	16.00
MS60	2.50	11.00	27.50	47.50	——	——	——
MS63	——	——	——	——	80.00	225.00	260.00
MS65	——	——	——	——	——	——	675.00

Comments: This date is notorious for being rare with full central bands. Like 1918-D, the lower diagonal band is often flat, as well. By and large, however, it is more often found with an overall good strike than is its contemporary from the Denver Mint. Another area of localized weakness is the date.

In studying the value history presented above, one interesting observation may be made. The published value of this issue in XF condition advanced from 1965 to 1975, remaining more or less steady for the next 30 years. Given the effects of inflation, its real value has thus declined. The Mercury Dime series offers a number of similar scenarios, mainly for semi-key coins in circulated grades. More dramatic examples will be highlighted for later dates in the series.

The San Francisco Mint used a mere 73 obverse dies and 66 reverse dies to produce more than 19 million 1918-S dimes. The reported average number of strikes was thus 274,794 per obverse die and 303,930 per reverse die.[9] This is much higher than for either Philadelphia or Denver. Since all of the dies were manufactured at the Philadelphia Mint, there's no ready explanation for this discrepancy. One possibility, however, is that San Francisco used a greater set distance between the dies, creating less stress and erosion, at the price of producing somewhat incomplete strikes.

1919

Mintage:
35,740,000
(Ranking 54/77)

Popular Varieties: Several rotated die positions are known. These are usually referred to as "rotated reverses", but this is a misnomer. Mercury Dimes were coined with the reverse die in the upper or "hammer" position within the press. Since only the lower or "anvil" die can work loose without falling from the press, it was this die which rotated. Known variances as viewed clockwise include 10, 16 and 26 degrees. While of some curiosity value to collectors, such pieces rarely command premium prices.

Rarity: This is an issue that is fairly common in all grades through MS-64. Even full band gems are usually available, though less so than for 'P' Mint dimes of the mid-1920s and later. Nine examples have been certified as MS-67 and none finer; all of these had full bands.

COMBINED NGC & PCGS POPULATION										
AU58	MS62	MS62FB	MS63	MS63FB	MS64	MS64FB	MS65	MS65FB	MS66	MS66FB
50	15	55	28	112	39	242	22	144	10	45

Values:

	1945	1955	1965	1975	1985	1995	2005
G	——	.25	.50	——	1.25	2.00	2.50
F	——	.75	1.50	1.25	3.00	3.25	4.00
XF	——	——	8.00	8.00	7.50	7.50	10.00
MS60	2.50	11.00	28.00	31.00	——	——	——
MS63	——	——	——	——	50.00	100.00	120.00
MS65	——	——	——	——	——	——	325.00

Comments: Well struck coins are the rule for this date. The luster is good, although it often exhibits a satin finish which is considered by many to be less desirable than the frosty look of earlier coins.

Note that the value of this date in Extremely Fine condition has remained almost stationary over the past 40 years. While the 1919(P) dime was almost certainly overvalued in 1965, it has experienced only a slight advance in recent years. Such developments tend to discourage the selling of Mercury Dime collections and make the locating of many dates a genuine challenge.

Some 521 obverse dies and 343 reverse dies were used in the coining of 1919(P) dimes. Again coming in low, the Philadelphia Mint produced only 71,050 strikes per obverse die and 107,921 per reverse die.[10]

Although World War I ended informally with the signing of an armistice on November 11, 1918, the economic build-up which had accompanied it continued its hectic pace for some months afterward. The lifting of wartime price controls led to immediate inflation, and this intensified the demand for fractional coinage. Mintages thus remained fairly high through 1920, though a gradual recession set in around the middle of 1919.

As the nation struggled to rebalance its post-war economy, the years 1919-20 were marred by labor strikes, urban race riots and an almost hysterical fear of Bolshevik incursions into American institutions.

While these concerns were followed closely by the general public, little notice was taken of the changes being made at the United States Mint. From a wartime high of slightly more than one thousand employees, the number of persons engaged at the various offices and factories of the U. S. Mint remained at 992 at the close of Fiscal Year 1919.[11] This number would decline steadily throughout the 1920s, despite increasing coinages again during the middle of that decade. Still more drastic cuts would be made during the Great Depression of the early 1930s, when the three mints nearly ceased operations.

1919-D

Mintage:
9,939,000
(Ranking 29/77)

Popular Varieties: A number of die crack formations are known *(photo)*, most notably the familiar wingtip to rim crack.

Rarity: 1919-D is common only in the lowest circulated grades and as mediocre Mint State coins. Although split band specimens are usually available, fully raised bands are rare. Since the certification services utilize a definition of FB which is slightly more liberal than the one presented in Chapter 4, the figures below for full bands likely include a few of the better split band coins, as well Not surprisingly, just a single example of this issue has been certified as MS-67 and none finer.

COMBINED NGC & PCGS POPULATION											
AU58	MS62	MS62FB	MS63	MS63FB	MS64	MS64FB	MS65	MS65FB	MS66	MS66FB
56	65	24	108	69	95	81	28	14	8	5

Values:

	1945	1955	1965	1975	1985	1995	2005
G	——	.35	1.35	1.10	2.75	3.00	5.00
F	——	1.25	6.00	5.00	5.50	7.00	12.00
XF	——	——	35.00	35.00	30.00	35.00	36.00
MS60	3.00	35.00	90.00	132.50	——	——	——
MS63	——	——	——	——	200.00	450.00	450.00
MS65	——	——	——	——	——	——	1500.00

Comments: Peripheral weakness is common, although less so than for 1918-D. The example which illustrates this date is exceptionally well struck.

Writing in 1980 for *The Coin Dealer Newsletter*, dealer Rick Sear reported having recently seen three and a half uncirculated rolls of this date.[12] As usual, many of these possessed split and only slightly rounded bands. The existence in roll quantities of any Mercury Dime dated earlier than the mid 1920s was unusual, even a quarter century ago, and it's a certainty that these coins have since been dispersed.

The Denver Mint used 51 obverse dies to produce an average of 196,776 dimes per die and 38 reverse dies to coin some 264,094 pieces per die.[13] A comparison of these figures with those from 1918 shows that while the average number of coins per die varied greatly from one mint to another, the number remained roughly equal at any given mint from one year to the next.

This die break from rim to rim would ultimately result in a cud when the affected ara works loose from the die.

1919-S

Mintage:
8,850,000
(Ranking 25/77)

Popular Varieties: None are reported.

Rarity: Scarce in all but the lowest circulated grades, this date is a challenge for both beginner and advanced specialist. Uncirculated specimens of any grade are difficult to locate, and fully struck gems are genuinely rare.

COMBINED NGC & PCGS POPULATION										
AU58	MS62	MS62FB	MS63	MS63FB	MS64	MS64FB	MS65	MS65FB	MS66	MS66FB
53	30	2	43	17	79	39	42	24	29	4

Values:

	1945	1955	1965	1975	1985	1995	2005
G	——	.35	1.50	1.10	2.75	3.00	3.50
F	——	1.00	6.00	5.00	5.50	6.00	8.00
XF	——	——	40.00	35.00	30.00	30.00	35.00
MS60	2.00	30.00	115.00	142.50	——	——	——
MS63	——	——	——	——	240.00	425.00	500.00
MS65	——	——	——	——	——	——	1000.00

Comments: An overall weakness of strike is particularly evident at the periphery of both obverse and reverse. When found, most examples in the higher circulated grades have been cleaned or dipped. Mint State coins are few and far between, gems even more so.

As usual, the San Francisco Mint proved the most frugal in its use of dies. A mere 26 obverse dies and 31 reverse dies provided an average die life of 342,884 dimes per obverse die and 287,580 per reverse.[14]

1919-S is an issue that has performed quite poorly is circulated grades. Notice that the value of this coin in Good has advanced quite modestly over the past 40 years, while Fine and Extremely Fine coins seem stuck in a rut. Adjusting for inflation, these figures represent a significant loss of value to the collector who purchased them at the height of the hobby's popularity in the early 1960s. This explains, at least in part, the very slow turnover of semi-key Mercury Dimes in these grades and their resulting scarcity in the marketplace.

An interesting chapter in American numismatic history was written in 1919-20, though both collectors and the general public took little note of it at the time. It actually began with a piece of legislation much better known to modern collectors—the Pittman Act of 1918. This called for the destruction of more than 270 million silver dollars, the bulk of this metal to be sold to America's ally in World War I, Great Britain.

The bullion was needed to flood the market in India and depress its price to a manageable level. (It must be remembered that India was then part of the British Empire, its "Jewel in the Crown.") The world price of silver, which had been fairly steady during the immediate pre-war years at around fifty cents per ounce, had risen dramatically during the period 1916-19. India, which craved silver, was thus undergoing the harmful effects of hoarding and speculation.

The mass melting of silver dollars mandated by the Pittman Act did not occur until 1919-20, after the war's end. The India crisis thus rendered less urgent, much of the recovered metal was diverted to the production of domestic subsidiary silver—dimes, quarters and halves.

Nevertheless, the price of silver continued to rise, peaking in November of 1919 at slightly over $1.38 per ounce.[15] Although the price fluctuated somewhat over the next few months, it remained at or above the point at which the bullion value of our silver coins exceeded their face value. Amazingly, this very real threat to the nation's coinage was addressed only in passing by both the general press and Congress. It received more attention from numismatists, Farran Zerbe raising the matter as a topic of discussion at the Pacific Coast Numismatic Society's meeting of November 25, 1919.[16] A study of the legislation proposed to address this crisis will be found in Chapter 1.

No contemporary reports can be found of persons hoarding and/or melting silver coins. The price of silver began to recede toward pre-war levels the following year, and this little remembered episode soon faded into history.

1920

Mintage:
59,030,000
(Ranking 65/77)

Popular Varieties: None are reported.

Rarity: 1920(P) dimes are common in all grades through MS-65, and full band examples are not especially scarce. Six pieces have been certified as MS-67 FB but none higher.

COMBINED NGC & PCGS POPULATION										
AU58	MS62	MS62FB	MS63	MS63FB	MS64	MS64FB	MS65	MS65FB	MS66	MS66FB
40	20	47	51	174	88	384	46	239	8	87

Values:

	1945	1955	1965	1975	1985	1995	2005
G	——	.25	.35	——	1.25	1.50	1.75
F	——	.50	1.00	.90	2.50	3.00	4.00
XF	——	——	3.00	4.00	6.00	7.00	8.00
MS60	2.50	4.00	11.00	17.50	——	——	——
MS63	——	——	——	——	30.00	70.00	75.00
MS65	——	——	——	——	——	——	250.00

Comments: The final digit of the date is often weakly struck, as a consequence of being too close to the coin's border for proper metal flow. This same phenomenon would appear with the Roosevelt Dime, a generation later. (In recent years the U. S. Mint has addressed this age old problem by moving all design elements away from the coin's border.)

Aside from this occasional handicap, 1920(P) is readily available in nearly any grade desired. The only limitation is one's budget.

Price appreciation for this issue in the circulated grades has been very modest over the past 40 years, not even compensating for inflation. Mint State coins, in contrast, have performed well, a fact that is generally true of all USA coin series. The evolving emphasis on obtaining quality specimens, rather than simply filling holes in a coin folder or album, accounts for this disparity in value advancement. The early-mid 1960s was the high watermark for collectors of silver coins from circulation, placing a greater pressure on the price of common, low-grade coins than the current coin market will support. With the exception of the few key dates, it's doubtful that Mercury Dimes in well worn condition will ever enjoy the strong following they did at that time.

1920-D

Mintage:
19,171,000
(Ranking 37/77)

Popular Varieties: Die cracks and breaks are even more prevalent than for 1919-D *(photos)*. This seems to have been a chronic problem with all denominations coined at the Denver Mint from the late teens through the mid twenties.

Rarity: Although common in all grades, the population of gem pieces is hampered by the striking problem described below in "Comments." Coins having full bands are available for a price.

Just seven examples have been certified as MS-67 and none finer.

COMBINED NGC & PCGS POPULATION										
AU58	MS62	MS62FB	MS63	MS63FB	MS64	MS64FB	MS65	MS65FB	MS66	MS66FB
63	39	33	71	73	82	124	45	52	13	17

Values:

		1945	1955	1965	1975	1985	1995	2005
	G	——	.35	.65	.65	1.50	2.00	3.00
	F	——	1.00	2.00	2.00	3.00	4.50	4.75
	XF	——	——	10.50	9.00	12.00	20.00	22.00
	MS60	3.00	12.50	31.50	50.00	——	——	——
	MS63	——	——	——	——	125.00	350.00	350.00
	MS65	——	——	——	——	——	——	775.00

Comments: The fade-away 0 in the date is a serious deterrent to finding a satisfying specimen, both for Mint State coins and those in the higher circulated grades. The placement of the date so close to the coin's border was a mistake that Weinman could not have anticipated, since he was conditioned to the creation of fine art medals that received multiple impressions from the dies.

The cracks frequently seen on otherwise serviceable dies used by the Denver Mint suggest that the die steel may have been improperly hardened. Also, the dies and collars may have been improperly set with respect to one another. While dies were made exclusively at the Philadelphia Mint's engraving department, collars often were machined on site. This could explain why cracks are more prevalent on Denver Mint dimes than on those of the other mints. It is no secret among series specialists that the dimes of each individual mint have unique qualities that made them readily identifiable, even before one checks the mintmark.

In a nationwide survey of thousands of Mercury Dimes taken from circulation during the late 1940s it was revealed that more than half of the pieces dated before 1923 had become worn to the point of being non-collectable:

> Eighty percent of these dimes in circulation were minted from 1935 to 1945. About fifteen percent were from 1923 to 1934 and the remaining five percent from 1921 back... Another surprising element was the condition of the dimes. In the group between 1916 and 1921 over half were so worn that the last figure of the date was impossible to read. On the reverse, the lettering and mintmark if any, were all but obliterated... The next thirty-five percent ran from Poor to Fair. The remaining fifteen percent ran mostly Good, a few Very Good and occasionally one Fine to Very Fine sneaked in without a passport.[17]

This study helps to explain the rarity of many early dates in the higher circulated grades. Recall also that the collecting of coins from circulation did not become popular until the mid-1930s. Since silver coins wore far more rapidly than the cupronickel clad pieces used today, the typical Mercury Dime would have worn down to no better than Good condition after just 20 years circulation.

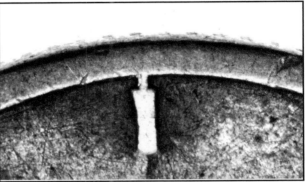

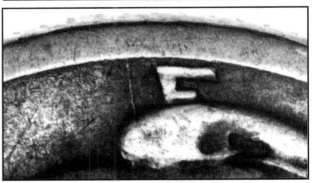

The three photos above depict the same coin with die cracks at the 2, 10 and 12 o'clock positions.
(Clark)

"Pigtail" die break
(Courtesy of Mark W. Clark)

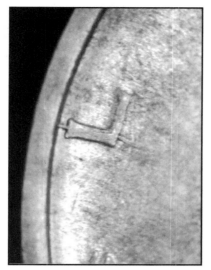

The same coin displays reverse die
clashing
(Courtesy of Bill Fivaz)

The three photos above depict a second
coin with die cracks

1920-S

Mintage:
13,820,000
(Ranking 33/77)

Popular Varieties: At least one obverse die shows clash marks *(photo)*. This common phenomenon simply represents one state of the die and adds no collector value.

Rarity: Scarce in all grades About Uncirculated and higher, Mint State examples are very scarce. Full band coins are not particularly hard to find among these pieces, but ones having both full bands and a sharp date are indeed rare, since numeral 0 is often indistinct. A mere three examples have been certified as MS-67, all having full bands. None have been graded higher by NGC and PCGS.

COMBINED NGC & PCGS POPULATION											
AU58	MS62	MS62FB	MS63	MS63FB	MS64	MS64FB	MS65	MS65FB	MS66	MS66FB
61	24	33	33	51	49	140	25	33	8	7

Values:

		1945	1955	1965	1975	1985	1995	2005
	G	——	.35	.65	.65	1.50	2.00	3.00
	F	——	1.00	2.25	2.00	3.00	4.00	5.00
	XF	——	——	9.25	9.00	12.00	17.00	19.00
	MS60	2.00	12.50	33.50	50.00	——	——	——
	MS63	——	——	——	——	100.00	275.00	275.00
	MS65	——	——	——	——	——	——	1300.00

Comments: The final digit of the date is again shy, as with 1920(P) and 1920-D. Unlike these two, which have the satiny luster typical for dimes of the twenties, the luster for 1920-S is usually quite frosty.

Collectors seeking XF-AU examples will find that nearly all of the few specimens available have been carelessly cleaned or dipped.

The dime illustrated for this issue offers a good example of the "broken nose" effect seen on many coins of this series. The result of over polishing of the dies, this low relief element of the design was partially obliterated. Such interruptions in Liberty's profile are so common that it's not worthy of mention for each date on which it appears. The reader may simply assume that it exists for virtually every date/mint combination in the series.

This was the last coinage of dimes at San Francisco until 1923.

An attempt to remove clash marks left Liberty with a "broken nose"
(Courtesy of Vic Rollo)

1921

Mintage:
1,230,000
(Ranking 3/77)

Popular Varieties: A prominent die clash is most visible on the obverse in front of Liberty's face *(photos)*. This variety is accompanied by extreme die erosion on both obverse and reverse. While merely die state phenomena that carry no premium value, they are nonetheless worth noting.

A reported 1921/0 overdate has never been verified and remains unlikely. Most such sightings occurred during the 1950s and 1960s, a time when collectors were just beginning to take a closer look at their coins but were as yet unknowledgeable about the minting and die making processes. A modern assessment of such coins usually reveals some form of post-mint damage.

Rarity: 1921(P) is common in grades Very Good and below, the result of widespread hoarding (see "Comments"). Grades Fine through About Uncirculated are scarce, due to unrelenting demand from collectors. Mint State coins are a little more available than one might expect, given this issue's low mintage. Still, true gems are rare, a consequence of die and striking deficiencies. Full band examples form the majority of Uncirculated survivors. A total of five MS-67 pieces have been certified, all of these having full bands. None have been graded higher.

COMBINED NGC & PCGS POPULATION						
VG-VF	XF40	XF45	AU50	AU53	AU55	AU58
160	33	31	26	12	29	31

COMBINED NGC & PCGS POPULATION									
MS62	MS62FB	MS63	MS63FB	MS64	MS64FB	MS65	MS65FB	MS66	MS66FB
1	35	2	62	5	158	2	129	1	49

Values:

	1945	1955	1965	1975	1985	1995	2005
G	——	.90	9.75	12.00	20.00	20.00	40.00
F	——	5.00	37.50	40.00	60.00	70.00	100.00
XF	——	——	85.00	200.00	325.00	400.00	500.00
MS60	30.00	10.00	275.00	900.00	——	——	——
MS63	——	——	——	——	1100.00	1300.00	1600.00
MS65	——	——	——	——	——	——	3400.00

Comments: Nearly all exhibit strong central details (full bands), while most are quite weak around their peripheries, both obverse and reverse. The major certification services have occasionally opted to ignore the strike on examples of this date and grade poorly struck coins as gems simply by virtue of having good luster and minimal marks. Since this condition describes a majority of the Mint State specimens extant, the population reports list a relatively large percentage of full-band gems. Buyers must therefore decide for themselves whether or not an offered coin meets their own criteria for gem status.

Values for this issue exploded between 1955 and 1965. Not surprisingly, this is about the same period during which it became impossible to find examples in circulation. The great influx of new coin collectors during the late 1950s and early '60s only fueled the higher demand, particularly with respect to lower grade specimens. These beginners were obsessed merely with filling the holes in their coin folders and were not too concerned about a coin's condition.

The high values for this date have long made it the target of those who would deceive. The most common technique involves removal of the numeral 4 from a 1941 dime. This is then replaced with a 2 from some common date such as 1942. Fortunately, this trick is easily exposed, as the numeral 9 on a genuine 1921 dime is quite distinctive from that on the 1941. The former is open, the latter closed. Study the close-up photo of the date on the genuine 1921 dime, and you will note that the two numerals 1 are also of a distinctive style, being quite thick and slightly concave. For examples of various alterations to 1921 from other dates, see Chapter 3.

The marketing of inexpensive boards for the collecting of coins from circulation, an industry which began in 1934, created an instantaneous market for dimes of this date, as well as for 1916-D and 1921-D. Coinciding with this development was the appearance of the first edition of Wayte Raymond's *Standard Catalogue of United States Coins*, the precursor of the "Red Book." As both the coin boards and Raymond's catalog provided mintage figures for USA coins, the rush was on to find these key dates. They were widely hoarded from circulation, so much so that they are only slightly scarce in low grades and are easily found at a typical coin show.

Most specimens thus saved graded Very Good and lower. Those persons not old enough to remember silver coins in circulation may be surprised to learn that dimes which had circulated only fifteen to twenty years could be so heavily worn. Yet, the inherent softness of silver, even when alloyed, left these coins subject to quick and thorough obliteration. For more on this subject, see "Comments" for 1920-D.

As with the quarters and halves of this date from all mints, the entire coinage of 1921(P) dimes occurred during the first half of the year.[18] The very large mintages of 1916-20, combined with a postwar economic recession, meant that the demand for new coins could be met entirely from existing supplies. Mint Director Raymond T. Baker made a direct reference to this slow down in a March 28 letter to Congressman William S. Vare: "The U. S. Mint at Philadelphia is now reducing its force on account of the slackening up of orders for new coins."[19]

This was the last coinage of dimes at Philadelphia until 1923.

Evidently of concern during 1921 was the potential threat to hygiene posed by our coins. Addressing this fear, tests were conducted by Drs. Charlotte B. Ward and Fred W. Tanner of the University of Illinois which proved conclusively that bacteria do not live for very long on coins after being handled by infected persons. It was their determination that caustic properties in the metal itself tended to kill these micro-organisms.[20]

Note style of date on
genuine 1921 dime

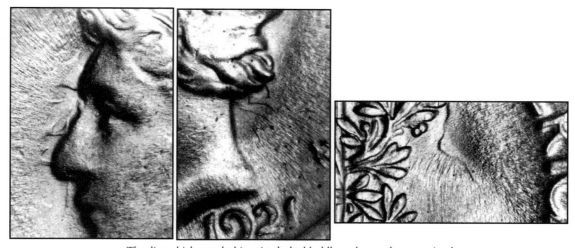

The dies which struck this coin clashed boldly and were then permitted
to suffer extreme wear, leaving deep metal flow lines
(Courtesy of John McIntosh)

1921-D

Mintage:
1,080,000
(Ranking 2/77)

Popular

Varieties: Like 1919-D and 1920-D, this date is frequently seen with one or more die cracks *(photos)*.

Rarity: Having a similar mintage, 1921-D has traditionally been treated as nearly a twin to 1921(P). Although 1921-D maintains a slight edge in rarity, this comparison holds up through most grades below the Mint State level. In unworn condition, 1921-D is notably scarcer. Just a single example has been certified above MS-66, this having graded MS-67 FB.

COMBINED NGC & PCGS POPULATION						
VG-VF	XF40	XF45	AU50	AU53	AU55	AU58
238	36	46	18	12	21	30

COMBINED NGC & PCGS POPULATION									
MS62	MS62FB	MS63	MS63FB	MS64	MS64FB	MS65	MS65FB	MS66	MS66FB
26	33	31	66	62	124	24	80	24	25

Values:

	1945	1955	1965	1975	1985	1995	2005
G	——	.75	11.00	19.00	30.00	30.00	55.00
F	——	3.50	39.00	50.00	85.00	90.00	150.00
XF	——	——	90.00	200.00	350.00	425.00	600.00
MS60	4.00	35.00	225.00	750.00	——	——	——
MS63	——	——	——	——	1100.00	1500.00	1850.00
MS65	——	——	——	——	——	——	3000.00

Comments: Peripheral weakness is a chronic problem with this date, although not to the degree seen with some 1921(P) dimes. Full band gems make up a good percentage of the total Mint State population and are usually available to those who can afford the asking price.

Prior to the 1940s this date, along with 1916-D and 1921(P), were the only Mercury Dimes regularly offered by dealers in less than Uncirculated condition. Typical was the advertisement placed by S. M. Koeppel of Los Angeles in the June 1939 issue of *The Numismatic Scrapbook Magazine*. In it, he offered any of these three dates at the following prices: G, 50¢; VG, 75¢; F, $1.

In what the author believes to have been the first comprehensive offering of Mercury Dimes for sale, John R. Stewart of Milwaukee placed the following valuations on Uncirculated examples in 1940: 1916-D, $9.50; 1921(P), $4.50; 1921-D, $2.[21] Note that 1921(P) was then worth more than twice as much as 1921-D. It was not until the mid-1940s that these figures began to level off, and they have more or less remained in this position ever since, with 1921-D maintaining a slight advantage.

In a survey undertaken by a reader of *The Numismatic Scrapbook Magazine* over a ten month period ending in September of 1938, some 5000 dimes then in circulation in the area of Rock Island, Illinois were examined. Out of these, nine were dated 1921(P), while only three 1921-D dimes were found.[22] This is surprising for a survey made in the Midwest, a region supplied its coins by the Denver Mint. The suggestion is that the 1921-D issue is indeed scarcer in low grades than its 'P' Mint cousin. By comparison, only a single 1916-D was found.

All 1921-D dimes were coined during the first half of the year.[23] No further production of dimes occurred at the Denver Mint until 1924, existing stocks being sufficient to meet the demand.

The recession of 1921-22 saw a near total suspension of coining at all three mints. The only coins produced for actual circulation during 1922 were a few million cents, these done up hastily at Denver to meet an unexpected shortage. The silver dollars coined that year were intended primarily to fulfill the terms of the Pittman Act of 1918 and to provide a reserve against outstanding silver certificates. Therefore, it was not anticipated that they would see wide use in commerce. So too were the gold double eagles of 1922 intended solely for foreign exchange and as a backing for the gold certificates in circulation. The only remaining coinage for 1922 was a small quantity of half dollars and gold dollars commemorating the centennial of Ulysses S. Grant's birth; these too were non-circulating coins.

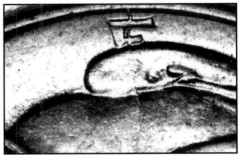

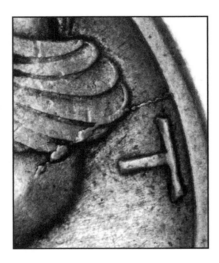

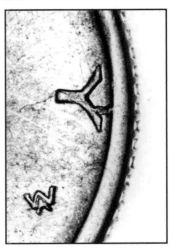

This date is often heavily cracked as is
shown in these photos above.

A second variety features similar cracks
as shown in these photos above.

1923

Mintage:
50,130,000
(Ranking 61/77)

Popular Varieties: The familiar die crack from wingtip to rim is known for this date. The only other variety reported is one in which numeral 3 of the date is scarcely visible, apparently as the result of a filled die. Both of these phenomena are so common to the series that they carry no premium.

Rarity: 1923(P) is common in all popular grades, including full bands gem. Some 70 examples have been certified as MS-67, most having full bands, while a single MS-68 coin is listed.

COMBINED NGC & PCGS POPULATION											
AU58	MS62	MS62FB	MS63	MS63FB	MS64	MS64FB	MS65	MS65FB	MS66	MS66FB
46	11	55	17	182	42	443	31	372	28	214

Values:

		1945	1955	1965	1975	1985	1995	2005
	G	——	.25	.35	——	1.25	1.50	2.00
	F	——	.35	.80	.90	2.50	4.00	4.00
	XF	——	——	2.25	3.50	5.00	6.00	7.00
	MS60	2.00	3.50	12.00	17.50	——	——	——
	MS63	——	——	——	——	27.50	45.00	45.00
	MS65	——	——	——	——	——	——	125.00

Comments: The 1923 Philadelphia Mint dime is an attractive issue in unworn condition. This issue seems to have slightly broader rims than most dates in the series, an unexplained curiosity. As the population reports suggest, full band coins make up a majority of the Uncirculated pieces extant.

This was the first issue of dimes coined at the Philadelphia Mint since the spring of 1921. Indeed, a full two years had passed before dime coinage resumed. By the end of June, only 5,380,000 1923(P) dimes had been coined, the bulk of this year's production occurring in subsequent months.[24] The Mint Director's Report shed some further light on the subject:

> During the first half of the fiscal year the demand for small coins—quarters, dimes nickels, cents—in the territory served by the Philadelphia Mint was such that the stocks of those coins were exhausted and it was necessary to operate the Philadelphia Mint on a 24 hours per day basis. It is thus evident that notwithstanding the enormous issues of small coins during the five year period 1917-21 there is no redundancy of coins below the dollar.[25]

A daring daylight robbery which occurred at the Denver Mint in 1922 alerted officials to the security threat that existed wherever large amounts of cash and bullion were handled. It was soon determined that the robbery had been planned by the thieves on the basis of information obtained during a previous visit to the mint in the guise of tourists. Perhaps overreacting, the director's office ordered that the three mints be indefinitely closed to visitors.

Following closely on the death of Dr. T. Louis Comparette, longtime curator of the U. S. Mint's coin collection, this closing no doubt hastened the decision by Treasury Secretary Andrew W. Mellon to relocate the collection from its traditional home at the Philadelphia Mint to the Smithsonian Institution in Washington, D.C. A formal acceptance of this gift was made by the Smithsonian's secretary, Dr. Charles D. Walcott, on February 19, 1923.[26]

The actual transfer of the coins, medals and other artifacts was delayed by protests from numismatic societies in the Northeast and from local newspapers. The American Numismatic Association, however, stood firmly behind the transfer, Editor Frank G. Duffield providing the following observations in a May 1923 editorial:

> Taking a broad view of the matter, the National Museum in Washington is the logical place for the coin collection. It has been termed the Mint collection, though, strictly speaking, it is the national collection. The National Museum already has a collection of medals, and the merging of the two collections will be advantageous.
>
> The construction of the Mint Cabinet is such that it would be impossible to enlarge the space for the collection without remodeling the entire rotunda. This fact would prevent the material growth of the collection...
>
> There is one phase of the matter that is worthy of reflection, but which may not have received consideration by the Treasury officials in reaching their decision. The late Dr. Comparette...is said to have been greatly concerned...about the apparent deterioration of the condition of the coins in the collection. The cause of this...was believed to be due to an atmospheric condition...with the collection resting on The Mall in Washington, all such conditions will be removed.[27]

This last comment is subject to some doubt, as the climate of Washington is not measurably different from that of Philadelphia. Perhaps, Editor Duffield was making reference to the level of industrial pollutants within their respective atmospheres. In any case, his parting comments related greater concern over the closing of the three mints to visitors than over the transfer of the National Coin Collection. Despite continued local protests, the entire collection was shipped via registered mail from Philadelphia to Washington, accompanied by Secret Service agents, and was formally accessioned by the Smithsonian Institution on June 13, 1923.[28]

1923-S

Mintage:
6,440,000
(Ranking 17/77)

Popular Varieties: None are reported.

Rarity: Usually available in low grades, 1923-S becomes scarce in grades VF and higher. When seen, XF and AU pieces typically display signs of harsh cleaning and/or dipping. The number of Mint State survivors is relatively small, and these are often plagued by flat central and lower diagonal bands, as well as the peripheral weakness so common to most dimes of the 1920s.

A lone example has been certified as MS-67 FB, but none finer.

COMBINED NGC & PCGS POPULATION										
AU58	MS62	MS62FB	MS63	MS63FB	MS64	MS64FB	MS65	MS65FB	MS66	MS66FB
58	29	24	50	43	89	64	25	33	8	5

Values:

	1945	1955	1965	1975	1985	1995	2005
G	——	.35	1.25	.75	1.50	2.00	3.00
F	——	2.00	4.00	3.25	4.00	5.00	7.00
XF	——	——	22.50	25.00	18.00	45.00	60.00
MS60	3.50	25.00	85.00	115.00	——	——	——
MS63	——	——	——	——	150.00	350.00	400.00
MS65	——	——	——	——	——	——	1200.00

Comments: In estimating the rarity of this issue with full bands, it may be instructional to quote from two detailed analyzes of the Mercury Dime series published by *The Coin Dealer Newsletter Monthly Summary* in 1977 and 1980, respectively. In March 1977, the late Allen Harriman had this to say: "This issue appears in the top twelve or fourteen 'most elusive with full bands' list of several major dealers. The 23-S is rather easy to find in any grade thru average strike MS-65—and 'sliders' are relatively common." Three years later, Rick Sear did a follow-up study: "For years this was an underrated date—but no longer. Still, it is a difficult issue to find well struck; both flat bands and fadeaway are often seen."

The author agrees with these findings, with only one exception. Harriman indicated that "sliders," or AU-58 coins, are relatively common. With a number of both collectors and dealers actively seeking such coins in original, uncleaned condition and having little luck, it seems that this comment is in error. Perhaps, what he intended to suggest was that such coins are frequently offered as Uncirculated, rather than being correctly labeled as AU-58. Of course, both articles quoted above predate the arrival of certified encapsulations, which have largely eliminated the practice of passing off sliders as Uncirculated coins.

1923-S dimes were widely hoarded in low grades during the 1940s and 1950s. This is true of most low mintage coins of the 1920s, particularly those made at San Francisco. Overvalued in the heated market of 1965, the 1923-S dime has not performed well since that time in grades below XF. Only in Mint state has its value kept pace with or exceeded inflation. A scan through the listings of other mintmarked dimes of the 1920s will reveal some similar histories.

This was the first minting of dimes at San Francisco since 1920, and all were coined during the second half of the year.[29] No dimes were coined at the Denver Mint during 1923. The counterfeits dated 1923-D are described in detail in Chapter 4.

1924

Mintage:
24,010,000
(Ranking 45/77)

Popular
Varieties: One obverse die is deeply scratched between the Y of LIBERTY and the designer's monogram *(photo)*.

Rarity: This date is common in grades Good through Fine, noticeably scarce in VF and higher. Mint state coins with partial or split bands are frequently available, although it's doubtful that the original rolls reported by Allen Harriman in 1977[30] still survive intact. Some 18 MS-67 examples have been certified, most having full bands, and a lone MS-68 FB.

COMBINED NGC & PCGS POPULATION											
AU58	MS62	MS62FB	MS63	MS63FB	MS64	MS64FB	MS65	MS65FB	MS66	MS66FB
24	13	28	30	88	79	227	65	172	40	90

Values:		1945	1955	1965	1975	1985	1995	2005
	G	——	.25	.35	——	1.25	1.50	1.75
	F	——	.50	.95	.90	2.50	3.00	4.00
	XF	——	——	3.75	3.50	6.50	9.00	10.00
	MS60	2.00	4.50	15.00	31.00	——	——	——
	MS63	——	——	——	——	65.00	100.00	100.00
	MS65	——	——	——	——	——	——	200.00

Comments: Full band gems are somewhat scarce; all lesser grades are available with patience.

Of the millions of dimes coined at the three mints during 1924, a total of just 45 were tested during the Mint's Annual Assay in February of 1925.[31]

The deep lines between letter Y and the monogram are scratches in the die, while the fainter lines were caused by vigorous die polishing done in an attempt to remove the scratches

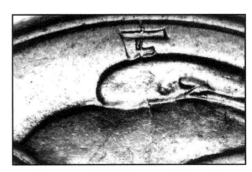

The same coin displays a small die crack

1924-D

Mintage:
6,810,000
(Ranking 20/77)

Popular

Varieties: None are reported.

Rarity: Common in low grades, problem-free XF and AU coins are scarce, as nearly all have been harshly cleaned. Mint State coins are not particularly scarce and have a higher than usual occurrence of full band examples, a finding which is consistent with the population report data.

Of the 16 coins graded MS-67, all but one possessed full bands. None have been graded higher.

COMBINED NGC & PCGS POPULATION										
AU58	MS62	MS62FB	MS63	MS63FB	MS64	MS64FB	MS65	MS65FB	MS66	MS66FB
43	12	39	17	101	44	221	14	106	3	59

Values:

		1945	1955	1965	1975	1985	1995	2005
	G	——	.35	.85	.65	1.25	1.50	3.00
	F	——	1.00	2.50	2.25	4.00	4.50	7.00
	XF	——	——	9.00	16.00	16.50	40.00	50.00
	MS60	3.00	11.00	52.50	140.00	——	——	——
	MS63	——	——	——	——	190.00	300.00	475.00
	MS65	——	——	——	——	——	——	1200.00

Comments: 1924-D is another date reported by Allen Harriman to be common in "slider" or AU-58 condition.[32] His emphasis was on the fact that such coins were frequently offered as Uncirculated. Since 1986, the widespread use of certification services which grade and encapsulate coins has largely eliminated such abuses. But where then are these sliders? The author's attempts to find such coins for this date have produced only damaged and/or harshly cleaned examples. When queried about this phenomenon, dealers usually assert that the unavailability of better-date sliders is due to limited price movement in recent years. Put simply, collectors don't want to sell their coins at current price levels. It is only when an estate is dispersed that these better dates become available, albeit for a very short time. Ironically, the most original and attractive About Uncirculated 1924-D dime that the author has examined is an error coin, the example with multiple clips which appears in Chapter 2.

As of June 30, 1924, a mere 400,000 dimes had been coined at the Denver Mint, the first since the spring of 1921.[33] This figure represents approximately 6% of its total output for the year.

1924-S

Mintage:
7,120,000
(Ranking 22/77)

Popular Varieties: No true varieties are reported, but various die states may be observed *(photo)*.

Rarity: As with nearly all Mercury Dimes, this date is common in low grades. Unlike most branch mint dimes of the 1920s, it is usually available in grades VF and XF, provided that one is not fussy about strike and surfaces. Only problem-free coins are scarce below the AU level. Low end Mint State coins are likewise more available than the population reports suggest. Fully struck gems, however, are indeed rare.

The highest graded specimen to date is a single MS-67 coin lacking full bands.

COMBINED NGC & PCGS POPULATION											
AU58	MS62	MS62FB	MS63	MS63FB	MS64	MS64FB	MS65	MS65FB	MS66	MS66FB
74	33	57	36	71	89	121	32	17	6	3

Values:

		1945	1955	1965	1975	1985	1995	2005
	G	——	.35	.85	.65	1.25	2.00	3.00
	F	——	1.25	2.75	2.25	4.00	4.00	5.00
	XF	——	——	18.50	16.00	15.00	35.00	45.00
	MS60	2.50	22.50	71.50	140.00	——	——	——
	MS63	——	——	——	——	200.00	525.00	500.00
	MS65	——	——	——	——	——	——	1200.00

Comments: It's the author's opinion that a greater number of specimens would be shown in the population reports were it not for the generally poor quality of most 1924-S dimes, a condition predetermined by the slipshod manner in which they were coined. Knowledge that one's prize will likely come back with a disappointing grade tends to discourage submissions.

The only XF and AU coins of this date which are found with some frequency are cleaned and/or damaged examples struck from heavily worn dies. Prospective buyers are inclined to pass on such disappointing coins, rendering them more available than this issue's low mintage would suggest. With dates such as 1924-S, the author is tempted to provide two rarity estimates for grades XF-AU, one for well-struck, problem-free coins having original surfaces and another for the typical examples found.

The specimen illustrated for this issue exhibits a peculiar inward curving of its edge, giving the coin sharply peaked rims. In a previous book on Buffalo Nickels, the author described this phenomenon as "San Francisco Roll" There seems no reason to discard this term, as it is evident on several of the S-Mint dimes of the 1920s appearing in this book. Its use in authenticating dimes coined at San Francisco comes immediately to mind. Of course, while the presence of this peculiarity helps to identify the mint of origin, its absence should not be taken as proof that a coin has been counterfeited or altered.

1924-S dimes were widely hoarded in low grades during the 1940s and 1950s.

The close-up photo reproduced below displays the sort of badly eroded dies which typify 1924-S. Many dimes of this date were coined from dies which had clashed and were then severely repolished, or "lapped," to efface these clash marks. Added to this loss of low relief detail is the erosive effects of utilizing dies well beyond their intended lifespan. This practice is typical for all branch mint coins of the 1920s, with the possible exception of gold pieces. By increasing the set distance between the obverse and reverse dies, further die erosion could be minimized, and it seems that this was done with some coins during this period, particularly the five cent piece.

The reason for this de-emphasis of quality seems to have been purely one of economy. The presidential administrations of Warren Harding (1921-23) and Calvin Coolidge (1923-29) set the tone for budget cutting throughout all divisions of the federal government. The U. S. Mint, of course, was not immune to these cutbacks. From the circumstantial evidence obtained through study of the coins themselves, it may be concluded that a deliberate policy of die economy was in effect during this period. The author believes that reverse dies were particularly targeted, as they could be used beyond their year of manufacture. Obverse dies, on the other hand, bore dates and were thus suitable for use only during the year in which they were current. The fact that the greatest evidence of die erosion and failure is found on the reverse of Mercury Dimes during this period lends credence to this theory.

Worn dies often exhibit a radiant
pattern of metal flow lines and
distorted lettering

1925

Mintage:
25,610,000
(Ranking 48/77)

Popular Varieties: The only reported variety is the seemingly inevitable die crack from wingtip to rim.

Rarity: Much like 1924(P), this date is common only in the lower circulated grades and in the lower Mint State grades. XF-AU coins are slightly scarce, as are well struck Uncirculated pieces grading MS-65 and higher.

While it was still possible to encounter an original roll of this issue as late as the 1980s, it's doubtful that any of these still exist. The debut of certification and encapsulation services at that time provided great incentives to break up these rolls.

Presently, the highest certified grade for this date is MS-67 FB, two examples being published, along with a single coin of that grade lacking full bands.

COMBINED NGC & PCGS POPULATION											
AU58	MS62	MS62FB	MS63	MS63FB	MS64	MS64FB	MS65	MS65FB	MS66	MS66FB
26	14	24	22	56	63	154	39	107	11	33

Values:		1945	1955	1965	1975	1985	1995	2005
	G	——	.25	.35	——	1.25	1.50	1.75
	F	——	.35	.95	.90	2.50	2.50	3.75
	XF	——	——	2.50	3.50	6.00	7.00	8.00
	MS60	1.50	4.00	15.00	35.00	——	——	——
	MS63	——	——	——	——	55.00	70.00	75.00
	MS65	——	——	——	——	——	——	200.00

Comments: Philadelphia Mint dimes of the 1920s are, as a rule, fairly well struck. 1925(P) is an exception. Although full band coins are not great rarities, nearly all coins of this date display an overall softness, both centrally and peripherally. A common problem spot is the date, in which the final digit may be flat and indistinct. This likely accounts for the smaller than expected population of gems.

1925-D

Mintage:
5,117,000
(Ranking 14/77)

Popular Varieties: No true varieties are reported, although the poor striking quality of many 1925-D dimes makes for some interesting effects *(photo)*.

Rarity: This is another date which is not particularly rare in low grades, but it's much less often available than its mintmarked contemporaries from the 1920s. Examples grading Fine are scarce, while VF and higher grade specimens are even more so. In Mint State, 1925-D is among the tougher dates in the series to locate, as the population report suggests. Finding an example having full bands is not the greatest deterrent, as the rest of the coin may be quite disappointing with respect to strike.

While five examples have been certified as MS-67 FB, none are graded higher.

COMBINED NGC & PCGS POPULATION										
AU58	MS62	MS62FB	MS63	MS63FB	MS64	MS64FB	MS65	MS65FB	MS66	MS66FB
48	21	33	24	87	18	143	3	35	2	36

Values:

	1945	1955	1965	1975	1985	1995	2005
G	——	.35	2.00	2.00	4.00	3.50	4.00
F	——	1.00	6.00	6.50	7.50	9.00	12.00
XF	——	——	50.00	60.00	60.00	90.00	100.00
MS60	3.50	11.00	300.00	265.00	——	——	——
MS63	——	——	——	——	300.00	500.00	700.00
MS65	——	——	——	——	——	——	1800.00

Comments: Weakness of strike in the central obverse and peripheral reverse are the rule for 1925-D. Areas particularly noted for this are the curls framing Liberty's face, the final digit of the date and, most notably, the E in ONE. The proximity of the mintmark to this position may cause it to be nearly invisible *(photo)*.

The value of this date makes it a likely target for those who would add a D mintmark to a 1925(P) dime. Although no such alterations have come to the author's attention, shoppers should be alert to this possibility.

1925-D is another issue that has performed poorly in circulated grades over the past 40 years. It was probably overvalued in 1965, but it seems to be a bit undervalued in 2005.

Extreme peripheral weakness has flattened both date and mintmark
(Courtesy of David & Ginger Pike)

1925-S

Mintage:
5,850,000
(Ranking 16/77)

Popular Varieties: None are reported, aside from the usual die polishing and erosion problems *(photo)*.

Rarity: Common in all grades through Fine, this issue is slightly scarce in VF and higher circulated grades. Mint State coins are not especially rare, but nearly all suffer from terrible strikes. This will affect the desirability of XF-AU coins, as well.

Ten pieces have been certified as MS-67 and none higher. As one might expect with this date, none of the ten have full bands.

COMBINED NGC & PCGS POPULATION										
AU58	MS62	MS62FB	MS63	MS63FB	MS64	MS64FB	MS65	MS65FB	MS66	MS66FB
43	12	19	20	56	30	160	17	66	12	29

Values:

		1945	1955	1965	1975	1985	1995	2005
	G	——	.35	.95	.65	1.25	2.00	3.00
	F	——	1.00	3.00	2.25	4.00	4.00	7.00
	XF	——	——	20.00	20.00	16.50	40.00	60.00
	MS60	2.50	20.00	85.00	130.00	——	——	——
	MS63	——	——	——	——	250.00	425.00	475.00
	MS65	——	——	——	——	——	——	1500.00

Comments: In the opinion of the author and many others, 1925-S holds the record for most poorly made date in the series. Both obverse and reverse and plagued by heavy die polishing and erosion and a generally weak strike throughout. This is especially noticeable around the reverse periphery. Some of the letters in UNITED STATES OF AMERICA may be indistinct, particularly at their tops, a characteristic suspiciously common to 1924-S, as well (leftover dies?).

The deficiencies of strike seen in 1925 dimes from all three mints suggest that the problem may have originated with the common master die for that year. This phenomenon occurs with the nickels of 1925, the date being weak in the same place for all three mints, regardless of strike. Added to this fundamental problem is the overall obverse fuzziness which characterizes the 1925-S alone. Ironically, such coins may have fully struck central bands on their reverse, as this area of the coin is the one least affected by the above described problems.

1925-S dimes were widely hoarded in low grades during the 1940s and 1950s. As a result, such coins remain common to this day. Overvalued in 1965, this date and several other S-Mint issues of the 1920s have performed poorly since that time in grades below XF.

Why is this? The explanation may be found in the changing nature of the hobby. In the early 1960s, when coin collecting was at the peak of its popularity, the typical collector of Mercury Dimes still began his or her set by obtaining as many different dates as possible from circulation. Since all but the more recent issues were heavily worn by that time, little emphasis was placed on a coin's grade. Every attempt was made to upgrade the collection with further circulation finds, but most dates were destined to remain in VG or lower condition. When the dates which had eluded discovery were ultimately obtained from a dealer or fellow collector, they were apt to be in a similarly low state of preservation.

It was only with the disappearance of silver from circulation after 1965 that a new generation of collectors was compelled to acquire their coins exclusively by purchasing them from dealers. With the coins now costing a premium, their buyers quickly learned to become conscious of quality. As they had no previous association with lower grade coins, these new buyers gravitated toward the naturally more attractive examples in grades VF and higher. These had historically proved to be better investments, and this condition fed on itself as evermore collectors switched to higher grade coins. The old concept of simply filling the holes in one's album with whatever became available, a trend which had dominated the hobby from 1934 to 1965, was rendered obsolete as the demand for low grade coins disappeared. As there were always more than enough of these pieces to meet the demand, their value fell dramatically after the mid-1960s. Now that most collectors are at least conscious of their holdings as potential investments, the future for low grade Mercury Dimes of any but the rarest dates looks bleak.

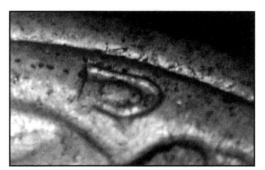

Burnishing of the die left letter R and part of
Liberty's cap detached and resulted in an
extremely brilliant patch known as "die burn"

1926

Mintage:
32,160,000
(Ranking 53/77)

Popular Varieties: One variety has a die crack through the back of Liberty's neck and into numeral 2 of the date. On the reverse of this same variety, a crack begins near the top of the fasces, passing above the blade and through letter A in STATES. Still another variety has a die crack from the underside of Liberty's chin and connecting the letters OD of the motto. Readers are cautioned that die cracks and other die-state phenomena carry little or no premium value, though they are collectable.

Rarity: 1926(P) is common in all grades through MS-64, with a fair number of gems being available, too.

Of the 18 examples certified as MS-67, all but two have full bands. None have been graded higher.

COMBINED NGC & PCGS POPULATION										
AU58	MS62	MS62FB	MS63	MS63FB	MS64	MS64FB	MS65	MS65FB	MS66	MS66FB
54	29	43	55	129	114	324	41	184	21	73

Values:

		1945	1955	1965	1975	1985	1995	2005
	G	——	.25	.35	——	1.25	1.25	1.50
	F	——	.35	.95	.90	3.00	2.50	2.50
	XF	——	——	2.50	3.50	5.00	6.00	7.00
	MS60	2.00	3.00	10.50	18.50	——	——	——
	MS63	——	——	——	——	25.00	50.00	60.00
	MS65	——	——	——	——	——	——	250.00

Comments: With its generous mintage, this date is as common as one would expect. All grades are available, although most XF-AU coins have been abrasively cleaned or dipped.

Since its inception the Mercury Dime featured a date style in which numeral 9 was merely an arc, rather than having a closed loop. 1926 is the first year in which numerals 6 and 9 of the date are nearly closed. This style remained in effect through 1927, while later issues show these numerals fully closed. No documentation is known to account for this change. As with the numeral 1 of peculiar style used in 1921, numismatists are left to their own imaginations.

It's the author's opinion that the closed style of 6 and 9 was favored by the Mint's new chief engraver, John R. Sinnock, who assumed this title following the death of George

T. Morgan in 1925. Examination of the silver half dollar and gold quarter eagle issued for the Sesquicentennial of American Independence in 1926 tends to corroborate this explanation. These were the first coins designed by Sinnock, and both feature closed 6's and 9's. In a further argument that this change was made merely as a matter of taste, one need only note the absence of any technical problems attributable to the open style numerals.

Another change is evident beginning in this year, although it was probably unintentional. The reverse master hub seems to have become slightly damaged sometime between the sinking of 1925's master die and that for 1926. All dimes dated 1926 through the end of the series have a portion of the olive branch missing when compared with earlier coins. The two stems leading to the upper diagonal band where it disappears behind the right side of the fasces appear connected to the band on pre-1926 dimes, while they hang disjointedly in space on later coins. This peculiarity was first published by Frank S. Robinson more than 30 years ago.[34] Earlier issues that display such hanging stems were the result of die polishing, or lapping, and simply represent later states of dies that were complete when first placed into the press.

The solution to this problem was to create a new master hub from the sculptor's original model, an activity now practiced frequently by the U. S. Mint. In 1926, however, the introduction of a new master hub would have been perceived as too radical a measure. Instead, both obverse and reverse hubs were permitted to deteriorate throughout the remainder of the series, losing evermore detail. Several other stems would ultimately be affected in a similar manner through continued wear and/or damage to the master hubs. This is why even the best struck dimes of the 1940s, including proofs, will not have the wealth of fine detail evident on well struck dimes dated 1916 through about 1924.

1926-D

Mintage:
6,828,000
(*Ranking 21/77*)

Popular Varieties: The familiar die crack from wingtip to rim is again evident on some dimes of this date and mint.

Rarity: More common than its low mintage would imply, 1926-D is usually available in all circulated grades through XF. Coins grading AU are slightly scarce, particularly if one is seeking only examples which have original, uncleaned surfaces. Mint State coins are almost always available with peripheral weakness on the reverse; often these possess full bands. Finding one with both full bands and a fully struck legend UNITED STATES OF AMERICA will be challenging.

The highest graded 1926-D dimes are two examples certified as MS-67, one having full bands and the other lacking them.

COMBINED NGC & PCGS POPULATION										
AU58	MS62	MS62FB	MS63	MS63FB	MS64	MS64FB	MS65	MS65FB	MS66	MS66FB
44	28	32	36	110	63	220	19	94	6	18

Values:

	1945	1955	1965	1975	1985	1995	2005
G	——	.25	.75	.65	1.25	2.00	2.75
F	——	2.00	2.25	2.00	3.00	4.00	5.00
XF	——	——	9.25	15.00	15.00	16.00	25.00
MS60	4.00	11.00	45.00	75.00	——	——	——
MS63	——	——	——	——	125.00	225.00	250.00
MS65	——	——	——	——	——	——	600.00

Comments: At one time placed in the same category with 1925-D and 1925-S, this date is far more available in any desired grade and is consistently more appealing. 1926-D dimes seemed to have been manufactured with more care than most denominations of this date and mint, the nickels being particularly bad.

1926-D has been another poor performer in circulated grades over the past 40 years, a condition common to most Mercury Dimes with the exception of the few key dates. In contrast, Mint State coins typically have kept pace with inflation. There is a lesson to be learned in this: Common coins will always be common and will always exist in numbers greater than the demand for them from collectors.

This said, however, there is still a lot of enjoyment to be derived from the collecting of Mercury Dimes in the grades of Fine through Extremely Fine. Locating problem-free examples that have original, uncleaned surfaces is quite challenging for all but the most common dates. With a rich variety of coin albums appearing in recent years, it is evident that many people are still collecting this series in circulated grades. What effect this will have on values in the coming years is impossible to predict.

1926-S

Mintage:
1,520,000
(Ranking 5/77)

Popular Varieties: None are reported, though heavy lapping of the dies did provide for some die state collecting possibilities *(photo)*.

Rarity: Fairly common in grades Good through Fine, grades VF and higher are genuinely scarce. True Mint State coins are likewise difficult to locate, although lower end Uncirculated examples are about tied in availability with average quality AU coins. Choice, original AU specimens are very scarce and often are more desirable than MS-60 and MS-61 coins. In grades MS-63 and higher the situation shifts dramatically. Choice and gem specimens, even those merely having split bands, are frustratingly rare.

The highest graded coins of this issue are four pieces certified as MS-67, with only one of these displaying full bands.

COMBINED NGC & PCGS POPULATION										
AU58	MS62	MS62FB	MS63	MS63FB	MS64	MS64FB	MS65	MS65FB	MS66	MS66FB
46	9	16	26	37	84	70	33	27	14	16

Values:

	1945	1955	1965	1975	1985	1995	2005
G	——	.50	3.00	5.00	8.00	5.50	7.00
F	——	3.50	9.50	11.50	15.00	15.00	20.00
XF	——	——	45.00	70.00	85.00	190.00	225.00
MS60	6.50	35.00	150.00	425.00	——	——	——
MS63	——	——	——	——	625.00	1500.00	1500.00
MS65	——	——	——	——	——	——	3000.00

Comments: A full bands gem of this date is easily among the most difficult coins in the entire series to locate. Despite its rarity with full bands, the overall strike for 1926-S is superior to that of 1924-S and 1925-S. It's possible that the low mintage for this year did not require using dies beyond the limits of their desirability, the coin at right being an exception.

A worn die left these leaves detached.

As befits a date of such low mintage, the demand for specimens in the better circulated grades is relentless. While the usual badly cleaned and/or damaged XF-AU coins are seen at most large coin shows, truly desirable examples are few and far-between.

1927

Mintage:
28,080,000
(Ranking 52/77)

Popular

Varieties: None are reported.

Rarity: This issue is common in all popular grades through full bands gem. Among 'P' Mint issues of the 1920s only 1926 and 1929 are easier to find in this top condition.

Some 17 examples have been certified as MS-67, all but one having full bands. None have been graded higher.

COMBINED NGC & PCGS POPULATION										
AU58	MS62	MS62FB	MS63	MS63FB	MS64	MS64FB	MS65	MS65FB	MS66	MS66FB
30	15	20	32	79	71	257	41	225	14	87

Values:

		1945	1955	1965	1975	1985	1995	2005
	G	——	.25	.35	——	1.25	1.25	1.50
	F	——	.35	.65	.90	2.00	2.25	3.00
	XF	——	——	1.75	3.50	5.00	6.00	7.00
	MS60	2.00	3.00	9.50	16.50	——	——	——
	MS63	——	——	——	——	25.00	50.00	55.00
	MS65	——	——	——	——	——	——	135.00

Comments: As the population reports indicate, enough Mint State coins exist with full bands to meet the demand. Perhaps more importantly, this issue is usually well struck in all other respects. The great emphasis placed on the presence of full bands should not make one careless about examining the overall coin for its quality of strike, since many full band dimes may reveal weakness of strike at their peripheries.

1927-D

Mintage:
4,812,000
(Ranking 12/77)

Popular Varieties: The "broken nose" effect, caused by excessive lapping of the obverse die, is known for this date, as it is for most coins in the series.

Rarity: 1927-D is scarce in grades Fine and higher. XF and AU coins are very elusive and when found usually have been badly cleaned. Mint State coins are also quite scarce, although full band gems are occasionally available.

This issue is notorious for its poor overall quality, and not a single coin has been certified above MS-66.

COMBINED NGC & PCGS POPULATION										
AU58	MS62	MS62FB	MS63	MS63FB	MS64	MS64FB	MS65	MS65FB	MS66	MS66FB
39	35	15	46	25	67	53	46	28	16	9

Values:

	1945	1955	1965	1975	1985	1995	2005
G	——	.50	.85	1.00	2.75	3.00	4.00
F	——	5.00	4.00	4.50	5.00	5.00	6.00
XF	——	——	40.00	35.00	30.00	40.00	60.00
MS60	6.00	100.00	210.00	230.00	——	——	——
MS63	——	——	——	——	300.00	400.00	400.00
MS65	——	——	——	——	——	——	1300.00

Comments: This issue is somewhat better struck than most Denver Mint dimes from the 1920s. Even so, it will usually display the characteristic pattern of weakness seen in so many Mercury Dimes—flatness in the highest portions of Liberty's hair, flat tops to the letters in LIBERTY and UNITED STATES OF AMERICA and flatness in the central and lower diagonal bands.

Writing in 1980, Rick Sear reported that 1927-D, once thought to be as scarce in gem condition with full bands as 1925-D, had proved to be more available. Since that time, the population reports have indicated a reversal of this notion. The certified population of 1927-D is significantly lower in grades MS-65 FB and MS-66 FB than the corresponding grades for 1925-D.

This revelation is in keeping with the conclusion of an earlier generation of collectors and dealers that 1927-D was a key rarity in Uncirculated condition. Its value of $6 in 1945 was a very high figure for a coin then just 18 years old, and it was exceeded only by the values for 1916-D, 1921(P), 1926-S and 1942/41(P). An assumption was made then that circulated examples were just as rare, which proved to be untrue, at least for those in the lower circulated grades. The values for coin grading less than Mint State were too optimistic, and they have largely stalled over the past 40 years.

Despite increasing mintages throughout the second half of the 1920s, the number of employees on the U. S. Mint's payroll continued to decline. While a portion of this reduction may be attributed to increasing efficiency and the employment of new technology, the principal reason seems to have been one of simple economy. The Coolidge Administration, with the concurrence of Congress, continued its budget slashing throughout the federal service.

From a wartime high of more than a thousand employees for the entire Mint system, this figure had been reduced to only 738 in 1923 and a mere 685 by 1927.[35] One's natural inclination is to associate the poor quality of many coins struck during the 1920s with these cutbacks in staffing. Even so, the poorest products of the United States Mint were coined before 1927, while the number of employees continued to decline after this date. The suggestion here is that the deficiencies which characterize many coins dated 1920-26 were due not to shortfalls in manpower, but rather to economy of equipment. The use of aged dies, spaced too far apart in the press in an effort to extend their lifespan, is the most likely explanation.

1927-S

Mintage:
4,770,000
(Ranking 11/77)

Popular Varieties: At least one die is known having a die crack from the base of letter A in STATES through the top of the fasces *(photo)*. The frequently seen die crack from wingtip to rim also appears with this date.

Rarity: Fairly common in grades Good through Fine, VF and higher grade examples are always scarce. Having a low certified Mint State population, the rarity of this date in Uncirculated condition is readily apparent. Full band gems of this date are among the keys to this series. No examples of 1927-S have been certified higher than MS-66.

COMBINED NGC & PCGS POPULATION										
AU58	MS62	MS62FB	MS63	MS63FB	MS64	MS64FB	MS65	MS65FB	MS66	MS66FB
42	28	6	47	22	83	59	45	23	12	10

Values:

	1945	1955	1965	1975	1985	1995	2005
G	——	.35	.75	.65	1.75	2.00	3.00
F	——	2.50	3.25	2.25	3.00	3.50	5.00
XF	——	——	22.00	20.00	13.50	15.00	24.00
MS60	3.50	35.00	85.00	142.50	——	——	——
MS63	——	——	——	——	150.00	350.00	550.00
MS65	——	——	——	——	——	——	1500.00

Comments: In terms of striking sharpness this issue is superior overall to 1924-S and 1925-S and about equal in quality to 1926-S. The sole exception is in the area of full bands, wherein 1927-S is frequently deficient. Flat band or partially split band pieces are the rule. A low mintage, combined with a particularly low survival rate for Mint State coins, provide very few coins from which to search for full band specimens. Occasional comparisons with the popular 1926-S dime are invalid, as 1927-S in Mint State beats it on most counts. The number of Uncirculated coins, both with and without full bands, is notably lower for 1927-S.

In grades Fine through AU, these dates are comparable, although the dramatically lower mintage for 1926-S has always made it more highly sought. 1927-S thus seems to be undervalued in all circulated grades Fine and higher. This is a date which should command far greater respect from collectors and dealers than it currently does.

Widely hoarded in low grades during the 1940s and 1950s, the likelihood of price appreciation for such coins is slim.

Die crack

1928

Mintage:
19,480,000
(Ranking 39/77)

Popular

Varieties: One or more dies have the often seen die crack from wingtip to rim.

Rarity: 1928(P) is common in all circulated grades. Mint State pieces are sufficiently available that an original roll or two may still exist, though any such rolls that surface would quickly be broken up for submission to the grading services.

Of the 18 examples certified MS-67, all but one have full bands.

COMBINED NGC & PCGS POPULATION										
AU58	MS62	MS62FB	MS63	MS63FB	MS64	MS64FB	MS65	MS65FB	MS66	MS66FB
26	11	19	33	71	44	164	41	252	14	97

Values:

		1945	1955	1965	1975	1985	1995	2005
	G	——	.25	.25	——	1.25	1.25	1.50
	F	——	.50	.55	.90	2.00	2.00	3.00
	XF	——	——	2.00	3.50	4.25	6.00	7.00
	MS60	1.50	2.50	9.50	16.50	——	——	——
	MS63	——	——	——	——	25.00	50.00	50.00
	MS65	——	——	——	——	——	——	130.00

Comments: Fully struck gems form enough of the Uncirculated population to meet demand. Although the mintage for this date is lower than for most 'P' Mint dimes of the 1920s, there seems to be no shortage of these coins.

The reader should bear in mind when examining the current retail values for 1928(P) and other common dates that such coins in Good condition seldom bring the published price. The current valuation of $1.50 includes a reasonable service charge applied only when a dealer takes the trouble to individually package a coin and advertise it by date and mint. More often, such low value coins are tossed into a box containing other silver dimes offered at fixed prices ranging from 50 cents to $1, depending on the average quality of the coins contained in it and on the prevailing spot price of silver.

1928-D

Mintage:
4,161,000
(Ranking 9/77)

Popular Varieties: None are reported.

Rarity: 1928-D is common only in low grades. VF through AU specimens are as scarce or more so than those in the lower Uncirculated grades. In fact, AU examples are seldom encountered. Both choice and gem Mint State examples are very scarce, even without the qualifier of full bands.

Of the 17 pieces graded MS-67, just six possess full bands. No examples of this issue have been graded higher than MS-67.

COMBINED NGC & PCGS POPULATION										
AU58	MS62	MS62FB	MS63	MS63FB	MS64	MS64FB	MS65	MS65FB	MS66	MS66FB
39	16	24	20	65	39	136	17	63	7	21

Values:

	1945	1955	1965	1975	1985	1995	2005
G	——	.35	.80	.75	1.50	3.00	4.00
F	——	1.25	2.75	4.00	4.00	7.00	8.00
XF	——	——	20.00	25.00	30.00	40.00	45.00
MS60	2.50	17.50	90.00	130.00	——	——	——
MS63	——	——	——	——	200.00	300.00	350.00
MS65	——	——	——	——	——	——	900.00

Comments: The relatively high percentage of certified full band specimens probably reflects a greater tendency to resubmit such coins over those not having full bands. More of a problem than incomplete bands, however, is a particular susceptibility to flatness in the legends. This phenomenon appears with nearly all dates in this series, but 1928-D rarely appears without it. The grading services do not place a great emphasis on over-all quality of strike, and only in the most extreme cases will this problem result in a lowered grade.

Given the rarity of this date in grades XF and AU, it seems somewhat undervalued at the present time. It's likely that the value for MS-60 coins has imposed a ceiling on the higher circulated grades, though most collectors prefer a choice AU coin to a mediocre Mint state piece. This phenomenon occurs with most mintmarked Mercury Dimes from 1918 through 1931 and accounts in part for the difficulty in locating such coins. There exists little incentive to offer nice XF and AU coins when their values have been nearly frozen for years. This condition sums up both the frustration and the challenge of assembling a nice, original XF-AU collection.

1928-S

Mintage:
7,400,000
(Ranking 23/77)

**Popular
Varieties:** This issue is found with both the Small S of 1917-41 and a much larger S, used only in 1928 *(photos)*. An illustration published in the March 1963 issue of *The Numismatic Scrapbook Magazine* shows an alleged 1928-S Small S over Large S dime. The poor quality of reproduction doesn't allow for positive verification, but it does seem to be just what is claimed. If genuine and accurately described, this would be a very rare item.

A die crack is noted through the mintmark and to the rim.

Rarity: A relative lightweight among 'S' Mint dimes of the 1920s, only 1929-S is more common. This issue is readily available in grades Good through MS-63. Fully struck gems are slightly scarce, though not comparable to preceding dates from the San Francisco Mint.

The finest examples certified are seven pieces grading MS-67 and four at MS-67 FB.

COMBINED NGC & PCGS POPULATION										
AU58	MS62	MS62FB	MS63	MS63FB	MS64	MS64FB	MS65	MS65FB	MS66	MS66FB
39	29	19	48	37	115	87	102	77	56	36

Values:		1945	1955	1965	1975	1985	1995	2005
	G	——	.25	.50	.65	1.25	1.50	2.00
	F	——	1.00	2.00	1.50	3.00	3.00	4.00
	XF	——	——	14.00	15.00	12.00	10.00	15.00
	MS60	3.00	17.50	55.00	62.50	——	——	——
	MS63	——	——	——	——	90.00	175.00	250.00
	MS65	——	——	——	——	——	——	500.00

Comments: 1928-S dimes were better made than most products of the San Francisco Mint during the 1920s, though examples having full bands form a minority of the surviving Uncirculated population. Worn examples are fairly common, since the introduction of cheap boards for collecting this series from circulation was just a few years away.

In 1928 the dime was part of an anomalous issue of coins which also involved cents, quarter dollars and half dollars coined at San Francisco. A Large S punch was employed for a portion of the coinage bearing this date. The reasons for this one-time action are not known, since all working documents pertaining to this period of the Mint's history have been destroyed.

As mintmarks were added to each die at the Philadelphia Mint before the dies were sent west to Denver and San Francisco, the source of this curious issue is ultimately the eastern mint and, more specifically, its engraving department. A noticeably larger S, having a thick center section and tall serifs, appears on a certain percentage of the 1928-S dimes. This mintmark does not appear on any coin before or after 1928.

In the first edition of this book it was reported that about 20% of 1928-S dimes carry the Large S. This was far too conservative a figure, the author not wanting such coins to become objects of exploitation. Now that this variety is better known to the numismatic community, it may be revealed that its real rarity is much greater. Some idea of this rarity may be gleaned from a study published in 1961 by Jack H. Tod, who became aware of the Large S varieties early on and searched for examples throughout the 1940s and '50s. His experience revealed that approximately one in 100 1928-S dimes taken from circulation bore a Large S mintmark. This compares with his findings of one in 25 cents, one in 15 quarters and one in six half dollars having the Large S.

It may be assumed that the Large S coins were minted in the latter part of 1928, as the silver dollar, coinage of which ceased early in the year, is not known with this distinctive mintmark style. The nickel, too, is unknown with the Large S, and any such coin would prove to be an instant rarity.

1928-S dimes were widely hoarded in low grades during the 1940s and 1950s. Pieces grading Fine through XF have faired poorly over the past 40 years, perhaps as a result of being somewhat overpriced in 1965. As a consequence of this correction, XF and AU coins are now slightly undervalued.

Small S
(Courtesy of Bill Fivaz)

Large S
(Fivaz)

1929

Mintage:
25,970,000
(Ranking 49/77)

Popular

Varieties: The only known variety is the usual die crack from wingtip to rim.

Rarity: Common in all grades, this issue may still exist in original rolls. Any such roll coming into the market quickly would be broken up for certification of the individual pieces.

COMBINED NGC & PCGS POPULATION									
MS63	MS63FB	MS64	MS64FB	MS65	MS65FB	MS66	MS66FB	MS67	MS67FB
48	67	170	272	255	371	120	200	16	41

Values:		1945	1955	1965	1975	1985	1995	2005
	G	——	.25	.25	——	1.25	1.25	1.50
	F	——	.50	.55	.65	2.00	2.25	3.00
	XF	——	——	1.50	2.75	4.25	5.00	6.00
	MS60	.75	2.00	6.25	13.00	——	——	——
	MS63	——	——	——	——	20.00	30.00	35.00
	MS65	——	——	——	——	——	——	75.00

Comments: 1929(P) is tied with 1926(P) as the most common dime of the 1920s in fully struck gem condition. Both luster and strike typically are excellent.

1929 was the final year of high mintages before the onset of the Great Depression. Five years would pass before the mint was again summoned to meet such a large demand for dimes.

Dimes dated 1929(P) were among the coins which could be purchased directly from the Treasury Department by mail at the time of issue and for several years thereafter. This process was an informal affair in which collectors simply wrote letters requesting the coins desired and enclosing a sum sufficient to cover face value, plus postage.

Prior to 1948, when sets of Uncirculated coins dated 1947 were offered for sale to collectors in cardboard holders manufactured expressly for that purpose, the United States Mint had never undertaken a formal program of providing regular coinage for hobbyists. In the early years of the Mint's history, numismatists could purchase specimens at face value by visiting one of its facilities in person. As coin collecting grew in popularity after 1850, this policy was informally extended to include mail orders, provided that sufficient postage was included with one's payment.

By the late 1920s, however, an ever increasing demand on the Mint's limited resources amid the nation's unprecedented postwar growth had done much to eradicate the friendly relationship which had long existed with the numismatic community. Collectors and dealers were feeling increasingly unwelcome at the Mint's doors since the onset of World War I. This editorial from 1932 relates how pressure from hobby leaders was being placed on the bureaucrats:

> A special effort has been made during recent weeks by Nelson T. Thorson, chairman of the Board of Governors of the ANA, through influential men in Washington, to have the Treasury Department furnish, upon request, Uncirculated United States coins to collectors, dealers or others. This action was taken by Mr. Thorson, it is said, by the refusal of the Treasury Department to furnish a dealer with such coins.

> In the correspondence it was pointed out that the government philatelic agency in Washington employs a number of clerks regularly in the selection of the finest specimens of postage stamps for sale to collectors or dealers, by mail or over the counter, and a similar arrangement was sought for collectors of coins.

> So far results have not been very favorable. The Treasury Department says it does, however, undertake to provide specimens of coins for collectors when it is possible to do so in order to aid them in completing collections, but it is not intended to lend aid to dealers in coins for profit.[36]

In August of 1932 *The Numismatist* was able to announce that a number of older coins, as well as those still current, could be ordered directly from the Treasurer of the United States per the following terms:

> These applications must state definitely the coins desired, the mint by which manufactured, the amount and denomination, as well as the purpose for which desired, and they must be accompanied by a remittance in cash or money order payable to the Treasurer of the United States for the full face value of the coins, plus an amount sufficient to cover the postage thereon by first-class mail and the registration fee, if it is decided the shipment must be registered.

> In case coins are desired from all three mints it is necessary to include postage, etc., for three different shipments.[37]

1929-D

Mintage:
5,034,000
(Ranking 13/77)

Popular Varieties: Wexler and Flynn include a very minor doubled-die obverse.[38]

Just as this book was about to go to press, Larry Briggs showed the author a variety long rumored but unconfirmed until now. This is a 1929-D dime having the 'D' mintmark style of 1916-17. This mintmark puncheon was supposed to have been retired after its final use on the 1917-D Type of 16 dimes, but at least one reverse die bearing this style mintmark was employed during 1929. That this was a newly punched die, rather than a leftover from 1916-17, is evident from the condition of the reverse hub. The flaws which first appeared in this hub on the 1926 coinage (see page 123) are evident in the 1929-D dime having the old style mintmark *(photo)*. As old reverse dies were employed as long as they were useable, collectors are urged to check their 1931-D and 1934-D dimes for possible appearances of the 1916-17 style 'D' mintmark.

A bold example of mechanical or strike doubling is illustrated *(photo)*. Most alleged doubled-die varieties turn out to be nothing more than simple machine doubling, as shown. This phenomenon is particularly common on the obverse of the Mercury Dime and occurs with virtually every date/mint combination. For additional illustrations, see 1916-S and 1917(P).

Rarity: Common in the lower circulated grades and the lower mint state grades, VF through AU coins are elusive. Fully struck gems are far more common than for any other branch mint issue of the 1920s. Original rolls may yet exist.

COMBINED NGC & PCGS POPULATION									
MS63	MS63FB	MS64	MS64FB	MS65	MS65FB	MS66	MS66FB	MS67	MS67FB
62	153	288	626	239	448	70	142	15	23

Values:

	1945	1955	1965	1975	1985	1995	2005
G	——	.25	.55	.65	1.25	2.50	3.00
F	——	.75	1.35	1.75	3.00	5.00	6.00
XF	——	——	3.50	6.00	6.00	12.00	15.00
MS60	1.50	3.00	12.00	18.50	——	——	——
MS63	——	——	——	——	65.00	40.00	38.00
MS65	——	——	——	——	——	——	75.00

Comments: So-so uncirculated coins are very common. Many display peripheral weakness and filled or shallow mintmarks. These flaws are the likely source of rumored Small D and Large D varieties. Gems are relatively common, as the population reports suggest.

Historically, 1929-D has been a common coin in Mint State. During the late 1930s it was among the very few dates in this series that was almost always to be found within listings of Uncirculated Mercury Dimes for sale. 1929-D was frequently offered by the roll, as well, suggesting that this issue was not released to circulation at the time of coining. Such a scenario is quite possible, since the same phenomenon occurs with the five-cent piece. The Great Depression, though traditionally associated with the 1929 stock market crash, really began with a slowdown of economic activity in the Midwest as early as the mid-1920s. The greater than expected availability of Mint State 1929-D dimes and nickels, coins which are scarce in XF-AU, is consistent with the notion that these dates were withheld from circulation owing to a lack of demand at the time of striking. When released, probably circa 1934-35, they were quickly secured by collectors and dealers before entering circulation in large numbers.

1929-D dimes were among the coins which could be purchased from the Treasury Department at face value, circa 1932. This was the last coinage of dimes at the Denver Mint until 1931.

Strike doubling
(Courtesy of Bill Fivaz)

Small D, style of 1916-17
*(David J. Camire photo,
coin courtesy of Larry Briggs)*

1929-S

Mintage:
4,730,000
(Ranking 10/77)

Popular Varieties: A doubled-die obverse variety is known (photos).[39] Also found are one or more varieties having the familiar die crack from wingtip to rim.

Rarity: 1929-S is common in all grades short of fully struck gem, these being slightly scarce. Even so, 1929-S is still the most common 'S' Mint dime of the 1920s in all grades.

A lone example has been certified as MS-68, though it lacks full bands.

COMBINED NGC & PCGS POPULATION									
MS63	MS63FB	MS64	MS64FB	MS65	MS65FB	MS66	MS66FB	MS67	MS67FB
31	39	84	118	82	147	53	102	7	30

Values:

	1945	1955	1965	1975	1985	1995	2005
G	——	.25	.60	.65	1.25	1.50	2.00
F	——	.75	1.50	1.75	3.00	3.00	4.00
XF	——	——	5.00	6.00	6.00	7.00	8.00
MS60	1.50	5.00	16.75	24.00	——	——	——
MS63	——	——	——	——	75.00	45.00	45.00
MS65	——	——	——	——	——	——	125.00

Comments: Less often available in top condition than its Denver Mint cousin, 1929-S still appears with some frequency. Attractive Mint State coins are not too difficult to locate.

As with other coins of this date and mint, circulated 1929-S dimes were widely hoarded during the 1940s and 1950s. San Francisco Mint coins have long possessed a peculiar mystique among collectors, particularly for those in the eastern states. As a result, any coin bearing the magical 'S' was subject to immediate retrieval from circulation whenever found. Collectors in the western states knew that these same coins could be located in low grades without much effort, but they too were tempted to hoard S-Mint coins of the 1920s by the premium prices that were already being offered. Now that the experience of collecting coins from circulation is a fading memory for some and ancient history for most, these heavily worn coins have lost much of their former appeal.

1929-S dimes were among the coins which could be purchased from the Treasury Department at face value, circa 1932.

1929-DDO-1
(Fivaz)

DDO-1
(Fivaz)

1930

Mintage:
6,770,000
(Ranking 18/77)

Popular Varieties: Claims of a 1930/29 overdate are without foundation.

This date is another which may be found with cracks from wingtip to rim.

Rarity: 1930(P) is common only in the lower circulated grades. Although the modest values assigned don't reflect this fact, it is slightly scarce in all grades Very Fine and higher. The number of fully struck gems seems insufficient to meet the demand. Along with 1931(P) this issue is the only 'P' Mint dime dated 1926-45 which is not likely to exist in original rolls.

COMBINED NGC & PCGS POPULATION									
MS63	MS63FB	MS64	MS64FB	MS65	MS65FB	MS66	MS66FB	MS67	MS67FB
24	59	94	188	104	154	51	93	8	11

Values:

	1945	1955	1965	1975	1985	1995	2005
G	——	.35	.45	——	1.25	1.50	1.75
F	——	.75	1.00	1.00	2.00	2.50	3.00
XF	——	——	3.00	4.50	4.50	6.00	8.00
MS60	1.00	3.00	11.50	20.00	——	——	——
MS63	——	——	——	——	30.00	45.00	50.00
MS65	——	——	——	——	——	——	125.00

Comments: With its low mintage for a Philadelphia Mint dime, 1930(P) is more correctly comparable to branch mint issues of similar vintage. In fact, Uncirculated examples are as scarce as 1930-S. The 'S' Mint coins were largely withheld from release until several years after striking, ensuring their survival in Mint State. 1930(P) dimes, however, appear to have entered circulation almost immediately.

Dimes of this date and mint were among the coins which could be purchased from the Treasury Department at face value, circa 1932.

As the effects of the Great Depression grew more evident, demand for new coinage fell off drastically. The low mintage of dimes during 1930 reflects this lessened activity. Already diminished, the Mint's roster of employees further plummeted to only 652 persons as of June 30, 1930.[40]

A total of 114 dimes were tested by the Assay Commission when it met early in 1931.[41] These coins represented a small percentage taken from each delivery of dimes during 1930.

1930-S

Mintage:
1,843,000
(Ranking 7/77)

Popular Varieties: One or more minor varieties display die cracks from wingtip to rim.

Rarity: Fairly common in grades Good through Fine, and slightly scarcer in VF and XF, 1930-S is genuinely difficult to locate in AU. Mint State coins are more available than AU pieces, and an original roll or two may yet exist. Only as a fully struck gem is this issue truly, scarce. Some of the examples certified as having full bands in fact have merely split bands. Such coins will not satisfy the purist who seeks fully raised bands.

COMBINED NGC & PCGS POPULATION									
MS63	MS63FB	MS64	MS64FB	MS65	MS65FB	MS66	MS66FB	MS67	MS67FB
30	32	113	121	105	157	50	71	6	8

Values:

		1945	1955	1965	1975	1985	1995	2005
	G	——	.35	1.75	2.50	3.25	2.75	3.00
	F	——	1.00	3.50	4.50	4.50	4.50	5.00
	XF	——	——	9.00	15.00	11.00	12.00	15.00
	MS60	1.25	12.00	40.00	53.00	——	——	——
	MS63	——	——	——	——	135.00	100.00	110.00
	MS65	——	——	——	——	——	——	200.00

Comments: Widely hoarded in Mint State, it seems likely that this issue was not released in quantity before 1934-35. By then, alert collectors and speculators were waiting eagerly to receive them. The same is true for cents and nickels of this date, which are likewise fairly common in Mint State. The only 1930-S coins which are truly scarce are the quarter dollars. This statement excludes, of course, the ill-fated gold pieces which were almost entirely destroyed after 1933.

1930-S dimes were among the coins which could be purchased from the Treasury Department at face value, circa 1932.

No dimes were coined at the Denver Mint during 1930, yet a number of counterfeit dimes dated 1930-D began to surface during the 1940s. These turned up in ordinary circulation where they were spotted by alert collectors, due to their fictitious combination of date and mint. Being better made than the typical cast counterfeits of the time, it took some years before their spurious nature was confirmed. These and the similar 1923-D dimes are described in some detail in Chapter 4.

1931

Mintage:
3,150,000
(Ranking 8/77)

Popular

Varieties: At least one die is known with the familiar die crack from wingtip to rim.

The die lapping phenomenon known as the "broken nose" is found with this date, as it is for many other dates.

Rarity: 1931(P) is slightly scarce in lower grades, although not enough to be a problem. VF through AU coins are elusive, as are all Mint State grades. Full band specimens are scarce, split bands of varying degree being the norm for this date. Further signs of overall weakness are also evident on many examples.

COMBINED NGC & PCGS POPULATION									
MS63	MS63FB	MS64	MS64FB	MS65	MS65FB	MS66	MS66FB	MS67	MS67FB
49	49	129	145	127	140	34	55	5	8

Values:

	1945	1955	1965	1975	1985	1995	2005
G	——	.35	.90	.75	1.25	1.25	1.50
F	——	.75	2.00	2.00	2.00	3.50	4.00
XF	——	——	4.00	6.50	9.00	10.00	12.00
MS60	1.00	3.50	20.00	40.00	——	——	——
MS63	——	——	——	——	50.00	55.00	60.00
MS65	——	——	——	——	——	——	150.00

Comments: 1931(P) provides an example of why collectors seeking to complete a set of Mercury Dimes in the better circulated grades find so few coins from which to choose. Given the current wholesale and retail values for this scarce date in grades VF through AU, what incentive exists for persons having such coins to offer them for sale? Unfortunately, the values for low end Mint State specimens creates a ceiling through which the values for circulated coins can never penetrate, at least not on paper. In actuality, an experienced collector may pay more than MS-60 money for a particularly choice AU example.

Curiously, this demand for Fine through AU specimens contradicts a claim made by the late Walter Breen in his epic *Encyclopedia of U.S. and Colonial Coins:*

Beginners collect these (dimes) in GOOD or VG; advanced collectors prefer UNC. Intermediate grades tend to be neglected save for the key dates 1916 D, 1921, 1921 D, and overdates.

While this may have indeed been true while silver was still circulating, as witnessed by many advertisements offering only the three key dates in lower grades, current dealers in circulated coins acknowledge a demand for all dates 1916-31 in grades Fine through AU. They further report that these coins are nearly impossible to locate, with but a few exceptions. When found, specimens are almost always badly cleaned and/or damaged.

1931(P) dimes were among the coins which could be purchased from the Treasury Department at face value, circa 1932.

This was the last coinage of dimes at the Philadelphia Mint until 1934, the national economy being so slow that additional coins simply were not needed.

1931-D

Mintage:
1,260,000
(Ranking 4/77)

Popular

Varieties: One doubled-die obverse is known *(photo).*

Rarity: Scarce in all circulated grades, 1931-D is genuinely rare in XF-AU. Mint State coins are relatively abundant, and a high percentage of these possess full bands. Due to its peculiar release pattern, as described below, original rolls may yet exist. While in years past such rolls would have traded hands intact, they are now routinely broken up for submission to grading services.

COMBINED NGC & PCGS POPULATION									
MS63	MS63FB	MS64	MS64FB	MS65	MS65FB	MS66	MS66FB	MS67	MS67FB
12	73	77	320	87	370	34	149	6	32

Values:

		1945	1955	1965	1975	1985	1995	2005
	G	——	.35	3.25	5.00	7.50	5.00	6.00
	F	——	.75	6.00	8.00	11.00	9.00	10.00
	XF	——	——	14.25	20.00	27.50	30.00	35.00
	MS60	1.50	3.75	50.00	60.00	——	——	——
	MS63	——	——	——	——	150.00	100.00	110.00
	MS65	——	——	——	——	——	——	225.00

Comments: As a rule, 1931-D dimes are well struck overall, and many feature full bands.

This issue was coined seemingly as an afterthought. No dies had even been delivered to the Denver Mint as of June 30, 1931.[42] Since few if any of the dimes struck there were released before 1934, this coinage may have been performed merely to keep idled workers busy.

Along with 1929-D, this date was almost always available within any advertised offering of Uncirculated Mercury Dimes during the late 1930s and early 1940s. This indicates a delayed release, probably circa 1934-35, with the customary hoarding by speculators.

Despite the introduction of coin boards for Mercury Dimes in 1935, enabling the public to collect this series from circulation, precious few XF-AU 1931-D dimes are known. They were then and ever afterward rare in circulation. The few uncertified AU 1931-D dimes found at coin shows are often optimistically labeled MS-something-or-other or have been cleaned beyond any further desirability.

That 1931-D dimes were always rare in circulation is illustrated by a survey published in 1938.[43] This study of 5000 dimes taken randomly from circulation in the area of Rock Island, Illinois reveals that a mere seven specimens turned up within just a few years of minting. Excluding 1937-S, which presumably had not had sufficient time to work its way eastward, only three other dates proved more elusive. These were 1916-D, with one example found, 1921-D, three pieces located and 1926-S, for which just six coins turned up during a ten month period ending September 20, 1938.

1931-D dimes were among the coins which could be purchased from the Treasury Department at face value, circa 1932. This was the last coinage of dimes at Denver until 1934.

DDO-1
(Fivaz)

1931-S

Mintage:
1,800,000
(Ranking 6/77)

Popular Varieties: A very slight doubled die obverse is noted *(photo)*. Another variety has a tiny die crack through letter O in the word OF.

Rarity: 1931-S is more common in circulated grades than either 1931-P or 1931-D, due probably to widespread hoarding during the 1940s and 1950s. XF examples are slightly scarce, AU coins are more so. Mint State examples are less common than for 1931-D. The percentage of full band specimens for this date is notably low.

A single example has been certified as MS-68, without full bands.

COMBINED NGC & PCGS POPULATION									
MS63	MS63FB	MS64	MS64FB	MS65	MS65FB	MS66	MS66FB	MS67	MS67FB
71	25	128	63	120	54	70	35	7	4

Values:

	1945	1955	1965	1975	1985	1995	2005
G	——	.35	2.00	2.50	3.25	3.00	4.00
F	——	.75	4.00	4.50	5.00	5.00	6.00
XF	——	——	10.00	15.00	10.00	13.00	15.00
MS60	1.25	6.50	45.00	60.00	——	——	——
MS63	——	——	——	——	135.00	75.00	100.00
MS65	——	——	——	——	——	——	250.00

Comments: Though generally well struck, with the exception of the central and lower diagonal bands, this date is challenging to locate in top grades.

1931-S dimes were among the coins which could be purchased from the Treasury Department at face value, circa 1932. This was the last coinage of dimes at San Francisco until 1935.

No dimes were struck at any mint during 1932-33, though there have been occasional bursts of excitement when some collector or dealer announced the discovery of a 1933-dated dime from one or another of the mints. Most of these reports date from the 1940s through the early 1960s, a time when general ignorance of coinage technology prevented detection of alterations made to dimes originally dated 1938. The Mint itself was of no assistance. In fact, it often added to the problem by routinely denying any and all new discoveries and by occasionally confiscating specimens submitted to it for analysis on the grounds that they were counterfeit. The hobby now enjoys a much more open and productive relationship with the U. S. Mint.

A total of 612 Mint employees were on the roster as of June 30, 1931.[44] These persons were occupied largely with the assaying and refining of bullion into bars. Little in the way of coinage was produced during calendar year 1931.

DDO-1
(Courtesy of Peter K. Beane)

1934

Mintage:
24,080,000
(Ranking 46/77)

Popular Varieties: At least one obverse die displays a break through the date *(photo)*.

Also found is a die crack from wingtip to rim, something of a hallmark for Mercury Dime coinage. 1934(P) also comes with one or more "broken nose" varieties.

Rarity: Common in all circulated grades, low end Mint State coins are similarly abundant. Full band gems, once considered scarce, have since been certified in fairly large numbers. Original rolls may still exist, but their number would be very limited.

A total of 24 MS-68 examples has been certified, and only one of these lacks full bands.

COMBINED NGC & PCGS POPULATION									
MS63	MS63FB	MS64	MS64FB	MS65	MS65FB	MS66	MS66FB	MS67	MS67FB
11	76	80	360	143	504	111	423	28	186

Values:

	1945	1955	1965	1975	1985	1995	2005
G	——	.15	.25	——	1.25	——	——
F	——	.20	.50	.65	1.50	.75	1.20
XF	——	——	1.30	2.00	3.00	2.00	3.50
MS60	.75	1.50	6.00	13.50	——	——	——
MS63	——	——	——	——	37.50	15.00	30.00
MS65	——	——	——	——	——	30.00	50.00

Comments: The biggest problem with this date is quite literally the date itself. Often ill-defined, this weakness is particularly noticeable in numeral 4. Of course, faded dates are a problem with most coins in the series and with the type that followed, the Roosevelt Dime. Shallow elements placed closed to a coin's border tend to fall victim to inadequate metal displacement, leaving them flat and sometimes invisible.

This was the first coinage of dimes at Philadelphia since 1931.

The year 1934 marked a return to the high production figures which had characterized the 1920s. Although the Great Depression would drag on for another seven years before finally being overcome through wartime prosperity, the economic paralysis of 1930-33 was past. Even so, most of 1934's coinage was produced during the second half of the year. In fact, no dimes had been struck at Philadelphia as of June 30.[45]

During those bleak years the combined U. S. Mint roster reached its lowest figures of the 20th Century: 561 persons at the end of Fiscal Year 1932[46] and just 538 employees as of June 30, 1933.[47] Despite increased coinage during 1934 the recovery of jobs was slow. A mere 69 persons were added to the Mint's payroll for a total figure of 607.[48]

1934 witnessed the introduction of inexpensive punch boards for the collecting of coins from circulation, a product described more fully in Chapter 2. Devised by J. K. Post, who later sold his rights to Whitman Publishing Company, these coin boards revolutionized the hobby, making numismatics an activity for the whole family and one which could be pursued at very little expense.

Sold through novelty shops, five-and-ten-cent stores and hobby shops, these boards introduced coin collecting to the general public on a scale never before imagined. Millions were sold by Whitman and its competitors, which included the Colonial Coin &. Stamp Company and the Daniel Stamp Company, better known today as Dansco. By 1940 the familiar, one-piece 11" x 14" format began to give way to the now standard folding boards. That any Mercury Dimes survive between the grades of Good and Uncirculated is due in large part to the widespread popularity of these products.

Another important innovation which appeared in 1934 was *The Standard Catalogue of United States Coins*, published by veteran dealer Wayte Raymond. For the first time a complete, illustrated and priced listing of U. S. coins, including mintage figures, could be purchased in a single volume. This work added greatly to the enthusiasm with which collectors pursued their hobby. Its only drawback was the cover price. Adjusting for inflation, the cost of this book today would be around $35, placing it beyond the realm of the casual collector of coins from circulation. It was not until 1946, with the introduction of R. S. Yeoman's *A Guide Book of United States Coins*, that the most humble of collectors could command a working knowledge of our nation's numismatic heritage. Priced at just $1.50 in its early editions, this volume became an immediate best seller. After more than fifty years, the familiar "Red Book" remains a fixture in the hobby, while Raymond's catalog was last published in 1957.

Die break
(Courtesy of Bill Fivaz)

1934-D

Mintage:
6,772,000
(Ranking 19/77)

Popular Varieties: This date is found with both the Small D of 1917-34 and the Large D of 1934-45 *(photos)*. The former is slightly scarcer, though not enough to warrant any premium.

At least one of the Small D die pairings features a die crack across Liberty's face *(photo)*. Another Small D variety is known with the mintmark repunched.[49] One variety of the Large D has the mintmark repunched *(photo)*. It has been cataloged as Large D over Small D in some references, but this is now known to be erroneous.

A retained cud affecting the word AMERICA is another Large D variety *(photo)*.

Rarity: Common in all circulated grades through Very Fine, pieces grading XF and AU are a challenge to locate. Mint State examples are not rare, but those having full bands are in the minority. When reviewing the certified population figures below, keep in mind that full band coins are more likely to be submitted for certification than those lacking this feature, and that skews the data somewhat.

The highest certified example is a single specimen grading MS-68 FB.

COMBINED NGC & PCGS POPULATION									
MS63	MS63FB	MS64	MS64FB	MS65	MS65FB	MS66	MS66FB	MS67	MS67FB
37	37	229	222	264	280	133	125	21	27

Values:

		1945	1955	1965	1975	1985	1995	2005
G		——	.20	.55	.65	1.25	——	——
F		——	.25	1.15	1.00	1.50	.75	1.70
XF		——	——	2.50	3.50	5.50	5.00	7.50
MS60		1.00	1.75	10.50	31.00	——	——	——
MS63		——	——	——	——	45.00	30.00	60.00
MS65		——	——	——	——	——	65.00	85.00

Comments: So many 1934-D dimes are prooflike that this feature should not command a premium unless accompanied by full bands and an overall sharp strike. The mirror finish of these coins was no doubt caused by severe polishing, or lapping, of the dies in an attempt to remove clash marks. In addition to giving the dies a remarkable brilliance, such polishing often results in Liberty having a "broken nose" and in a weakening of certain design elements. These include the date and the motto IN GOD WE TRUST on the obverse and the mintmark and leaves on the reverse. All of these elements are in low relief to begin with and are therefore quite subject to the negative effects of die polishing.

An amusing letter published in 1939 reveals that collectors of that time were cognizant of various irregularities in the current coinage, although not especially knowledgeable about the minting process:

> Have in my possession a dime of 1934, D mint, with the figure four almost invisible. This coin has not been smashed for there are no marks on the coin. I wonder if this is a common die break?[50]

Aside from misattributing poor metal displacement to a die break, this letter reveals that the occurrence of flat or missing 4's for this date was noticed early on by collectors. Like 1934(P), this issue is plagued by incomplete dates, as well as by the weak peripheral elements found with so many Mercury Dimes.

The reason for introducing a new mintmark punch for Denver Mint dies may be found in examining the few 'D' Mint coins produced during the early 1930s. Although 1931-D dimes and double eagles usually have a very distinct mintmark, many Washington Quarters dated 1932-D and most of the small D 1934-D dimes reveal shallow or entirely filled D's. This suggests that some deterioration was occurring with this punch and that a replacement was inevitable. By making the new punch slightly more open, the chance of it again becoming filled was thereby reduced. The Large D puncheon debuted on the cents and Oregon Trail Half Dollars of 1933 and was used without interruption through the end of the Mercury Dime series.

This was the first coinage of dimes at Denver since 1931. Only 673,000 pieces had been struck as of June 30.[51]

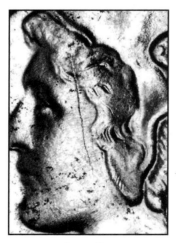

Die crack, small D reverse

Retained cud from 2 to 3 o'clock
*(Sam Thurman Collection,
courtesy of Arnold Margolis)*

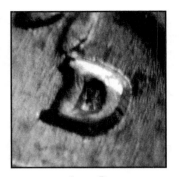

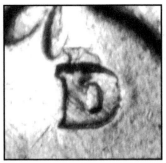

Small D
(Fivaz)

Large D
(Fivaz)

Large D, RPM-1
(Fivaz)

1935

Mintage:
58,830,000
(Ranking 64/77)

Popular Varieties: Two doubled-die obverse varieties are known, and the more prominent of these is illustrated *(photo)*.[52]

Rarity: 1935(P) is common in all circulated grades. Mint state pieces are likewise common, even those having full bands. Original rolls may still exist of this issue.

Six examples have been certified as MS-68, all having full bands.

COMBINED NGC & PCGS POPULATION									
MS63	MS63FB	MS64	MS64FB	MS65	MS65FB	MS66	MS66FB	MS67	MS67FB
15	59	101	319	235	825	293	821	103	251

Values:

	1945	1955	1965	1975	1985	1995	2005
G	——	.15	.20	——	1.25	——	——
F	——	.20	.50	.65	1.50	.75	1.20
XF	——	——	.75	1.50	3.00	2.00	2.00
MS60	.75	1.00	3.50	6.00	——	——	——
MS63	——	——	——	——	25.00	12.00	15.00
MS65	——	——	——	——	——	33.00	37.00

Comments: The low mintages of 1930-33 across all denominations, combined with a delay in the release of many of these coins until 1934 and later, led to a speculative market in Uncirculated rolls. After 1934 the regular saving of Uncirculated coins by the roll became an institution with many collectors. Consequently, from 1934 onward there are no United States regular issue coins which are truly rare in Uncirculated condition, though exceptions are made by error and variety specialists.

Some dates from within the last ten years of the Mercury Dime series have proved to be elusive with full bands. These will be identified as such, but it may otherwise be assumed that all dates 1935-1945 are common in Mint State. These issues are universally common in circulated grades, too, thanks to the advent of coin boards in 1934 and the hoarding of all silver coins beginning in 1965. Where no prices are given for circulated grades, it may be concluded that such coins trade at or slightly above their bullion value. The high values shown for circulated dimes in 1985 were the result of an inflated market in silver during the early 1980s.

As the number of coins being struck during 1935 rose, so too did the number of Mint employees. In fact, this figure more than tripled, reaching some 1,853 persons by the end of Fiscal Year 1935.[53] This would be the highest such figure recorded before America's entry into World War II.

DDO-1
(Fivaz)

1935-D

Mintage:
10,477,000
(Ranking 31/77)

Popular

Varieties: One repunched mintmark is noted *(photo)*.

Rarity: Gem specimens are limited in number by problems of strike, both in the central bands and along the periphery.

               No examples of 1935-D have been graded higher than MS-67 FB.

COMBINED NGC & PCGS POPULATION									
MS63	MS63FB	MS64	MS64FB	MS65	MS65FB	MS66	MS66FB	MS67	MS67FB
28	49	146	154	157	206	70	86	13	16

Values:		1945	1955	1965	1975	1985	1995	2005
	G	——	.15	.30	——	1.25	——	——
	F	——	.20	.65	1.00	1.50	.75	1.70
	XF	——	——	2.50	3.50	6.50	3.00	8.00
	MS60	1.00	2.50	20.00	35.00	——	——	——
	MS63	——	——	——	——	80.00	35.00	45.00
	MS65	——	——	——	——	——	65.00	80.00

Comments: Even a collector who is not particular about full center bands will have a tough time with this date, as both obverse and reverse often reveal indifference to quality control. This seems to be true of all denominations coined at Denver during 1935. On the plus side, 'D' Mint dimes of the 1930s typically have excellent luster.

RPM-1
(Courtesy of Tom Miller)

Circular die polishing lines

1935-S

Mintage:
15,840,000
(Ranking 35/77)

**Popular
Varieties:** Two repunched mintmark reverses are known,[54] along with another reverse variety featuring a prominent cud in the ten o'clock position *(photos)*.

Rarity: Common in all grades short of full bands gem, these are relatively scarce.

Of the three pieces certified as MS-68, all lack full bands.

COMBINED NGC & PCGS POPULATION									
MS63	MS63FB	MS64	MS64FB	MS65	MS65FB	MS66	MS66FB	MS67	MS67FB
29	15	151	141	263	209	169	169	34	78

Values:

		1945	1955	1965	1975	1985	1995	2005
	G	——	.15	.35	——	1.25	——	——
	F	——	.20	.60	.65	1.50	.75	1.20
	XF	——	——	1.50	2.00	4.25	3.00	4.00
	MS60	1.00	2.00	7.50	11.50	——	——	——
	MS63	——	——	——	——	37.50	20.00	30.00
	MS65	——	——	——	——	——	45.00	40.00

Comments: In the first edition of this book, published in 1993, it was noted that just 48% of the certified Mint State population possessed full bands. The figures above, gathered more than ten years later, reveal that the percentage is now much higher. It may be that full band dimes are more likely to be submitted and then resubmitted to the grading services than are flat or partial band dimes. It may be true, too, that the grading services have relaxed their standards for designating a Mercury Dime as having full bands. Both scenarios are likely true, and thus the actual percentage of full band dimes of this date is probably lower than the population reports suggest.

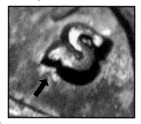

RPM -1
(Miller)

Writing in *The Coin Dealer Newsletter Monthly Summary* for May of 1980, Rick Sear had this to say about the 1935-S dime:

> The major difference in availability between this and the 1935-D is that there are many more "flat split" 1935-S's available. A few years ago an occasional roll would surface with perhaps a third of the coins having a "technical" split. Much as the 1919-D, the availability of flat-split specimens has distorted perception of how many "rounded-bands" gems are around.

1935-S was the first coinage of dimes at San Francisco since 1931.

Cud die break
*(SamThurman Collection, courtesy
of Arnald Margolis)*

1936
Mintage:
87,500,000
(Ranking 72/77)

Popular Varieties:

The great number of dies required for this year's high mintage resulted in no less than eight known doubled-die obverses. The most distinctive and prominent of these is illustrated *(photo)*, and it is included in *The Cherrypickers' Guide to Rare Die Varieties*, by Bill Fivaz and J. T. Stanton. Variety specialists will want to study the less well known DDO varieties, as published in the book *Treasure Hunting Mercury Dimes*, by John A. Wexler and Kevin Flynn.

Die break
(Courtesy of Bill Fivaz)

In the realm of lesser varieties, a prominent crack may be found through the date *(photo)*.

Rarity:

1936(P) is common in all popular grades, including full bands gem. Original rolls may still exist.

Of the ten pieces certified as MS-68, all but two have full bands.

COMBINED NGC & PCGS POPULATION									
MS63	MS63FB	MS64	MS64FB	MS65	MS65FB	MS66	MS66FB	MS67	MS67FB
30	54	240	298	513	695	503	552	147	163

Values:

	1945	1955	1965	1975	1985	1995	2005
G	——	——	——	——	1.25	——	——
F	——	——	——	——	1.50	.75	1.20
XF	——	——	——	.80	3.00	2.00	3.00
MS60	.50	.50	1.80	4.25	——	——	——
MS63	——	——	——	——	24.00	16.00	18.00
MS65	——	——	——	——	——	30.00	30.00

Comments:

This issue is notable for its great availability in Mint State. The quality of these coins is highly variable, but enough nice ones survive to satisfy the demand.

The sale of proof coins to the public was resumed in this year, following 20-year hiatus. This is the earliest date in the Mercury Dime series generally available as a proof striking. For more on these specialty coins, see Chapter 7.

DDO–1
(Courtesy of J.T. Stanton)

1936-D

Mintage:
16,132,000
(Ranking 36/77)

Popular Varieties: At least five repunched mintmarks have been reported, and three of these are illustrated *(photos)*.

Rarity: Mint State examples are not rare, but the quality conscious buyer will be dismayed. Lustrous, fully struck coins are scarce. Original rolls may yet exist, but these will ultimately be broken in search of gem singles for submission to the grading services.

Four 1936-D dimes have been certified as MS-68 FB.

COMBINED NGC & PCGS POPULATION									
MS63	MS63FB	MS64	MS64FB	MS65	MS65FB	MS66	MS66FB	MS67	MS67FB
9	38	82	143	122	344	74	220	17	72

Values:

	1945	1955	1965	1975	1985	1995	2005
G	——	——	——	——	1.25	——	——
F	——	——	——	.65	1.50	.75	1.70
XF	——	——	2.50	3.00	4.50	3.00	5.00
MS60	.75	2.00	16.50	28.50	——	——	——
MS63	——	——	——	——	55.00	25.00	30.00
MS65	——	——	——	——	——	40.00	45.00

Comments: Many 1936-D dimes are plagued by deep and irregular die polishing lines. Although mint made, these flaws may impair a coin's luster and are visually distracting. They will also have a negative impact on the coin's certified grade, since this is so heavily dependent on surface quality.

Note the significant drop in value for MS-63 between 1985 and 1995. What happened? A likely explanation is that the rarity of such coins was widely misunderstood before the advent of certified grading population reports. These debuted in the late 1980s and quickly dispelled many myths about the relative rarity of popular coins. The author was collecting choice and gem Mercury Dimes in the mid-1970s until the market in these coins exploded around 1978. Prices for dates from 1934 onward seemed to quadruple in just a couple of years, leading this writer and many others to look elsewhere for a collectable series. The high prices for gem Mercury Dimes largely survived the overall market setback of 1980-82, but they could not survive the revelation by certified population reports that they were not so rare, after all. Values for these later dates in the series have never fully recovered their pre-certification price levels.

RPM-1
(Courtesy of Tom Miller)

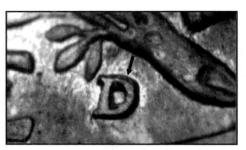

RPM-2
(Miller)

RPM-5
(Courtesy of Bill Fivaz)

1936-S

Mintage:
9,210,000
(Ranking 26/77)

Popular Varieties: At least one die displays the common crack from wingtip to rim. Another appears on the reverse from the top of the A in STATES to the rim. The only other thing which might qualify as a variety is the so-called "broken nose" *(photo)*.

Rarity: 1936-S is fairly common in most grades, including fully struck gem. Original rolls may exist.

A single coin grading MS-68 FB has been certified.

COMBINED NGC & PCGS POPULATION									
MS63	MS63FB	MS64	MS64FB	MS65	MS65FB	MS66	MS66FB	MS67	MS67FB
4	32	32	392	98	1168	102	695	19	118

Values:		1945	1955	1965	1975	1985	1995	2005
	G	—	—	—	—	1.25	—	—
	F	—	—	—	.65	1.50	.75	1.20
	XF	—	—	2.50	2.00	3.00	2.00	3.00
	MS60	.75	2.00	8.00	12.50	—	—	—
	MS63	—	—	—	—	30.00	15.00	25.00
	MS65	—	—	—	—	—	35.00	35.00

Comments: 1936-S dimes frequently are seen with evidence of erratic and excessive lapping of the dies, which left brilliant patches that contrast dramatically with the normal frosty luster of the coin. This phenomenon sometimes is described as "die burn," though this term has no official status. It seemed to occur most often on the obverse, either in front or in back of Liberty's head. Another frequent consequence of this aggressive polishing is the "broken nose" effect seen on so many Mercury Dimes. More conventional die polishing lines are also illustrated for contrast *(photo)*.

A certain number of 1936-S dimes have a slightly prooflike quality. This finish was caused by the same lapping of the dies that created die burn, but here applied in an overall, balanced manner. This can be quite attractive, and it's often associated with San Francisco Mint dimes of the late 1930s and 1940s.

Burnishing of the die left Liberty with a "broken nose" and a "burned" patch

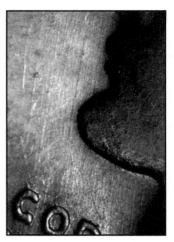

Die polishing lines

1937

Mintage:
56,860,000
(Ranking 63/77)

Popular

Varieties: At least seven doubled-die obverses are known.[55] Most of these are very minor and of interest only to variety specialists. The most popular one is illustrated *(photo)*.

While not strictly qualifying as a variety, photos are included here of a dime whose dies suffered a clashing. The dies struck one another, due perhaps to a failure of the feeder fingers to set a planchet between them. Each die received an inverted impression of its opposite, and these shallow, raised lines were then imparted to each coin struck from the dies until the clash marks were removed through lapping.

Rarity: Common in all popularly collected grades, original rolls may exist.

COMBINED NGC & PCGS POPULATION									
MS64	MS64FB	MS65	MS65FB	MS66	MS66FB	MS67	MS67FB	MS68	MS68FB
181	622	543	1879	1087	1941	439	711	22	32

Values:		1945	1955	1965	1975	1985	1995	2005
	G	——	——	——	——	1.25	——	——
	F	——	——	——	——	1.50	.75	1.20
	XF	——	——	——	.80	3.00	2.00	2.25
	MS60	.50	.40	1.80	3.75	——	——	——
	MS63	——	——	——	——	22.00	15.00	15.00
	MS65	——	——	——	——	——	25.00	30.00

Comments: This is perhaps the most common Philadelphia Mint dime of the 1930s in Mint State condition. A large coinage accounts in part for this availability, but a more important factor is the number of pieces saved by the roll. Unlike in earlier years, when Mercury Dimes were saved primarily as singles, the practice of roll collecting was firmly in place by the mid-1930s.

Advertisements from the 1930s and early '40s usually were directed toward the selling of recent date, Uncirculated coins, either as singles or by the roll. With only a few exceptions, Uncirculated Mercury Dimes dated before 1929 were rarely to be found within these ads. The only ones which could be purchased with ease were 1916(P), 1916-S and 1917(P). Periodic offerings of Philadelphia Mint dimes from the pre-1929 period were seen, but mintmarked examples from the years 1918 through 1928 were seldom advertised. To the author's knowledge, the first comprehensive offering of Uncirculated Mercury Dimes was the ad placed by dealer John R. Stewart of

Milwaukee in the January 1940 issue of *The Numismatist*. It's likely that most dealers could supply the desired coins upon request, but they did not maintain sufficient inventory to warrant advertising these scarcer dates.

DDO-1
(Courtesy of J.T. Stanton)

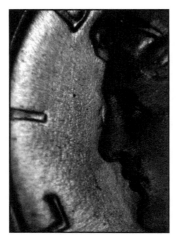

Clash marks

Clash marks

1937-D

Mintage:
14,146,000
(Ranking 34/77)

Popular Varieties: A single variety with repunched mintmark is known *(photo)*.

Rarity: Common in all popular grades, original rolls may exist.

COMBINED NGC & PCGS POPULATION									
MS64	MS64FB	MS65	MS65FB	MS66	MS66FB	MS67	MS67FB	MS68	MS68FB
47	276	102	610	108	639	26	265	3	22

Values:

		1945	1955	1965	1975	1985	1995	2005
	G	——	——	——	——	1.25	——	——
	F	——	——	——	.65	1.50	.75	1.20
	XF	——	——	1.25	1.25	3.00	2.00	3.50
	MS60	.50	1.00	5.00	9.50	——	——	——
	MS63	——	——	——	——	37.50	20.00	28.00
	MS65	——	——	——	——	——	45.00	45.00

Comments: As with all dates from 1936 through 1945, the supply of Uncirculated examples likely exceeds the demand. Even so, the number of gem pieces having full bands is small enough to provide some challenge. Like all denominations struck at Denver in 1937, both luster and strike are generally superior to that seen in earlier products of this mint. Semi-prooflike examples may be found.

An episode related by Harry Boosel in his "Capital Comment" column sheds a humorous light on the ceaseless struggle by collectors of that time to secure newly minted coins:

> A recent visit to the Treasury department to secure two of the new 1937 Denver half-dollars, left your correspondent a bit flabbergasted. One dollar was paid for the two halves, and they were brought out on a cardboard. We inquired about two envelopes for the coins, and were told that the Treasury Department no longer furnishes envelopes except for those coins sent out. After a little persuasion, we were able to get two small pieces of paper to wrap the coins in. Moral: When securing coins from the Treasury Department, bring you own envelopes.[56]

In reading this account it must be remembered that the Treasury Department's sales of Uncirculated year sets, commonly called "mint sets" by collectors, did not begin until 1948. Today's hobbyists are thus spared a great deal of inconvenience. With progress, however, comes some cost. The coins, now readily available and attractively packaged, are no longer furnished at face value.

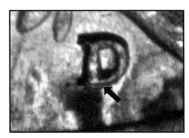

RPM -1
(Courtesy of Tom Miller)

Heavy die polishing lines
(Fivaz)

1937-S

Mintage:
9,740,000
(Ranking 28/77)

Popular

Varieties: A single repunched mintmark was reported years ago, but its existence now appears doubtful. A minor doubled-die obverse is confirmed.[57]

Rarity: Fairly common in all grades through partial or split bands gem, examples having full bands are considerably scarcer. Original rolls may still exist, but this likelihood has diminished since the debut of encapsulation services in 1986.

COMBINED NGC & PCGS POPULATION									
MS64	MS64FB	MS65	MS65FB	MS66	MS66FB	MS67	MS67FB	MS68	MS68FB
120	154	333	344	392	169	150	70	3	2

Values:

		1945	1955	1965	1975	1985	1995	2005
	G	——	——	——	——	1.25	——	——
	F	——	——	——	.65	1.50	.75	1.20
	XF	——	——	1.25	1.25	3.00	1.25	3.00
	MS60	.75	1.25	5.75	9.00	——	——	——
	MS63	——	——	——	——	27.50	18.00	28.00
	MS65	——	——	——	——	——	35.00	35.00

Comments: The percentage of full bands coins is relatively low, and this is true of all 'S' Mint dimes through the end of the series. The certified population is skewed in favor of coins having full bands, since these are more likely to be submitted one or more times.

Like other 'S' Mint dimes dated 1936-42, this issue often comes semi-prooflike, particularly on the obverse. If this brilliant polishing doesn't cover the entire surface of either obverse or reverse, then isolated hot spots called "die burn" may result.

The San Francisco Mint building of 1874 was the oldest operating coin factory within the United States Mint system. By 1935 it was deemed obsolete, and the cornerstone for a new structure was laid that year. The new San Francisco Mint opened for business in May of 1937. Regrettably, no commemorative medals were issued for the occasion, nor is there any way to distinguish between 1937-S coins minted at the different locations.

1938

Mintage:
22,190,000
(Ranking 43/77)

Popular

Varieties: None are reported.

Rarity: · Common in all grades excepting full bands gem, original rolls may exist.

COMBINED NGC & PCGS POPULATION									
MS64	MS64FB	MS65	MS65FB	MS66	MS66FB	MS67	MS67FB	MS68	MS68FB
93	272	333	715	485	673	243	258	10	5

Values:

	1945	1955	1965	1975	1985	1995	2005
G	——	——	——	——	——	——	——
F	——	——	——	——	1.25	.50	1.20
XF	——	——	——	.95	3.00	1.25	2.75
MS60	.50	.40	2.50	5.75	22.00	——	——
MS63	——	——	——	——	——	15.00	15.00
MS65	——	——	——	——	40.00	25.00	25.00

Comments: While common in gem condition, 1938(P) dimes have a far lower percentage of full band coins than their Denver Mint counterparts. 'D' Mint dimes are the most consistently well struck of the three mints, not just with respect to the central bands, but in their entirety. Philadelphia Mint dimes typically place second, with 'S' Mints being the most difficult to find having full bands. This pattern generally is true for all Mercury Dimes from the mid-1930s through the end of the series.

After three years of extremely large coinages, the Philadelphia Mint relaxed a bit. The recession which had set in during the latter part of 1937 slowed the nation's economy throughout 1938. This fact is reflected in lower production figures for all five denominations.

Two interesting stories date from 1938. The first of these was the inception of the March of Dimes, a fundraising campaign devised for the treatment and eventual cure of polio. President of the United States Franklin D. Roosevelt was certainly the most well known figure disabled by this virus, and he became indelibly associated with the program. In fact, his death in 1945, occurring while he was still in office, led to the adoption of a circulating commemorative dime which succeeded the familiar Mercury type. The dime denomination was chosen as a direct reference to his participation in the March of Dimes campaign.

The end of Mercury Dime coinage might easily have come even sooner, if some persons had had their way. Their were occasional protests over America's "fascist dime,"[58] a reference to the use of a fasces by Italian leader Benito Mussolini's Fascist Party as its symbol. In addition, a movement began around 1938-39 to have the portrait of Benjamin Franklin placed on our ten-cent piece. At the behest of Mint Director Nellie Tayloe Ross, studies were actually made by Chief Engraver John Ray Sinnock for such a coin, though this work doesn't seem to have survived. Despite the forced interruption of World War II, the idea of a Franklin Dime persisted. It seems that only the sudden death of President Roosevelt and the subsequent placement of his portrait on the dime caused this plan to be cancelled.

At the continued urging of Director Ross, Benjamin Franklin's profile ultimately was placed on the new half dollar of 1948. In the few years that passed between the conception and realization of the Franklin coin, Sinnock had died, and the actual sculpting for the half dollar was performed by his successor, Gilroy Roberts. The new Chief Engraver seemingly based his work on Sinnock's preliminary studies, and it was the initials 'JRS' that actually appear on the coins.

1938-D

Mintage:
5,537,000
(Ranking 15/77)

Popular Varieties: A single repunched mintmark variety is known *(photo)*.

Rarity: 1938-D is common in all popular grades, including fully struck gem. Original rolls may exist.

COMBINED NGC & PCGS POPULATION									
MS64	MS64FB	MS65	MS65FB	MS66	MS66FB	MS67	MS67FB	MS68	MS68FB
26	438	103	1202	128	1260	35	330	2	12

Values:		1945	1955	1965	1975	1985	1995	2005
	G	——	——	——	——	——	——	——
	F	——	——	——	.65	1.25	.75	2.00
	XF	——	——	1.25	1.75	3.00	2.00	3.00
	MS60	.50	.60	5.50	11.00	40.00	——	——
	MS63	——	——	——	——	——	17.00	20.00
	MS65	——	——	——	——	70.00	35.00	32.00

Comments: 1938-D dimes consistently are among the most appealing issues in this series. Excellent luster and generally full strikes are the norm. This is true of Denver Mint dimes in general from the late 1930s through the end of the series.

A number of semi-prooflike specimens may be found, such reflective fields being more typically associated with the San Francisco Mint. This finish resulted from vigorous lapping of the dies, which may or may not have been performed in an effort to remove some flaw such as clash marks.

Although 1938-D has the lowest mintage from 1934 through 1945, it is certainly not the scarcest coin. Like other Denver Mint dimes from 1937 onward, this issue was widely saved by the roll. While all Mercury Dimes after 1934 were retained in roll quantities, 'D' Mint coins seem to have been targeted in greater numbers. Numismatic journals of the 1930s published the monthly production figures from the three mints, and a lower than usual mintage such as that reported for 1938-D would certainly have attracted the interest of speculators.

Another possible factor in the availability of this date and mint is the geographical spread of the coin collecting hobby during the 1930s. Contemporary advertisements from *The Numismatist* and *The Numismatic Scrapbook Magazine* reveal a greater number of dealers from the Midwest than from any other region. It's only logical that these individuals would have more opportunities for acquiring new rolls of Denver Mint dimes than they would for those of the other mints.

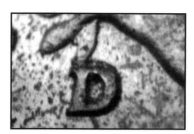

RPM -1
(Courtesy of Tom Miller)

1938-S

Mintage:
8,090,000
(Ranking 24/77)

Popular Varieties: 1938-S is known with the familiar die crack from wingtip to rim.

Rarity: Most Mint State grades are fairly common, though the figures below tend to exaggerate the number of coins having full bands. Original rolls may exist.

COMBINED NGC & PCGS POPULATION									
MS64	MS64FB	MS65	MS65FB	MS66	MS66FB	MS67	MS67FB	MS68	MS68FB
153	262	224	466	254	424	69	141	2	12

Values:

	1945	1955	1965	1975	1985	1995	2005
G	——	——	——	——	——	——	——
F	——	——	——	.65	1.25	.50	1.20
XF	——	——	1.50	1.75	3.00	1.25	3.00
MS60	.50	1.25	5.50	9.00	30.00	——	——
MS63	——	——	——	——	——	15.00	20.00
MS65	——	——	——	——	45.00	30.00	32.00

Comments: Like other 'S' Mint dimes of the period, semi-prooflike examples are not unusual. If well struck and relatively free of marks, these may command a premium.

The Mercury Dime had been designed during a period in which American art thrived, reaching its greatest glory in the use of neo-classical realism. By 1938 that period had already closed, to be succeeded by several generations in which a simpler, less ornamental art came to prominence. This changing aesthetic was reflected in the Washington Quarter Dollar of 1932 and the Jefferson Nickel which debuted in 1938.

Already discarded were three of the Mercury Dime's contemporaries—the Buffalo Nickel, the Standing Liberty Quarter Dollar and the Peace Silver Dollar. Also terminated were the radical gold designs instigated by President Theodore Roosevelt and brought to fruition by sculptors Augustus Saint-Gaudens and Bela Lyon Pratt. Soon, too, Adolph Weinman's dime and half dollar would succumb to the sterile and severe tastes of a more international society. It ultimately remains for numismatists alone to preserve and cherish these lasting testaments to the finest flourishing of American art.

1939

Mintage:
67,740,000
(Ranking 70/77)

Popular Varieties: With its large mintage, this issue produced at least five doubled-die obverses.[59] All of these are quite minor, the most popular one being illustrated *(photo)*.

Rarity: Common in all grades short of full bands gem, original rolls may exist.

A single example has been certified as MS-69, but it lacks full bands. 1939-D and 1945-S are the only other issues in the series to have received this lofty grade.

COMBINED NGC & PCGS POPULATION									
MS64	MS64FB	MS65	MS65FB	MS66	MS66FB	MS67	MS67FB	MS68	MS68FB
493	155	1028	298	1381	288	1474	97	125	4

Values:

	1945	1955	1965	1975	1985	1995	2005
G	——	——	——	——	——	——	——
F	——	——	——	——	1.25	.50	1.20
XF	——	——	——	.85	3.00	1.25	2.50
MS60	.35	.40	1.85	3.75	15.00	——	——
MS63	——	——	——	——	——	11.00	12.00
MS65	——	——	——	——	25.00	25.00	25.00

Comments: The rarity of fully struck coins is emphasized by the low percentage of certified examples designated as FB. In all other respects, however, Mint State 1939(P) dimes typically are quite attractive coins.

DDO-1
(Fivaz)

1939-D

Mintage:
24,394,000
(Ranking 47/77)

Popular Varieties: A doubled-die reverse was reported, but it remains unconfirmed. At least three repunched mintmark reverses are known.[60] These are quite minor and of interest only to variety specialists.

Rarity: Common in all grades through fully struck gem, original rolls may exist. Full band examples comprise the majority of surviving Mint State coins.

Some 16 examples have been certified as MS-69 FB, making 1939-D the most "common" Mercury Dime in this grade.

COMBINED NGC & PCGS POPULATION									
MS64	MS64FB	MS65	MS65FB	MS66	MS66FB	MS67	MS67FB	MS68	MS68FB
128	492	429	1587	740	1712	302	702	6	83

Values:

	1945	1955	1965	1975	1985	1995	2005
G	——	——	——	——	——	——	——
F	——	——	——	——	1.25	.50	1.20
XF	——	——	——	.85	3.00	1.25	2.50
MS60	.35	.50	2.50	4.75	16.00	——	——
MS63	——	——	——	——	——	12.00	12.00
MS65	——	——	——	——	27.00	25.00	25.00

Comments: To the degree that 1939(P) and 1939-S are scarce with full bands, 1939-D is common. This issue is the quintessential type coin, being perhaps the most consistently attractive Mercury Dime in the entire series. 1939-D has graced many a high-grade type set, including the famous Knoxville Collection. This writer had the pleasure of cataloging those coins, and the Knoxville Collection's 1939-D dime graces the cover of this book.

A small percentage of Mint State examples are semi-prooflike, as in 1938.

1939-S

Mintage:
10,540,000
(Ranking 32/77)

Popular Varieties: The often-seen die crack from wingtip to rim is known, as is a die break connecting numerals 1 and 9 in the date.

Rarity: 1939-S is slightly scarce in all Mint State grades and is genuinely rare with full bands. The widespread search for gem singles has largely eliminated the possibility of encountering an original roll.

COMBINED NGC & PCGS POPULATION									
MS64	MS64FB	MS65	MS65FB	MS66	MS66FB	MS67	MS67FB	MS68	MS68FB
242	119	463	130	370	99	126	28	2	1

Values:

		1945	1955	1965	1975	1985	1995	2005
	G	——	——	——	——	——	——	——
	F	——	——	——	.65	1.25	.50	1.50
	XF	——	——	1.25	1.75	3.00	2.00	3.00
	MS60	.50	1.25	5.25	14.00	37.00	——	——
	MS63	——	——	——	——	——	20.00	25.00
	MS65	——	——	——	——	60.00	45.00	40.00

Comments: 1939-S seems to have been somewhat overlooked in the mania for saving rolls which was so much a part of the hobby from 1934 through 1964. Uncirculated examples of this date are more scarce than for nearly all other dates in the 1934-45 sequence, only 1934-D, 1935-D, 1935-S and the two overdates being tougher to find.

Partial or split bands are scarce enough for this date that such coins may have to suffice for the budget minded collector. A gem having fully rounded bands is a rarity, and a number of the ones so graded by the certification services will fail to convince the purist. A certain relaxation of the accepted definition for full bands may be in order with this date.

Like other 'S' Mint dimes of this period, a minority are found semi-prooflike.

The opening of a new San Francisco Mint in 1937 led to a number of interruptions in coinage over the next few years, as related in this news item from 1939:

> The San Francisco Mint is occupied with the last of the removal of precious metals from the old Mint at 5th and Mission Sts., so has halted coinage for the time.[61]

1940

Mintage:
65,350,000
(Ranking 69/77)

Popular

Varieties: None are reported.

Rarity: Common in all popular grades, including fully struck gem, some original rolls likely exist. Coins having full bands form a minority of the overall population, but a majority of the certified population.

COMBINED NGC & PCGS POPULATION									
MS64	MS64FB	MS65	MS65FB	MS66	MS66FB	MS67	MS67FB	MS68	MS68FB
175	371	510	1026	740	1092	632	435	11	12

Values:

	1945	1955	1965	1975	1985	1995	2005
G	——	——	——	——	——	——	——
F	——	——	——	——	1.25	.50	.90
XF	——	——	——	.85	3.00	1.25	1.50
MS60	.35	.40	1.50	3.75	10.00	——	——
MS63	——	——	——	——	——	8.00	10.00
MS65	——	——	——	——	18.00	20.00	24.00

Comments: While the majority of certified 1940(P) dimes have full bands, these figures are a bit misleading. Full band coins are far more likely to be submitted for grading than their weaker companions. Also, the majority of common-date Mercury Dimes are submitted by dealers, rather than collectors. These dealers are likely to submit such coins in large quantities utilizing the pre-screen option offered by both of the leading grading services. This option permits the dealer to specify a minimum grade below which the coins will not be graded at all, but rather will be returned raw (uncertified) in tubes. More likely than not, the submitter will specify to not encapsulate coins that don't have full bands, greatly skewing the certified population of these common dates.

Dimes struck at the Philadelphia Mint from 1936 through 1945 are more likely to be found without full bands. This diminishing of quality seems to have intensified as mintages grew, reaching its worst point during 1944-45. Fortunately, enough uncirculated 'P' Mint Mercury Dimes survive from the years 1936-45 that a satisfactory number of full band specimens exists for all dates except 1945(P).

Another aspect of this lower quality, particularly for 'P' Mint dimes dated 1940-45, was the generally poorer maintenance evident in dies used at Philadelphia. While the dies for all three mints were manufactured there alone, those employed for coining at Philly seem to have been the ones most abused by the Coining Department.

It's possible that the unprecedented mintages brought on by a wartime economy simply overtaxed the mint's capacity to produce new dies. This, in turn, would have led to prolonged use of the existing dies with a corresponding increase in wear. Furthermore, employees may have been tempted to offset the rate of wear by increasing the set distance between the dies. While indeed achieving their immediate goal of reduced die wear, this action would also have diminished the amount of high point detail in evidence as the planchet metal failed to completely fill the dies. 'P' Mint dimes dated 1940-45 often reveal the effects of both worn dies and increased set distances.

Most 1940(P) dimes were coined during the second half of the year, only 22,265,633 pieces having been struck as of June 30.[62]

1940-D

Mintage:
21,198,000
(Ranking 40/77)

Popular

Varieties: 1940-D dimes provide a rich hunting ground for variety enthusiasts. Some eight doubled-die obverses and three doubled-die reverses are known.[63] In addition, no fewer than seven repunched mintmarks are known, of which three are illustrated here *(photos)*.

Rarity: This date is common in all grades through MS-66 FB. Original rolls likely exist.

COMBINED NGC & PCGS POPULATION									
MS64	MS64FB	MS65	MS65FB	MS66	MS66FB	MS67	MS67FB	MS68	MS68FB
69	395	218	1067	395	1161	150	382	4	20

Values:

	1945	1955	1965	1975	1985	1995	2005
G	——	——	——	——	——	——	——
F	——	——	——	——	1.25	.50	.90
XF	——	——	——	.85	3.00	1.25	1.50
MS60	.35	.45	1.75	7.50	22.00	——	——
MS63	——	——	——	——	——	13.00	14.00
MS65	——	——	——	——	35.00	25.00	25.00

Comments: The percentage of coins having full bands is quite high with this date, and nearly all have at least split bands. 1940-D is among the more common Mercury Dimes in gem, fully struck condition.

The coining of silver at the Denver Mint seems to have been something of an afterthought during 1940. No silver pieces had been struck as of mid-year,[64] and the dimes alone were destined to be made in substantial numbers. Fewer than three million quarters were coined, while the year would end with no halves being produced at all there.[65]

Dimes dated 1940 once enjoyed some whimsical notoriety, as related in the following account by C. B. Edwards of Wichita, Kansas:

> Our story begins August 1, 1950. It seems that Mrs. Tucker, Sherman, Texas manufacturer and distributor of oleomargarine, decided to celebrate the removal of the tax on Oleo. Mrs. Tucker's oleomargarine was brought into being in 1940. She decided to collect 1940 dimes, P, D, or S mint—no thought of condition—just the date. During August and September she was the greatest volume coin collector in the country, even though the collection was made only in three states of Texas, Oklahoma and Kansas. Literally thousands of 1940 dimes both new and old poured into her coffers. Mrs. Tucker gave one pound of Oleo for each 1940 dime presented to a grocer carrying her product. The grocer was paid the purchase price of

the product for each dime. Everybody was happy—but—the story does not end there. Housewives, kids, men, everyone searched for 1940 dimes. Collectors and coin dealers got into the game. 1940 dimes were a low issue. About three per cent of dimes in circulation today are 1940 date—since the sale the percentage has gone to about "zero" in the tri state area. People got the coin collecting habit and started dime collections of all dates and mint marks—some fine 1916D and 1921P were unearthed. Dealers all over the country received orders for uncirculated 1940 P, D or S dimes in rolls and many of them have sold out.

As a result, uncirculated 1940 dimes, P, D or S mint mark in rolls will be "circulated singles" when Mrs. Tucker dumps her hoards into the Federal Reserve Banks. If she continues the sale in other states the Brilliant Uncirculated 1940 P D S dimes will become as scarce as "hens teeth," and that "my children" in this instance, is how an uncirculated "sleeper" was born.[66]

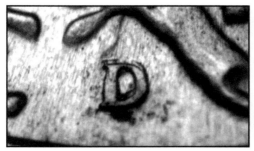

RPM-1
(Courtesy of Tom Miller)

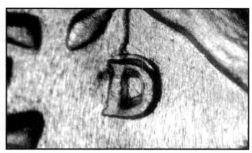

RPM-2
(Courtesy of Bill Fivaz)

RPM-3
(Miller)

1940-S

Mintage:
21,560,000
(Ranking 41/77)

Popular Varieties: At least six obverse doubled-die varieties are known, along with three doubled-die reverses.[67] The most distinctive of the DDO varieties is illustrated *(photo)*. A single repunched mintmark is known, along with a nice cud die break on the reverse *(photos)*.

In one or more instances, lapping of the die has given Liberty a "broken nose." In addition, 1940-S is often seen with multiple die cracks and/or bold die-clash marks *(photos)*.

Rarity: Common in Mint State, 1940-S has a fairly low percentage of full band examples. Original rolls likely exist.

COMBINED NGC & PCGS POPULATION									
MS64	MS64FB	MS65	MS65FB	MS66	MS66FB	MS67	MS67FB	MS68	MS68FB
269	273	708	622	1080	573	347	163	5	3

Values:		1945	1955	1965	1975	1985	1995	2005
	G	——	——	——	——	——	——	——
	F	——	——	——	——	1.25	.50	.90
	XF	——	——	——	.85	3.00	1.25	1.50
	MS60	.35	.45	2.00	4.50	12.00	——	——
	MS63	——	——	——	——	——	11.00	15.00
	MS65	——	——	——	——	20.00	25.00	25.00

Comments: As is true of many 'S' Mint dimes of this period, 1940-S is occasionally found with brilliant, semi-prooflike fields. This brilliance, though not always uniform, seems to be particularly high for 1940-S.

One may speculate that the reason for such excessive lapping of the dies is to be found in the frequency of deep clash marks. The only way to remove these flaws is to abrade the die faces until enough metal has been lifted that the surfaces are again smooth. This effect, while it diminishes low relief elements such as the designer's monogram and the motto IN GOD WE TRUST, can often add greatly to a coin's beauty. Unless done with care, however, the result of this operation will be heavy, irregular polishing lines which impair the luster of coins struck from such dies. All of these problems, whether found singly or collectively, are characteristic of 1940-S dimes.

As with 1940-D, all were struck during the second half of the year.[68]

Die cracks

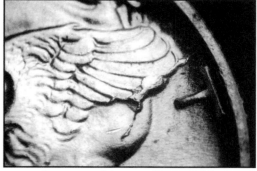

Later state of the same die seen at left
(Courtesy of Bill Fivaz)

Die cracks

Heavy die clash
(Courtesy of Bill Fivaz)

DDO-1. This dime also has a die crack from the rim
at 6 o'clock to Liberty's neck.

Cud die break
*(Sam Thurman Collection, courtesy of
Arnold Margolis)*

S/S/S, RPM-1
(Courtesy of Tom Miller)

1941

Mintage:
175,090,000
(Ranking 74/77)

Popular Varieties: A doubled-die obverse is reported but remains unconfirmed. Also found is the common "broken nose" variety, which is more correctly described as just a die state.

Rarity: Common in all popular grades including full bands gem, original rolls likely exist.

COMBINED NGC & PCGS POPULATION									
MS64	MS64FB	MS65	MS65FB	MS66	MS66FB	MS67	MS67FB	MS68	MS68FB
220	431	929	1031	1247	1158	653	446	2	5

Values:

		1945	1955	1965	1975	1985	1995	2005
	G	——	——	——	——	——	——	——
	F	——	——	——	——	1.25	.50	.90
	XF	——	——	——	.85	3.00	1.25	1.50
	MS60	.25	.30	1.15	3.00	10.00	——	——
	MS63	——	——	——	——	——	8.00	12.00
	MS65	——	——	——	——	16.00	20.00	35.00

Comments: Typical of Philadelphia Mint dimes of the 1940s, this issue is generally lower in overall quality than its Denver and San Francisco cousins. Full band examples are plentiful only because of the large number of Mint State coins from which to choose, but they are distinctly within the minority.

America's entry into World War II came too late in the year to account for the tremendous increase in coinage for 1941. Rather, it was the USA's supplying of the Allies with the tools of war which so stimulated the national economy. Also, the anticipation of American involvement led to a general buildup within the defense industry. This, in turn, revitalized the various supporting industries such as steel and railroading.

A record number of new hires was recorded by the United States Mint in 1940-41. While the figure for total employees at all three coining facilities and its various other offices had hovered around 1000-1200 during the years 1936-40, the total at the end of Fiscal Year 1941 more than doubled to some 2428 persons.[69]

It seems that at least a few of the Mint employees suffered from a touch of larceny:

At the U. S. Mint in Philadelphia imperfect coins have been dipped in a solution which is not visible when dry. The coins are thus labeled and will be discovered if mixed with perfect specimens.

An employee recently was charged with stealing a number of these imperfect dimes, and when the coins were subjected to the ultra-violet light they became fluorescent. The employee confessed, according to the report given by Mr. Dressel, the Superintendent of the Mint.[70]

1941-D

Mintage:
45,634,000
(Ranking 58/77)

Popular Varieties: One doubled-die obverse and three doubled-die reverse varieties are known.[71] Only the DDO is distinct enough to be desirable beyond the specialist arena *(photos)*. Three repunched mintmarks are noted,[72] and two of these are illustrated here *(photos)*. The familiar die crack from wingtip to rim is found with this date, as well.

Rarity: Common in all popular grades including full bands gem, original rolls probably exist.

COMBINED NGC & PCGS POPULATION									
MS64	MS64FB	MS65	MS65FB	MS66	MS66FB	MS67	MS67FB	MS68	MS68FB
46	765	139	2372	196	2116	61	747	0	20

Values:		1945	1955	1965	1975	1985	1995	2005
	G	——	——	——	——	——	——	——
	F	——	——	——	——	1.25	.50	.90
	XF	——	——	——	.85	3.00	1.25	1.50
	MS60	.25	.40	1.75	3.75	20.00	——	——
	MS63	——	——	——	——	——	10.00	15.00
	MS65	——	——	——	——	30.00	20.00	25.00

Comments: The high percentage of full band specimens is typical of Denver Mint dimes of the 1940s. The coins of this mint are found consistently better struck than those of either Philadelphia or San Francisco. Also typical, though for a smaller number of coins, are the semi-prooflike fields seen on some 'D' Mint dimes dated 1937-42.

1941-D dimes became the objects of an unusual promotion early in the year:

Gov. Ralph L. Carr of Colorado declared the week of Jan. 20 as "Silver Week" the time when the miners of the state gather in Denver for their annual meeting.

During the week, silver was virtually the only money in circulation and Denver merchants co-operated in an effort to make Denverites more silver-conscious.

Mark A. Skinner, supt. of the mint at Denver, released a quantity of 1941 D Dimes. During the week anyone who was fortunate enough to find one of these dimes could exchange it for a silver dollar at the headquarters of the Association.[73]

DDO-1
(Stanton)

DDO-1
(Fivaz)

RPM -1
(Miller)

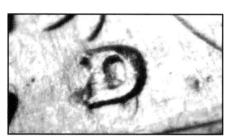

RPM -2
(Fivaz)

1941-S

Mintage:
43,090,000
(Ranking 57/77)

Popular Varieties:

Two entirely different mintmark puncheons were used for the San Francisco Mint dimes of 1941. Most 1941-S display the Small S with serifs used regularly since 1917. Introduced this year, however, was a new Large S having an upper serif which projects downward only and a lower lobe shaped like the bell of a musical instrument, from which this puncheon has received the designation "Trumpet Tail S" *(photos)*. This designation, as well as subsequent ones identified for later 'S' Mint dime, are attributed to variety expert Bill Fivaz, who documented their various appearances for coins of the 1940s across all denominations.

The Small S dimes include at least one "broken nose" die state and two repunched mintmarks. The second of these (RPM-2) is not entirely convincing and may be just a flaw in the die, but the first one (RPM-1, known in two die states) is a whopper. While not all that rare, it is very popular and especially desirable in its earlier die state (RPM-1a). See accompanying photos.

Trumpet Tail S varieties appear to be limited to the "broken nose" die state. Bill Fivaz notes two positional varieties for this mintmark, indicating that at least two dies used in 1941 bore this style of mintmark *(photos)*.

The common die crack from wingtip to rim may exist with either mintmark. Another crack parallels the numeral 1 in the date, making it seem to read 19411. Yet another is known connecting letters DI in DIME.

Finally, 1941-S is known with the reverse rotated either 90 or 135 degrees clockwise, relative to the obverse. Readers are reminded that Mercury Dimes were coined with the reverse die as the upper, or hammer, die. Since only the lower or anvil die can come loose in the press without falling from it, the obverse die is actually the one which rotated from its initial setting. One might therefore prefer to call these coins "rotated obverse" varieties rather than using the more popular expression "rotated reverse."

Rarity:

Common in all popular grades including fully struck gem, original rolls likely exist.

COMBINED NGC & PCGS POPULATION									
MS64	MS64FB	MS65	MS65FB	MS66	MS66FB	MS67	MS67FB	MS68	MS68FB
396	636	1013	1619	1434	1328	406	472	5	13

Values:		1945	1955	1965	1975	1985	1995	2005
	G	——	——	——	——	——	——	——
	F	——	——	——	——	1.25	.50	.90
	XF	——	——	——	.85	3.00	1.25	1.50
	MS60	.25	.40	2.00	3.50	15.00	——	——
	MS63	——	——	——	——	——	11.00	12.00
	MS65	——	——	——	——	25.00	25.00	30.00

Comments: A fair number of 1941-S dimes are semi-prooflike, in that they have brilliant fields, while others simply display annoying die-polishing lines.

If, indeed, just two reverse dies bore the Trumpet Tail S in 1941, this would account for the rarity of this popular variety. These two dies could be expected to coin no more than about half a million dimes between them, or about 1% of the total mintage for 1941-S. Having studied dimes drawn from circulation over a 20-year period during the 1940s and '50s, Jack H. Tod published his results in 1961.[74] He observed that just one in 30 1941-S dimes carried what he described as the "Large S." If this ratio was accurate, then there must be at least one other Trumpet Tail S reverse die awaiting discovery.

The exact reason for introducing a new mintmark punch for San Francisco Mint dies is uncertain, as the old punch seems to have been in good condition. Even so, this move followed by some years a similar action made with respect to Denver Mint dies when the 'D' punch had begun to fill. Both 'S' varieties appear for all denominations dated 1941-S, excepting the half dollar—its transitional varieties appear during 1942. In each instance the Small S is the more common variety. The degree to which this is true varies from one denomination to another, the halves being perhaps the most evenly divided.

(Readers are reminded that all dies were manufactured at Philadelphia and then shipped to the respective branches with mintmarks already punched. Thus, the decision to make such changes rested within the Engraving Department at Philadelphia. Only the manufacture of collars and the final polishing, or lapping, of the dies, was performed locally at each respective mint.)

Before the 1970s officials of the United States Mint routinely denied all reports of irregularities in its products. The efforts of collectors and the numismatic press to get at the truth were thwarted at every turn, particularly during the 1940s and '50s. Their inquiries typically ran afoul of Leland Howard. While his title was Acting Director, he seemed to have been designated as the Mint's unofficial information officer, and he held a deep suspicion and dislike of coin collectors. Persons furnishing examples of oddities and errors to the Mint for verification were typically given an uncompromising denial of authenticity. After a wait of months or even years, the coins' owners would ultimately be told that their lucky finds had been irretrievably lost to the Mint's furnaces in an official effort to secure against "counterfeits."

An example of such leaden thinking is to be found in this 1941 account by Lee F. Hewitt, editor and publisher of *The Numismatic Scrapbook Magazine:*

While touring the Mint last month we asked Mr. Sinnock, the chief engraver, about "large and small mint marks." He stated that only ONE punch for each mint was used so the mint marks had to be the same size—at least during his thirty years at the mint the same punches have been used. When a die wears the mint mark may appear to be thicker.[75]

As chief engraver, it's inconceivable that Sinnock didn't know about the introduction of a new 'S' mintmark punch that very year. Evidently, he believed it his duty to keep such "sensitive" information from coin collectors.

Small S
(Fivaz)

Small S, RPM-2
(Fivaz)

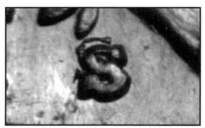
Small S, RPM-1a
(Stanton)

Small S, RPM-1b
(Fivaz)

Large, Trumpet Tail S, Die 1
with diagnostic die gouge
(Fivaz)

Large, Trumpet Tail S, Die 2
(Fivaz)

1942

Mintage:
205,410,000
(Ranking 76/77)

Popular Varieties: The principal variety for this issue is a doubled-die obverse, better known to collectors as the 1942/41 overdate. This enormously popular variety merits a separate listing, and it may be found on the following pages. A prominent cud variety is known for this date *(photo)*.

Also found are the usual irregularities such as the "broken nose" die state.

Rarity: 1942(P) is common in all popular grades including fully struck gem. Original rolls almost certainly exist.

COMBINED NGC & PCGS POPULATION									
MS64	MS64FB	MS65	MS65FB	MS66	MS66FB	MS67	MS67FB	MS68	MS68FB
385	354	1196	910	1677	922	760	291	12	4

Values:

	1945	1955	1965	1975	1985	1995	2005
G	——	——	——	——	——	——	——
F	——	——	——	——	1.25	.50	.80
XF	——	——	——	.85	3.00	1.25	1.50
MS60	.25	.30	.85	2.75	9.50	——	——
MS63	——	——	——	——	——	8.00	10.00
MS65	——	——	——	——	15.00	20.00	30.00

Comments: As with other Philadelphia Mint dimes of the 1940s the percentage of coins having full bands is fairly low, a fact the above table only suggests. Furthermore, the enormous mintage led to a number of coins having been struck from poorly polished dies with missing low-relief details (the "broken nose"). This is not a problem, however, as the enormous quantity of Mint State survivors provides a substantial field of candidates.

With America's entry into the war, our entire culture was directed toward this major undertaking. No aspect of everyday life was left untouched. Coins played an important part in this activity, since one's disposable income was ideally spent on Defense Stamps and Bonds. In an effort to promote this program, Sears, Roebuck & Company took out full page ads in Southern newspapers announcing their new slogan: "A Dime—Symbol of America."[76]

There's a certain irony in this retailer's choice of the Mercury Dime as a symbol of America, given the number of protests over the "fascist coin."

Cud die break
*(Sam Thurman Collection,
courtesy of Arnold Margolis)*

1942/41

Mintage:
(Included with 1942)

Rarity: Circulated examples through grade Very Fine are not particularly scarce, Fine and VF being perhaps the most available grades. Mint state survivors are far fewer in number and remain in constant demand.

Just a single example has been certified higher than MS-66. This remarkable coin grades MS-68 but lacks full bands.

COMBINED NGC & PCGS POPULATION										
VG-VF	XF40	XF45	AU50	AU53	AU55	AU58	MS60	MS60FB	MS61	MS61FB
634	183	163	107	82	137	153	3	1	22	2

COMBINED NGC & PCGS POPULATION										
MS62	MS62FB	MS63	MS63FB	MS64	MS64FB	MS65	MS65FB	MS66	MS66FB
42	9	22	13	24	9	10	11	3	8

Values:

	1945	1955	1965	1975	1985	1995	2005
G	——	——	65.00	——	——	——	——
F	3.50	8.50	100.00	125.00	225.00	210.00	600.00
XF	——	——	150.00	225.00	300.00	325.00	800.00
MS60	10.00	45.00	360.00	865.00	1700.00	——	——
MS63	——	——	——	——	——	2000.00	4000.00
MS65	——	——	——	——	2500.00	6000.00	12500.00

Comments: This is the most highly sought variety in the Mercury Dime series. Its popularity stems from being the most obvious and visually compelling variety. Also adding to the demand for this overdate is its notoriety over the past 60+ years, having been discovered and illustrated within months of its coining. The Philadelphia Mint overdate has been a fixture in the "Red Book" since early editions, and this has further guaranteed its place in numismatic legend. Until recently it was also the only one of the two overdates to be included in coin albums.

Almost overlooked by collectors, who focus primarily on the coin's date, is the fact that this variety is actually a doubled-die obverse *(photos)*. This type of mishap occurs during the die preparation process. Until the 1990s, when the U. S. Mint perfected the complete impression of dies in a single hubbing, the sinking of a working die from a working hub requires that two impressions be taken, with a break in between for annealing, or softening of the die. If the second impression is slightly misaligned with the first, the more common form of doubled die results (an example of this doubling is the 1941-D dime illustrated on page 187). But what happens when hubs of two different dates are employed for successive impressions of the die?

As early as September 1941, dies were being prepared at the Philadelphia Mint for coins dated 1942. A demand still existed for new dies dated 1941, and these too were in production. In at least two instances, a working hub dated 1941 was used for the initial impression of a new dime die, while the second impression came from a hub dated 1942. The result was a pair of overdate dies, one employed at Philadelphia, the other shipped west to Denver. Whether or not anyone at the respective mints noticed this peculiarity in the dies is unknown, but the same circumstances account for other 20th Century overdates such as the 1918/7-D and 1943/2 -P nickels, the 1918/7-S quarter dollar and the 1909/8(P) double eagle.

While the mints' employees may have failed to notice the overdate, collectors did not. The 'P' Mint variety was discovered in circulation by Arnold Cohn of Kingston, New York and reported to *The Numismatic Scrapbook Magazine* in time for its March 1943 issue. Despite the lessons learned from previous encounters with Mint officials, Scrapbook Editor Lee F. Hewitt submitted Mr. Cohn's dime to Chief Engraver John Ray Sinnock for evaluation. Although Sinnock did not attempt to deny the coin's authenticity, he did initially offer an explanation of its origin which a person in his position should have known to be impossible. His first suggestion as to how this variety came about was that a 1941 dime was overstruck with a 1942 die! Perhaps realizing the incredible nature of this explanation, he then presented readers of Hewitt's publication with a streamlined rendition of what is now known to have been the actual cause—the use of two differently dated working hubs in the sinking of a single working die.

In disputing the suggestion that a 1941 die might have been re-engraved to read 1942, Sinnock provided some background information which is worth including here:

> In September of each year we start engraving the numeral in the new master die for the following year. We have no punches for these numerals since they were sculptured in the first place we follow the individual style of each sculptor. From this master die a working "hub" is drawn. This is re-touched if necessary, then hardened. This hub is used to fabricate all the working dies for that year. About one thousand dies with new date must be ready by January 1st of each year.[77]

A few years later, Mint Director Nellie Tayloe Ross reaffirmed that institution's belief that the error had occurred during the final few months of 1941, when dies of both dates were being prepared:

> During that period when utmost vigilance was required to keep the dies segregated by respective years, a die may have been given one blow with a 1941 hub and then, by some accident, finished with a 1942 hub.
>
> All dies are usually inspected by a number of skilled workmen before they are delivered. Due to the heavy demands for coins, the Engraving Department had necessarily streamlined its operations and such an imperfect die apparently escaped detection.[78]

The May 1943 issue of *The Numismatic Scrapbook Magazine* included a photograph of the 1942/41(P) overdate. Thus alerted to this variety, collectors began examining each and every 1942 dime encountered. As a result, an adequate number of slightly circulated examples survive of the 'P' Mint overdate, though truly Mint State coins are rare.

Widespread publicity of the 1942/41 dime led to a rapid escalation in value. This, in turn, gave rise to the seemingly inevitable counterfeiting of such coins. Most are actually crude alterations of genuine 1941 and 1942 dimes which were made during the heyday of popular coin collecting, circa 1955-64. These are easily dismissed by persons armed with a little knowledge. More alarming are the sophisticated counterfeits created since that time. These are usually struck from transfer dies created by using a genuine coin as the subject. For examples of various counterfeit and altered overdate dimes see Chapter 3.

Two photographs of genuine 1942/41(P) dimes are included on this page for comparison with any examples which may be offered. Note the principal diagnostic for this variety—a raised lump between numerals 4 and 1 near their bases. Also useful is the fact that most 1942/41(P) dimes have a diagnostic die scratch between the fasces and the olive branch. This scratch appears at the left of the fasces, about one-third of the distance from the bottom of the rods to the lowest horizontal band. In this protected location, it should remain visible even on well worn specimens. Finally, any alleged overdate which simply doesn't look like the genuine examples shown must be a fake.

The diagonal die scratch which runs downward from the horizontal of the numeral 4, as seen in the photos, is common to most 1942 dimes and should not be used as a diagnostic for the overdate. Finally, it's worth noting that this overdate is, in fact, 1942/1941, the first two digits likewise being doubled to some degree.

Most of the 1942/41(P) dimes found by collectors were taken from circulation in New York City and its suburbs within a few years of coining. People who handled large amounts of change, such as transit company workers and telephone box collectors, were especially successful in finding quantities of this variety. The few specimens now encountered in Mint State were likely taken from rolls which had been saved by collectors as ordinary 1942 dimes and only later discovered to contain overdates. Numismatic scholar Walter Breen reported that such a discovery did occur in 1954, some four rolls being found at that time.[79] It's not clear from his account whether all of the dimes in these rolls were overdates, but the number of known Mint State survivors suggests that they were not.

DDO-1, 1942/ 41(P)
(Fivaz)

Genuine overdate with diagnostic lump
between bases of 4 and 1
(ANAAB)

1942-D

Mintage:
60,740,000
(Ranking 67/77)

Popular Varieties: John A. Wexler and Kevin Flynn list two doubled-die obverse varieties[80] One of these is, of course, the overdate, while the other is quite minor.

At least seven repunched mintmarks are known, one of which is found with the 1942/41-D overdate. For more information on this important variety, see the following pages.

One or more die cracks may appear, including the familiar position from wingtip to rim. The "broken nose" die state is likewise common.

Rarity: This date is common in all popular grades including fully struck gem, and original rolls probably exist.

COMBINED NGC & PCGS POPULATION									
MS64	MS64FB	MS65	MS65FB	MS66	MS66FB	MS67	MS67FB	MS68	MS68FB
74	665	281	2372	492	2387	306	892	26	20

Values:		1945	1955	1965	1975	1985	1995	2005
	G	——	——	——	——	——	——	——
	F	——	——	——	——	1.25	.50	.80
	XF	——	——	——	.85	3.00	1.25	1.50
	MS60	.25	.35	1.35	3.50	19.00	——	——
	MS63	——	——	——	——	——	10.00	15.00
	MS65	——	——	——	——	27.00	22.00	30.00

Comments: Typical of 'D' Mint dimes from the 1940s, well struck examples with full bands are readily available. Semi-prooflike fields are not uncommon, and the typical Mint State 1942-D dime is a very attractive coin.

RPM-1a, early die state
(Courtesy of Tom Miller)

RPM-1b, later die state
(Miller)

RPM-2
(Miller)

RPM-3
(Miller)

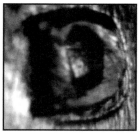

RPM-5
(Courtesy of J.T. Stanton)

RPM-6
(Miller)

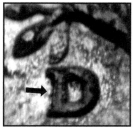

RPM-7
(Miller)

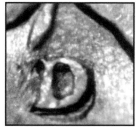

Wexler/ Flynn lists this
as WRP-002
(Fivaz)

1942/41-D

Mintage:
(Included with 1942-D)

Rarity: Very scarce in any grade, Mint State coins are genuinely rare. This variety is more rare than the Philadelphia Mint overdate in all grades, and it is more likely to be found well worn as a consequence of having evaded detection for 20 years.

While the table reveals that only 139 examples have been certified as Mint State, it will be noted that the majority of these coins have full bands. This is fairly typical of 1942-D dimes, irrespective of variety. None have been graded higher than MS-66 FB.

COMBINED NGC & PCGS POPULATION										
VG-VF	XF40	XF45	AU50	AU53	AU55	AU58	MS60	MS60FB	MS61	MS61FB
259	63	68	45	24	43	72	0	1	0	3

COMBINED NGC & PCGS POPULATION										
MS62	MS62FB	MS63	MS63FB	MS64	MS64FB	MS65	MS65FB	MS66	MS66FB
1	19	0	21	3	54	2	22	0	13

Values:		1945	1955	1965	1975	1985	1995	2005
	G	——	——	——	——	——	——	——
	F	——	——	——	150.00	225.00	210.00	600.00
	XF	——	——	——	——	325.00	400.00	800.00
	MS60	——	——	——	——	1900.00	——	——
	MS63	——	——	——	——	——	1800.00	3750.00
	MS65	——	——	——	——	2750.00	4500.00	8000.00

Comments: Although it may be difficult to identify with the naked eye, this is unquestionably a genuine overdate. The cause of this seeming accident is the same as for its 'P' Mint counterpart—the use of two differently-dated hubs in sinking this working die. Unlike 1942/41(P) this doubled-die obverse is also evident in the motto IN GOD WE TRUST *(photo)*. The single pair of dies used for this variety also features a repunched mint-mark *(photo)*. The fact that numeral 1 appears to have been partially effaced from the die suggests that someone at the Denver Mint was aware of the overdate and attempted to correct it. No such evidence is found when examining the 1942/41(P) variety.

Claims for discovery of this overdate have come from a number of persons, and the facts remain a bit cloudy. Walter Breen reported in his *Encyclopedia* that this variety was discovered by Delma K. Romines in 1962, and Romines has said that his efforts to have it publicized were interrupted by his military service. Q. David Bowers credits Frank S. Robinson with its discovery around that same time, while Bill Fivaz believes that James Greenwich was the first to make a public inquiry about this variety. In researching the present book, however, the author came across its discovery in the November 1960 issue of *The Numismatic Scrapbook Magazine*. A letter to the editor, submitted by a reader in West Baldwin, Maine identifying himself simply as "Days," revealed that a friend of his had recently shown him a 1942/41 dime. Instructed by his friend to turn it over, he was surprised to find a Denver mintmark. This then seems to be the earliest reporting of the 1942/41-D dime.

In any case, its first publication was in 1963 in Frank Spadone's *Major Variety and Oddity Guide*. The collecting of varieties and error coins was then still in its infancy, and first knowledge of the 1942/41-D dime for most in the hobby came with its appearance that same year in the "Collectors Clearinghouse" section of *Coin World*.[81] It was simply mentioned at that time, and few persons took much notice of it until more detailed coverage appeared in *Coin World* three years later.[82] It wasn't until the early 1970s that this variety achieved a listing in the Red Book and became widely acknowledged. Only since the 1990s has the 'D' Mint overdate been included in coin albums and display holders for the Mercury Dime series.

This variety is actually 1942/1941, all four digits being doubled to varying degrees. Unlike its eastern cousin, however, this variety has numeral 4 doubled to the left rather than to the right.

A number of peculiarities are known for non-overdate 1942-D dimes which may confuse inexperienced collectors. Among these is the great frequency with which this date is found having mechanical or strike doubling *(photo)*. This is true of all 1942-dated dimes, including those from the other mints. In addition, at least one obverse die for 1942-D was used when in an extremely eroded state. What is actually heavy erosion lines from the base of numeral 2 may be misinterpreted as the remains of a 1 *(photo)*.

DDO-1, 1942/41-D
(Stanton)

Close-up of date
(ANAAB)

DDO-1
(Stanton)

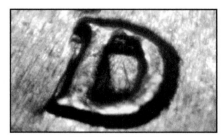

RPM-4, 1942/41-D
(Stanton)

Strike doubling on a normal die 1942-D
maybe mistaken fot the overdate
(Courtesy of Bill Fivaz)

Simple die erosion can simulate an overdate
(Courtesy of Vic Rollo)

1942-S

Mintage:
49,300,000
(Ranking 59/77)

Popular Varieties: Most 1942-S dimes feature the Trumpet Tail S that debuted in 1941. A somewhat lesser number display a new mintmark style that appeared for the first time this year. The Large S is nearly perfect in style, being quite symmetrical and having distinctive, matching serifs *(photos)*. The late Walter Breen reported rare examples having the Small S of 1917-41, but this is believed to be an error on his part.

Three repunched mintmarks are known, all exhibiting the Trumpet Tail S *(photos)*.

The usual die crack from wingtip to rim may be found, along with several variations of the "broken nose" die state.

Rarity: 1942-S is common in all grades through full bands gem, though its population drops off quite a bit above MS-66. Original rolls of this date may still exist.

COMBINED NGC & PCGS POPULATION									
MS64	MS64FB	MS65	MS65FB	MS66	MS66FB	MS67	MS67FB	MS68	MS68FB
187	270	484	573	611	521	222	113	1	0

Values:		1945	1955	1965	1975	1985	1995	2005
	G	——	——	——	——	——	——	——
	F	——	——	——	——	1.25	.50	.80
	XF	——	——	——	.85	3.00	1.25	1.50
	MS60	.25	.40	1.75	4.00	24.00	——	——
	MS63	——	——	——	——	——	12.00	15.00
	MS65	——	——	——	——	36.00	26.00	30.00

Comments: Like those of the Philadelphia Mint, dimes struck at San Francisco during the 1940s are not likely to have fully raised and rounded bands. Split bands are common enough and usually will be certified as FB, but this won't satisfy the specialist.

This is another 'S' Mint Mercury Dime which may often be found with semi-prooflike surfaces, these coins usually exhibiting a "broken nose." Both features are caused by aggressive polishing of the dies to remove clash marks, erosion lines and other flaws. Later dates are also known to possess semi-prooflike surfaces but are much scarcer after 1942.

Mechanical or strike doubling is very common on all 1942-dated dimes. This is particularly true of 1942-S, and such pieces have been mistaken by countless collectors and dealers for doubled dies.

RPM-1
(Fivaz)

RPM-2
(Tom Miller)

RPM-3
(Fivaz)

1943

Mintage:
191,710,000
(Ranking 75/77)

Popular Varieties:

A reverse cud is the only reported variety, and even this is really just a die state *(photo)*. Numerous examples of mechanical or strike doubling are known, but these carry no premium value.

Rarity:

Common in all grades through full bands gem, original rolls almost certainly exist.

COMBINED NGC & PCGS POPULATION									
MS64	MS64FB	MS65	MS65FB	MS66	MS66FB	MS67	MS67FB	MS68	MS68FB
429	431	1215	967	1833	1016	962	261	16	3

Values:

		1945	1955	1965	1975	1985	1995	2005
G		——	——	——	——	——	——	——
F		——	——	——	——	1.25	.50	.80
XF		——	——	——	.85	3.00	1.25	1.50
MS60		.25	.25	.75	3.00	9.50	——	——
MS63		——	——	——	——	——	8.00	12.00
MS65		——	——	——	——	15.00	20.00	25.00

Comments:

Typical of Philadelphia Mint dimes from this period, most examples are not fully struck at their centers. The low percentage of full band specimens is offset, however, by the sheer number of Uncirculated coins, making this date easy to locate in any popularly collected grade.

1943 may nearly be pinpointed as the year that coin collecting took hold in a big way. Famed coin dealer Abe Kosoff went so far as the state that it was his auction of the Michael F. Higgy Collection that launched the big wartime run-up in prices, though professional pride may have played a part in that assessment. Countless persons were already searching through their pocket change to fill coin boards and folders, but the greatest growth in the hobby occurred from 1943 through 1947 and again from 1955 through 1964. This is when dramatic price advances were occurring regularly, and every collector eagerly awaited the release of the latest annual edition of Richard S. Yeoman's *A Guide Book of United States Coins*, better known as the "Red Book."

For an idea of what Mercury Dimes cost at the outset of this period of phenomenal growth one need only look at the April 1944 issue of *The Numismatic Scrapbook Magazine.* An advertisement by Chicago dealer R. Green (actually Charles Green using his wife's initial) offered a complete, Uncirculated set of Mercury Dimes from 1916 through 1943, excluding the overdate, for a total of just $175.00!

Cud die break
*(Sam Thurman Collection, courtesy of
Arnold Margolis)*

1943-D

Mintage:
71,949,000
(Ranking 71/77)

Popular
Varieties: Three repunched mintmarks are known, and two of these are illustrated *(photos).*

The familiar wingtip to rim die crack is also found with this date, as well as one on the reverse connecting letters MERIC. In a similar vein, at least one obverse cud die break is known *(photo).*

Rarity: Common in all grades through full bands gem, original rolls probably exist.

COMBINED NGC & PCGS POPULATION									
MS64	MS64FB	MS65	MS65FB	MS66	MS66FB	MS67	MS67FB	MS68	MS68FB
59	1311	240	4442	322	4001	168	909	4	26

Values:		1945	1955	1965	1975	1985	1995	2005
	G	——	——	——	——	——	——	——
	F	——	——	——	——	1.25	.50	.80
	XF	——	——	——	.85	3.00	1.25	1.50
	MS60	.25	.35	.95	3.00	15.00	——	——
	MS63	——	——	——	——	——	10.00	15.00
	MS65	——	——	——	——	25.00	25.00	30.00

Comments: There's little to be said about this issue. Routinely well struck and lustrous, 1943-D dimes compare quite favorably with other 'D' Mint dimes of the period. For collectors seeking an ideal example for their type sets, this entry is highly qualified.

RPM-1
(Courtesy of Tom Miller)

Cud die break
(Sam Thurman Collection, courtesy of Arnold Margolis)

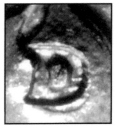

RPM-3
(Courtesy of Bill Fivaz)

1943-S

Mintage:
60,400,000
(Ranking 66/77)

Popular Varieties: Nearly all 1943-S dimes feature the attractive Large S mintmark introduced in 1942. An extremely small percentage exists having the Trumpet Tail S, and these are likely the product of a single reverse die *(photos)*. If that assumption is true, then this variety represents less than one half of one percent of the entire mintage.

Three repunched Large S mintmarks are recorded, and two of these are illustrated below *(photos)*. Again, the often seen die crack from wingtip to rim is known for this date. Other die crack locations are too numerous to list.

Rarity: 1943-S is common in all popular grades, with the exception of full band coins. These are slightly scarce, though enough have been certified to meet the needs of serious collectors. Original rolls may exist.

COMBINED NGC & PCGS POPULATION									
MS64	MS64FB	MS65	MS65FB	MS66	MS66FB	MS67	MS67FB	MS68	MS68FB
291	272	931	791	1448	834	669	284	6	19

Values:

	1945	1955	1965	1975	1985	1995	2005
G	——	——	——	——	——	——	——
F	——	——	——	——	1.25	.50	.80
XF	——	——	——	.85	3.00	1.25	1.50
MS60	.25	.40	1.35	3.00	16.50	——	——
MS63	——	——	——	——	——	10.00	15.00
MS65	——	——	——	——	26.50	25.00	30.00

Comments: Flat or split bands are the rule for this date, the actual percentage of coins having fully raised and rounded bands being considerably lower than the certified population suggests. An additional consideration is that 1943-S dimes having incomplete bands are not as likely to be submitted to the certification services as are ones expected to come back with the desired designation "FB." The widespread use by dealers of grading service pre-screen submissions, in which only those coins meeting a minimum grade are holdered, further skews the certified population in favor of FB coins.

This date may be found semi-prooflike, but it is much less often encountered with mirrorlike fields than are 1940-S, 1941-S and 1942-S. This brilliance usually is accompanied by heavy and distracting die-polishing lines and the familiar "broken nose."

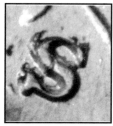

Large S, RPM-1
(Fivaz)

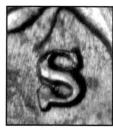

Large S, RPM-2
(Miller)

Trumpet Tail S
(Fivaz)

1944

Mintage:
231,410,000
(Ranking 77/77)

Popular

Varieties: A single, rather trivial, doubled-die obverse is reported.[83] Clashed and worn dies are far more common for this date *(photos)*. The most boldly clashed variety is described below under "Comments."

Rarity: Common in all grades short of full bands gem, the number of full band examples is definitely smaller than for any other date of the 1940s, excepting the infamous 1945(P). Original rolls most likely exist.

COMBINED NGC & PCGS POPULATION									
MS64	MS64FB	MS65	MS65FB	MS66	MS66FB	MS67	MS67FB	MS68	MS68FB
554	217	1779	569	2894	531	857	115	3	0

Values:

	1945	1955	1965	1975	1985	1995	2005
G	——	——	——	——	——	——	——
F	——	——	——	——	1.25	.50	.80
XF	——	——	——	.85	3.00	1.25	1.50
MS60	——	.25	.75	3.00	9.50	——	——
MS63	——	——	——	——	——	8.00	12.00
MS65	——	——	——	——	15.00	20.00	25.00

Comments: Quality control suffered mightily at the Philadelphia Mint in 1944. All denominations of coins frequently are seen with obvious signs of overextended die use and heavy polishing. Specific to the dimes is a very low percentage of pieces having full bands, even lower than the certified population reveals. Flat and partially split bands are the norm, and even the diagonal bands are shallow on many specimens. Other signs of die wear and polishing include "broken nose" obverses and indistinct lettering.

1944(P) dimes occasionally are found with a semi-prooflike obverse. Rarer still is the cameo effect, wherein Liberty is frosted against a prooflike field. Of the two major grading services, NGC presently is the only one designating Mercury Dimes as "PL" (prooflike), but no examples of this date have been so labeled. To receive this designation, the prooflike quality must be uniform and cover all field areas, while the typical prooflike Mercury Dime displays an uneven blend of prooflike brilliance with frosty luster.

One interesting oddity found with 1944(P) dimes received a great deal of publicity while this issue was still fresh from the mint. Dubbed the "Leaved" variety by its discoverer, Richard S. Caldwell of Pittsburgh, Pennsylvania, he described it as follows:

> This is a really remarkable "freak" specimen. On the obverse, cracks in the die have formed beautiful outlines of small clusters of leaves around the head. The leaves are discernible to the naked eye, and are to be found at the forehead, at the bridge of the nose, protruding from the nostril, under the chin, and at the back of the neck. There is also what would appear to be the branch or limb running parallel to and near the front of the neck.[84]

From the description provided, it's obvious that what Mr. Caldwell had found was a severely clashed obverse die. The two dies had come together without a planchet between them, and each die had received a bold impression of the other. This impression was then transferred to all coins struck from these dies, unless and until the dies were polished enough to remove the clash marks. Caldwell makes no mention of any peculiarities in the reverse of his coin, so that means that the reverse die had been lapped to remove the marks or had been declared unfit for further use and was replaced. In a follow-up to his original account, Mr. Caldwell correctly identified this die-clash phenomenon.[85]

Not content to simply inform the numismatic community of this oddity, Mr. Caldwell went on to place a full-page advertisement in the September 1944 issue of *The Numismatic Scrapbook Magazine* offering Uncirculated examples for sale, priced on request. In his ad, he made some remarkable claims for this variety. Among these was that only 16 specimens were known to exist, that its rarity was comparable to that of the 1894-S dime, that no collection of dimes was complete without one and, finally, that ownership of "an uncirculated 1944 P. Mint 'Leaved Dime' will be a source of genuine pride, and will prove a sound investment." In concluding, Caldwell noted that he had for sale "14 uncirculated specimens of this unique coin." (One wonders how many he might have had were it not unique.) It's doubtful that he got rich marketing these dimes, as the variety never again appeared in print.

The author's attempts to locate an early die state of this variety for photographing were unsuccessful, but it may be assumed that it resembles the boldly clashed 1945(P) dime illustrated on page 215. Since clashed dies are not at all rare for this series, similarly damaged dies will likely turn up for other dates. While an interesting addition to one's collection, clashed dies rarely command much of a premium.

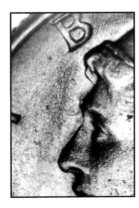 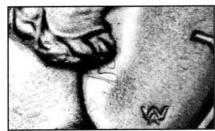 

Clash marks, late die state of the "leaved" variety
(Courtesy of Ralph Huntzinger)

1944-D

Mintage:
62,224,000
(Ranking 68/77)

Popular Varieties: A very minor doubled-die obverse is illustrated in Wexler/Flynn.[86] In addition, three repunched mintmarks are known *(photos)*.

A die crack runs from letter D in UNITED to the rim on one die.

Rarity: Common in all popular grades, original rolls almost certainly exist.

COMBINED NGC & PCGS POPULATION									
MS64	MS64FB	MS65	MS65FB	MS66	MS66FB	MS67	MS67FB	MS68	MS68FB
86	1031	327	3512	512	4243	190	1750	7	69

Values:

	1945	1955	1965	1975	1985	1995	2005
G	——	——	——	——	——	——	——
F	——	——	——	——	1.25	.50	.80
XF	——	——	——	.85	3.00	1.25	1.50
MS60	——	.30	.80	3.00	13.00	——	——
MS63	——	——	——	——	——	8.00	15.00
MS65	——	——	——	——	22.00	22.00	30.00

Comments: 1944-D is another issue that typically is found with excellent luster and a full or nearly full strike.

After several years in the 2000-2200 range, the number of employees staffing the United States Mint increased to 2941 during 1944.[87] This figure grew still higher during 1945 and helps, in part, to account for the decline in quality and the increase in irregularities experienced during the war years. Each facility was attempting to produce enormous quantities of coins using new and inexperienced staff. In addition, the need to continue using dies that were barely fit for further service just added to the number of poor quality coins. This loss of quality control was least evident in coins from the Denver Mint, which perhaps reflected a greater emphasis on quality by Denver's veteran employees.

Struck from worn dies
(Courtesy of Bill Frivaz)

RPM-1
(Fivaz)

RPM-2
(Courtesy of Tom Miller)

RPM-3
(Courtesy of J.T. Stanton)

1944-S

Mintage:
49,490,000
(Ranking 60/77)

Popular
Varieties: The majority of 1944-S dimes feature the Large S typical of 1943-S dimes. A significantly smaller number bear a new mintmark style that debuted this year. The Knob Tail S has a serpentine aspect to it, with prominent, rounded lobes at either end that give this puncheon its name. While scarce in the upper Mint State grades, the Knob Tail S is not genuinely rare overall.

The lower lobe of the Knob Tail S is slightly larger, and this helps to identify instances in which the mintmark was punched into the die in an inverted position. The collecting of inverted mintmark varieties is still a new and somewhat untested area that may not appeal to anyone but the most dedicated specialists.

At least two broken dies, or cuds, are also known *(photos)*.

No other varieties are reported, aside from the seemingly inevitable die crack from wingtip to rim.

Rarity: 1944-S dimes are common in all popular grades, with the exception of full band specimens. As is typical of 'S' Mint dimes from the 1940s, such examples are slightly scarce. Original rolls may still exist.

COMBINED NGC & PCGS POPULATION									
MS64	MS64FB	MS65	MS65FB	MS66	MS66FB	MS67	MS67FB	MS68	MS68FB
330	542	1293	1286	2635	1248	817	313	13	7

Values:

		1945	1955	1965	1975	1985	1995	2005
	G	—	—	—	—	—	—	—
	F	—	—	—	—	1.25	.50	.80
	XF	—	—	—	.85	3.00	1.25	1.50
	MS60	—	.35	1.00	3.00	13.00	—	—
	MS63	—	—	—	—	—	10.00	15.00
	MS65	—	—	—	—	22.00	25.00	30.00

Comments: 1944-S dimes occasionally are found with varying degrees of prooflike brilliance. Aside from their possible aesthetic value, no premium has been established for such coins. This may be a future area for collecting and promotion, now that NGC is applying the PL designation to coins that qualify. Thus far, no 1944-S dimes have been certified as MS PL, and only a scattering of other issues have been so graded.

Given the great increase in coinage during World War II, the following item makes for interesting reading:

> During 1944-45, a dual-die holder was invented by Joseph Steel, Supt. of Coining, and William P. Kruse, Machinist, of the S. F. Mint. This permitted a 90% increase in production. Used on all coins, foreign and domestic, quarter-dollar size or smaller, at all three mints. This is in addition to the acquisition of new presses to the capacity of the buildings.[88]

The actual conception of the dual-die holder occurred during 1943, but it was not immediately applied. This successful wartime invention was later extended to all five denominations and was ultimately developed into the quad-die holder used beginning in 1964 for coins of quarter dollar size and smaller. For their innovative thinking, Steel and Kruse were each awarded a $10,000 bonus in 1952, by which time it was estimated that their device had saved the U. S. Mint about two million dollars.[89]

Cud die break
*(Sam Thurman Collection,
courtesy of Arnold Margolis)*

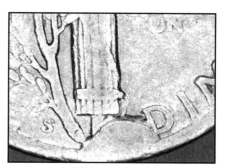

A different cud variety
(Thurman/Margolis)

Joseph W. Steel demonstrating the dual press to Mint Director Nellie Tayloe Ross, 1947

1945

Mintage:
159,130,000
(Ranking 73/77)

Popular Varieties: Two doubled-die obverse varieties and one doubled-die reverse are known.[90] All of them are quite minor, but one is illustrated here *(photo)*.

This issue seems to have been particularly plagued by die clashings. Shown here is the "Leaved" variety in which an inverted impression of the olive branch from the reverse die is seen on the obverse. Also commonly found are brilliant patches in the fields from vigorous lapping of the die *(photos)*. This phenomenon sometimes is called "die burn."

Other varieties include an obverse die dot of unknown cause and a reverse die cud, in which a piece of the die has actually broken away. Finally, at least one reverse die displays a crack from the top of the wreath to the rim.

Rarity: Common in all grades short of fully struck gem, original rolls likely exist. 1945(P) is the rarest coin in the series with full bands, and striking quality in general is less than desirable with this issue.

The rarity of 1945(P) dimes having full bands is such that it invites fraud. Beware of Denver and San Francisco Mint coins that have had their mintmarks removed. Also watch for bands which have been separated through cutting with a blade, machine tool or laser. All three operations have been employed, and buyers should stick to certified coins when purchasing a full bands example of this issue.

COMBINED NGC & PCGS POPULATION									
MS64	MS64FB	MS65	MS65FB	MS66	MS66FB	MS67	MS67FB	MS68	MS68FB
772	47	1930	36	2775	19	781	4	2	0

Values:

	1945	1955	1965	1975	1985	1995	2005
G	——	——	——	——	——	——	——
F	——	——	——	——	1.25	.50	.80
XF	——	——	——	.85	3.00	1.25	1.50
MS60	——	.25	.75	3.00	9.25	——	——
MS63	——	——	——	——	——	8.00	10.00
MS65	——	——	——	——	15.00	20.00	27.00

Comments: The reason for this issue being so rare with full center bands has never been satisfactorily explained. Since the dies for all three mints were prepared at Philadelphia, there was nothing fundamentally different about them. Even if some of the revere dies lacked center bands altogether, due to inadequate hubbing, their distribution would have been random among the three mints. The mints were likewise using very similar equipment in striking the coins, all presses of that period being electrically powered and having a knuckle action.

There were only two variables in the minting equation: One was the collars, as these typically were machined onsite at each of the different mints. The second variable is the upsetting mill, which applied a raised rim to each planchet before it was sent to the coin press. Slight differences in the diameter of the collar or the curvature of the rims could result in detectable variations in the finished coins. An excellent example of this influence is found in the 1921(P) dimes, which almost invariably have full bands, yet typically are weak at their peripheries.

Ironically, the coins of this date most likely to have split or full bands are error pieces. The unconventional displacement of metal associated with broadstruck, off-centered or struck-through dimes has left many with strong central details, including the center bands! For some examples of this curious phenomenon see Chapter 2.

Bold die clash, the popular "leaved" variety
(Courtesy of Bill Fivaz)

Die dot, cause unknown
(Courtesy of Ralph Huntzinger)

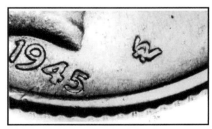

DDO-1
(Courtesy of Peter K. Beane)

Bold die clash, the popular leaved variety
(Fivaz)

Burnished patches of "die burn"

Cud die break
(Sam Thurman Collection, courtesy
of Arnold Margolis)

1945-D

Mintage:
40,245,000
(Ranking 55/77)

Popular

Varieties: Five repunched mintmarks are known. The most desirable of these features a first punching in which the mintmark was rotated 90 degrees clockwise so that it faces downward. Another die features a 'D' mintmark that was placed too high *(photos)*.

The "broken nose" die state is found, as is a die break in numeral 5 of the date.

Rarity: Common in all grades, including full bands gem, original rolls almost certainly exist.

COMBINED NGC & PCGS POPULATION									
MS64	MS64FB	MS65	MS65FB	MS66	MS66FB	MS67	MS67FB	MS68	MS68FB
265	695	1261	2375	2231	2062	628	408	4	11

Values:

	1945	1955	1965	1975	1985	1995	2005
G	——	——	——	——	——	——	——
F	——	——	——	——	1.25	.50	.80
XF	——	——	——	.85	3.00	1.25	1.50
MS60	——	.30	.80	3.00	12.00	——	——
MS63	——	——	——	——	——	8.00	12.00
MS65	——	——	——	——	20.00	22.00	30.00

Comments: Although the percentage of full bands specimens is lower than usual for a 'D' Mint dime of the 1940s, the overall number of Mint State survivors should provide enough examples from which to choose.

The number of people employed at the United States Mint's various facilities reached an all-time high for the period of Mercury Dime coinage. Some 3736 persons were laboring for Uncle Sam's coin mills as of June 30, 1945.[91]

With the enormous mintages of 1941-45 came a proportional increase in the number of pieces reserved for assay. When the Assay Commission met to test the silver coinage of 1945, early in the following year, a total of 79,565 dimes had been reserved from Philadelphia, 20,123 from Denver and 20,960 from San Francisco. Of course, only a very small portion of these coins, less than 1%, were actually weighed, melted and assayed. Of these, the coinage of the Philadelphia Mint revealed the greatest deviation from established standards, though it was not enough to exceed the legal margin of error.[S]

Highly placed D, this position not commonly used after 1917
(Courtesy of Bill Fivaz)

1945-D / Horizontal D
(Courtesy of J.T. Stanton)

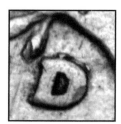

RPM-1
(Courtesy of Tom Miller)

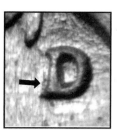

RPM-2
(Miller)

1945-S

Mintage:
41,920,000
(Ranking 56/77)

Popular Varieties:

1945-S is an extraordinary issue within the Mercury Dime series, as no less than three different mintmark punches were employed. The Knob Tail S used in 1944 is the most common and accounts for the two repunched mintmark varieties, one of which is S over horizontal S *(photos)*.

The Trumpet Tail S used 1941-43 appears again in 1945, and this is the rarest mintmark style for this date.

Finally, the popular Micro S is unique to this date alone. While not especially rare, it has long been collected as a mainstream variety and therefore is treated as a separate issue (see following page).

All three mintmarks are reportedly found mated to "broken nose" obverse die states. Also within the realm of such minor die state phenomena, a reverse die crack is known from the top of letter E in ONE to the rim. Also reported is the usual crack from wingtip to rim.

Rarity:

1945-S is fairly common in all grades, excepting full bands gem, and original rolls probably still exist. Flat, partial or split bands are the norm for this date, and some of the coins certified as FB will not satisfy the purist.

Aside from 1939(P) and 1939-D, this is the only issue in the Mercury Dime series to have been certified as MS-69, five examples achieving this grade. None of these has full bands, and two of them feature the Micro S mintmark.

COMBINED NGC & PCGS POPULATION									
MS64	MS64FB	MS65	MS65FB	MS66	MS66FB	MS67	MS67FB	MS68	MS68FB
568	200	1771	528	3176	443	1023	145	361	24

Values:

	1945	1955	1965	1975	1985	1995	2005
G	——	——	——	——	——	——	——
F	——	——	——	——	1.25	.50	.80
XF	——	——	——	.85	3.00	1.25	1.50
MS60	——	.30	1.00	3.00	12.00	——	——
MS63	——	——	——	——	——	8.00	12.00
MS65	——	——	——	——	20.00	25.00	30.00

Comments: 1945-S dimes typically have a very pleasing appearance, unless one is a stickler for sharpness of detail. The luster of these coins is usually very bright and deeply textured, as a consequence of the dies being used far too long. It is an axiom that the most sharply struck coins from fresh dies typically have somewhat mediocre luster, while those coined from severely worn dies are often dazzling to the eye. Since the professional grading services rely heavily on surface quality and luster in arriving at a numerical grade, 1945-S dimes often receive very high numbers.

Due to the deteriorated state of many of the reverse dies used to coin 1945-S dimes, it may be difficult to distinguish between those bearing the Trumpet Tail S and those having a Knob Tail S *(photos)*. Design elements that are near a coin's peripheries, such as the mintmarks on Mercury Dimes, often are distended or weak, as this is where the erosion process proceeds most rapidly. Therefore, little interest has been shown in these varieties by general collectors of the series. Conversely, the Micro S was spotted early on and quickly gained a following.

Trumpet Tail S
(Fivaz)

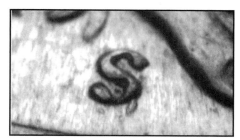

RPM-2, Knob Tail S
(Miller)

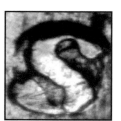

RPM-3, Knob Tail S
over horizontal S
(Stanton)

1945-S

Micro S

Mintage:
(Included with 1945-S)

Rarity: It appears that several working dies employed the Micro S puncheon, and Mint State examples are fairly plentiful. Circulated pieces may nearly be called common. Only with full bands is this variety difficult to find.

As a testament to the appealing visual quality of 1945-S dimes in general, two examples of the Micro S variety have been certified as MS-69.

COMBINED NGC & PCGS POPULATION									
MS64	MS64FB	MS65	MS65FB	MS66	MS66FB	MS67	MS67FB	MS68	MS68FB
343	112	1046	162	1655	101	259	11	6	2

Values:

	1945	1955	1965	1975	1985	1995	2005
G	——	——	——	——	——	——	——
F	——	——	1.50	.65	1.25	1.25	1.25
XF	——	——	3.50	3.00	3.00	4.00	5.00
MS60	——	——	15.00	10.00	20.00	——	——
MS63	——	——	——	——	——	25.00	35.00
MS65	——	——	——	——	37.50	65.00	90.00

Comments: Despite the use of two previous Small S punches from 1916 through 1941, the Micro S does not resemble either of these. It's about the same size of the puncheon used 1916-17, but it has more sweeping curves and pronounced serifs. Like that first Mercury Dime 'S' puncheon, it is almost perfectly symmetrical *(photo)*.

As noted above, the 1945-S Micro S dimes are not especially rare, but they enjoy a popular following. This is due in no small part to this variety's long term familiarity among collectors. The Micro S was discovered and reported by Bernard J. Maier only two years after being coined.[93] Beginning in 1955, a Mr. H. Dwight Ludlow began to keep track of this variety among dimes retrieved from general circulation. Though he did not specify his employment, he indicated that he handled large quantities of small change and had examined some 161,623 dimes by the time of publishing his results in 1962. Of this number, 776 were 1945-S dimes having the "regular" (Knob Tail or Trumpet Tail) S, while just 75 bore the Micro S.[94] This indicates that roughly 10% of the observed 1945-S dimes were of the Micro S variety.

Among USA regular-issue coins, the Micro S was used only in 1945 and for dimes alone. This puncheon had been created in 1907, when the size of the coins struck by the San Francisco Mint for use in the Philippine Islands was reduced. This tiny puncheon fit the small space available on dies of the ten- and twenty-centavos pieces. Last used in 1919, it was no doubt greased for protection from corrosion and set away in some tool locker at the Philadelphia Mint. The urgent need for evermore dies during the high production years of 1941-45 prompted the creation of two new 'S' mintmark puncheons, and it was at this time that the Micro S puncheon evidently was discovered and pressed into service. It was never used again after 1945.

This variety initially was assumed to be quite rare, and collectors took a great fancy to it while simultaneously overlooking truly rare issues such as the 1928-S Large S dimes. Its value, however, has not kept pace with inflation. Only a full bands specimen is highly priced in the current market, and only certain albums and display holders include a hole for this variety.

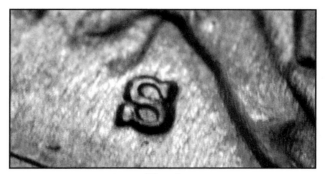

Micro S
(Fivaz)

Notes to Chapter 6

1 Breen, Walter. *Walter Breen's Complete Encyclopedia of United States and Colonial Coins.*

2 Wagner, Dick. "Delay Despoils Denver Dime Debut." *The Numismatic Scrapbook Magazine,* September 1973.

3 Robinson, Frank S. "Mercury Dime Questions Unresolved." *The Numismatic Scrapbook Magazine,* August 1970.

4 National Archives and Records Administration, Record Group 104, Bureau of the Mint, Letters Sent, Volume 417.

5 *Annual Report of the Director of the Mint, 1917.*

6 *Annual Report, 1918.*

7 *Annual Report, 1919.*

8 ibid.

9 ibid.

10 *Annual Report, 1920.*

11 *Annual Report, 1919.*

12 Sear, Rick. "A date by date analysis of Mercury Dimes." *The Coin Dealer Newsletter Monthly Summary.* April & May 1980.

13 *Annual Report, 1920.*

14 ibid.

15 Carothers, Neil. *Fractional Money.*

16 Archives of the Pacific Coast Numismatic Society, San Francisco.

17 *The Numismatic Scrapbook Magazine,* January 1949.

18 Annual Report, 1922.

19 NARA, RG-104, Letters Received, Box 315.

20 ibid.

21 *The Numismatist,* January 1940.

22 *The Numismatic Scrapbook Magazine,* November 1938.

23 *Annual Report, 1922.*

24 *Annual Report, 1924.*

25 ibid.

26 *Coin World Almanac.*

27 ibid.

28 ibid.

29 *Annual Report, 1923.*

30 Harriman, Allen. "An in-depth look at the Mercury Dime series." *The Coin Dealer Newsletter Monthly Summary,* March 1977.

31 *Annual Report, 1925.*

32 Harriman.

33 *Annual Report, 1925.*

34 Robinson, Frank S. "Mercury Dime Questions Unresolved." *The Numismatic Scrapbook Magazine,* September 1970.

35 *Annual Report, 1927.*

36 *The Numismatist,* January 1932.

37 ibid, August 1932

38 Wexler, John A. and Kevin Flynn. *Treasure Hunting Mercury Dimes.*

39 Fivaz, Bill and J. T. Stanton. *The Cherrypickers' Guide to Rare Die Varieties,* Third Edition.

40 *Annual Report, 1930.*

41 *Annual Report, 1931.*

42 ibid.

43 *The Numismatic Scrapbook Magazine,* November 1938.

44 *Annual Report, 1931.*

45 *Annual Report, 1934.*

46 *Annual Report, 1932.*

47 *Annual Report, 1933.*

48 *Annual Report, 1934.*

49 Wexler and Flynn.

50 *The Numismatic Scrapbook Magazine,* December 1939.

51 *Annual Report, 1934.*

52 Wexler and Flynn.

53 *Annual Report, 1934.*

54 Wexler and Flynn.

55 Wexler and Flynn.

56 *The Numismatic Scrapbook Magazine,* November 1937.

57 Wexler and Flynn.

58 *The Numismatic Scrapbook Magazine,* February 1938.

59 Wexler and Flynn.

60 Wexler and Flynn.

61 *The Numismatic Scrapbook Magazine,* March 1939.

62 ibid, August 1940.

63 Wexler and Flynn.

64 *The Numismatic Scrapbook Magazine,* August 1940.

65 Yeoman, R. S. *A Guide Book of United States Coins,* 58th Edition.

66 *The Numismatic Scrapbook Magazine,* October 1950.

67 Wexler and Flynn.

68 *The Numismatic Scrapbook Magazine,* August 1940.

69 *Annual Report, 1941.*

70 *The Numismatist,* December 1941.

71 Wexler and Flynn.

72 ibid.

73 *The Numismatic Scrapbook Magazine,* February 1941.

74 *The Numismatic Scrapbook Magazine,* August 1961.

75 ibid, September 1941.

76 ibid, January 1942.

77 *The Numismatic Scrapbook Magazine,* May 1943.

78 *The Numismatist,* August 1946.

79 Breen.

80 Wexler and Flynn.

81 *Coin World,* August 30, 1963.

82 ibid, August 10, 1966.

83 Wexler and Flynn

84 *The Numismatic Scrapbook* Magazine, July 1944.

85 ibid, September 1944.

86 Wexler and Flynn.

87 *Annual Report, 1944.*

88 *Annual Report, 1945.*

89 *The Numismatic Scrapbook Magazine,* July 1952.

90 Wexler and Flynn.

91 *Annual Report, 1945.*

92 *Annual Report, 1946.*

93 *The Numismatist,* March 1947.

94 *The Numismatic Scrapbook Magazine,* April 1962.

CHAPTER 7

Proof Coinage

For any coin enthusiast, the ultimate example of numismatic art is the proof coin. This is a coin created not for use within the channels of commerce but struck solely to impress the observer with its beauty and to display the artist's design in its perfect state. Special preparation of both dies and planchets is required, and each coin is struck two or three times to bring out every detail. In selecting a subtitle to his *Encyclopedia of United States and Colonial Proof Coins,* the late Walter Breen described these pieces as "A Coiner's Caviar." Despite the desirability of such coins, no proofs of the Winged Liberty or Mercury Dime were offered for sale by the Mint until 1936. Nevertheless, rumor and fact have merged to become legend regarding the proof dimes of 1916 and 1917.

Of the 1916, Breen provided pedigrees for three specimens in his proof coin encyclopedia, published in 1977. Eleven years later, his comprehensive encyclopedia of all United States coinage noted that as many as four or five were known, but no additional documentation was offered. To date, none have been certified by the various authentication/grading services.

Nevertheless, one confirmed proof survives within the National Numismatic Collection at the Smithsonian Institution's Museum of American History in Washington, DC. This was the first of Breen's pedigreed specimens, and it was the only irrefutable 1916 proof dime available for inclusion in this book. The author has examined this coin and agrees with Breen's attribution. Photographs of the Smithsonian coin may be found on page 231.

The existence of at least one proof dime dated 1917 is possible, based primarily on circumstantial evidence. The appearance of a complete proof set from cent through half dollar is documented by Breen in his 1977 work. This set was at one time owned by Philadelphia coin dealer Ira Reed, who sold it to an anonymous collector in 1942. It resurfaced in 1976, when it was purchased by dealer Joel Rettew, Sr. from the collection of Reed Hawn. As not even a rumor of 1917 proof coins had hitherto existed, the three silver pieces were subsequently sold to different buyers before their special nature was known. As a result, the dime was among the coins not actually seen by Walter Breen. His determination that all of the coins must have been proof specimens is based on his examination of the remaining cent and nickel. Thus, no absolute confirmation exists for a 1917 proof dime. Even so, two or three proofs were authenticated by Breen for each of the other denominations, and a proof dime of 1917 may exist, if only the single specimen once included in the complete set.

While a Breen authentication was once considered definitive and irrefutable, this is no longer the case. Great as Mr. Breen's achievements may have been, a number of his authentication letters, though still often included in subsequent sales of the coins they accompany, have been discounted by serious numismatists. To date, no 1917 dimes have been certified as proof by the various authentication/grading services. As Director of Research for Numismatic Guaranty Corporation, this author has examined several coins of 1917 that were submitted to NGC as possible proofs, including a dime, and none has measured up to verifiable proofs of earlier years.

The fact that proofs of the new Winged Liberty Dime were not offered for sale to collectors seems to have been largely a matter of bad timing. When this design was introduced in 1916, the sale of proof coins had been floundering for some years. More specifically, the sale of non-brilliant proof coins had floundered. The introduction of new coin designs beginning in 1907 had been accompanied by a new style of art in which the coins were modeled with irregular, textured fields that were concave, the fields rising up toward the rims. Previous types had possessed flat fields ideally suited to brilliant polishing. Thus, the preparation of mirror-finish proofs was not possible with the new coins, much to the dismay of collectors.

Ultimately, the original textured fields of the new coins were eliminated by the Mint's engraving staff, which had resisted this development from its inception. Until that time, however, several new methods of proof coin manufacture would be tested in an effort to utilize the existing hubs. Various finishes having either a satin glow or a matte dullness were employed beginning with the Saint-Gaudens gold coins of 1907. While favored by medallists, these proofs were met with resistance by collectors who protested that they were not sufficiently distinctive from ordinary coins. In the case of the matte proof gold coins of 1908 and 1911-15, some contended that they were just plain ugly. Sales dropped off after the first couple of years, a trend which was to recur as these finishes were employed with each successive new coin type. Collectors wanted brilliant proofs, and ever-greater numbers of non-brilliant proofs were left unsold at year's end.

The dimes, quarter dollars and half dollars of Barber's Liberty Head type were still coined as brilliant proofs through 1915. Being of antiquated designs, such polishing of the dies remained possible. After 1913, these three coins were the only brilliant proofs still being made at the U. S. Mint. Their sales remained fairly steady, while sales of proof cents, nickels and gold pieces declined. With the impending introduction of new dimes, quarters and halves, the Mint was thus faced with a dilemma. Realizing that the textured and concave fields integral to these coins would not permit the manufacture of brilliant proofs, the Mint opted to discontinue the sale of proof coins altogether, rather than attempt to market the new designs as matte or satin proofs.

The delay in readiness of the new designs led to a situation which has aroused the curiosity of collectors ever since. The question is often asked of why there were no proof dimes and quarters of the Barber Liberty Head type dated 1916 when such pieces were made for circulation. The answer lies in the fact that these coins were not struck for circulation until midway through the year and then only because the demand for additional dimes and quarters could not be met from existing stockpiles. The Mint never intended to coin silver pieces of the old type in 1916 and thus did not include them in the proof sets for that year.

The whole issue of silver proofs for 1916 was new to incoming Mint Director F. J. H. von Engelken when he assumed office on September 1 of that year. Philadelphia Mint Superintendent Adam M. Joyce, who was evidently tiring of inquiries from collectors, sent von Engelken the following letter on October 17:

> The issue of the silver coins of the new designs will complete the series of changes in the coin designs. The ground of all these designs is uneven, which makes it impossible to produce proof coins which are distinctive from the regular coins made on the coining presses from new dies, the only difference between proofs and the regular coins being the sharper edge and design.
>
> Formerly the full set of proofs was made in January or February and orders could be filled when received, but since the manner of manufacture and issuing the proofs has been changed so that some of the denominations may not be issued until late in the year (we are only allowed to make each denomination after the regular coins for circulation have been issued) great dissatisfaction has been shown by persons desiring these proofs and a seemingly

unnecessary amount of correspondence entailed on this office, returning orders and answering complaints.

In order to distinguish gold proofs from the regular issue, it has been necessary to give them a sandblast finish, which changes the appearance of the coins to such an extent that it is almost impossible to put them in circulation. This is something I am not sure we have a right to do.

The extra charge for the silver and minor proof coins, 5¢, does not cover the cost of manufacture.

I would, therefore, suggest for your consideration the advisability of ceasing the manufacture of proof coins.[1]

The following day, the Director gave his terse reply, "Effective at once, you will please discontinue the manufacture of proof coins."[2]

The Mint's position regarding the further manufacture and sale of proof coins was summed up a letter dated November 21, 1916 in reply to Commodore W. C. Eaton:

The coinage of the proof coins has been abolished by the order of the Director of the Mint at Washington, D. C. We will supply the proof nickel and cent only for 1916.

Respectfully,

A. C. Williamson, Medal Clerk[3]

Williamson's letter points out another interesting fact—that gold proofs were likewise unavailable for 1916. Still, there were those of taste and influence who desired proof specimens of the new coinage, and it's likely that one or more proofs were coined of the quarter dollar and half dollar, as well as the dime. Which parties received these coins and by what means is likely to remain a mystery, as such matters are rarely recorded for posterity. The only 1916 proof dime currently traced is at the Smithsonian Institution, transferred there with the balance of the U.S. Mint Collection when these coins were removed from Philadelphia in 1923. Presumably, the others must have gone to persons linked with their production. These may have included the artist Weinman, Chief Engraver Barber, Treasury Secretary William G. McAdoo and the successive Mint Directors R. W. Woolley and F. J. H. von Engelken, both of whom served during 1916. Other possible recipients include Philadelphia Mint Superintendent Adam M. Joyce and members of the Commission of Fine Arts. It's presumed that all 1916 and 1917 proof dimes will have a satin or slightly matte finish, as is the case with the Smithsonian coin.

As far as collectors are concerned, the coinage of proof Mercury Dimes began in 1936. Sales resumed that year as the result of the growing interest in coin collecting generally and as a consequence of influential persons who were sympathetic to the hobby being highly placed in Washington, D.C. On April 28 of that year, Treasury Secretary Henry Morgenthau authorized the resumption of proof coinage for sale to collectors. This action was prompted by President Franklin D. Roosevelt himself, reportedly after a suggestion from his personal secretary, Louis McHenry Howe.[4] Evidently assisting in this action was the fact the Morgenthau's brother, Ben, was an avid collector and numismatic columnist.

During the years that proof Mercury Dimes were offered by the Mint, 1936-42, all proof coins were sold individually. This accounts for the varying mintages from one denomination to another. As the quarter dollar was the least popular type, its mintage places a ceiling on the number of complete sets possible. All proofs of these years were coined exclusively at the Philadelphia Mint and carry no mintmarks.

A proof dime was priced at 20 cents, an additional 8 cents postage being required with all mail orders. During the first few years, coins sent by mail were packaged in cellophane sleeves which ultimately caused them to develop deep toning over time. This toning usually appears as a milky, beige film that is distributed more or less evenly over both sides. Though this distinctive toning is a badge of originality that some collectors prize, most find it unappealing, and the majority of 1936-42 proofs have been cleaned over the years with varying degrees of skill.

After a 20-year hiatus, there were few in the Mint's service who recalled the coining of brilliant proofs. Thus, the technique had to be relearned. This fact became all too evident when the first sales of proof coins prompted complaints from collectors that the coins were not equal to their pre-1916 brilliant proofs. Although superior in all respects to regular coinage, the first proofs of 1936 were only slightly mirrored, possessing a finish which has been described as satin-like. Ironically, this same problem would recur in 1950, when proof coinage was again resumed after a suspension of several years.

Subsequent proofs made during the latter part of 1936 and afterward through 1942 were fully brilliant. These look much like the later proofs of 1950 through 1964 in that they are brilliant and mirror-like throughout, with little or no contrast between fields and devices. Although satisfactory to most collectors, these enhanced proofs still elicited some negative remarks from old timers, who recalled the stunning contrast between brilliant fields and frosted devices which typified the proofs of a generation earlier. The response of Mint Director Nellie Tayloe Ross to these criticisms was published in *The Numismatist*:

> Your letter of June 13th, relative to Proof coins, has been referred to this bureau for attention. The superintendent submits the following explanation in regard to the method of preparing Proof coins:
>
> "Proof coins being struck at the Mint at the present time are made in every detail exactly as they have been made in the past, namely, the planchets are carefully selected and each one struck individually on a hydraulic press, and handled so that one coin cannot mar another. The dies are polished to a mirror finish at frequent intervals.
>
> "The difference between the recent proofs and those struck in the past is due to the difference in the design and the method used in preparing the master dies. All the present coins are made from sculptured models without retouching with a graver in any way in order to preserve the exact quality and texture of the original sculptor's work. This gives a more or less uneven background with less sharpness in the details. In other words, they are produced the same as small medals might be struck.
>
> "The master dies for the gold coins struck previous to 1907, and the silver coins struck prior to 1916, were prepared in the older and entirely different method, being lower in relief and much greater sharpness in detail by re-engraving, even though the original design was reduced from a sculptured model. The inscriptions were usually put into the master dies by means of punches. In addition, they were prepared with a 'basined' background or field, that is, the field was polished to a perfect radius on a revolving disc, which again produced a much clearer definition between motif and field, and this gave an entirely different appearance to the coin.

"With the present coins, the models were never prepared with the intention of 'basining' and it could not be done without many radical alterations in the relief of the present designs."[5]

This seemed to settle the matter at the time. We know, however, from our current proof coins that it is indeed possible to provide contrasting elements within coins having concave fields. The technology then available, combined with a general inexperience in coining proofs, may have made this an impossibility in the 1930s.

To a knowledgeable reader, the superintendent's explanation seems to raise more questions than it answers. His statement that the Mint preserved "the exact quality and texture of the original sculptor's work" was absolutely false, although he was doubtless unaware of it. All of the designs introduced since 1913 had had their original textured fields smoothed out by the Mint's engraving staff within their first year or two of coinage. The Mercury Dimes of 1917 are found with either their original textured fields or with modified smooth fields, these corresponding to the Types of 1916 and 1917, respectively (see Chapter 2).

The superintendent's description of the different methods employed in preparing the old dies versus the newer ones is essentially correct, though it doesn't directly address the matter of contrasting finishes between relief elements and fields. He comes closest with his reference to the old dies having a perfect radius, this evidently meaning that they were flat in their fields and thus subject to brilliant polishing.

The disappointing quality of the first 1936 proof coins hindered sales of this date, setting the stage for some future rarities. In his "Capital Comment" column, Harry Boosel recounted the hobby community's reaction:

> It seems that most collectors were disappointed with the early proofs of last year, and so avoided them. Later the proofs were improved but not many knew about it. As a result the number of proofs sold was comparatively small, and most dealers are asking $5 for a complete set.[6]

Lee F. Hewitt, editor of *The Numismatic Scrapbook Magazine*, supplemented this information with some further facts:

> After a "proof-less" era of some twenty years, the sale of proofs by the Philadelphia Mint was resumed in the summer of 1936. The coins struck during the first month or two in that year were very little better than those issued for general circulation—they were improved in the fall but it is felt that the poor quality of the early sets held down sales. In fact the Philadelphia Mint had a quantity of 1936 sets left on hand at the end of the year; a Chicago collector visiting Philadelphia in February of 1937 was able to buy ten sets at the Mint office.[7]

Although the greater brilliance of the enhanced proofs satisfied collectors, this feature came at a high cost to the overall quality of the coins. In repeatedly polishing the dies, the Mint caused much of the low relief detail of the Mercury Dime to become weakened or even obliterated. Elements such as the motto IN GOD WE TRUST, the designer's monogram AW, the date and the leaves in the olive branch were all lessened to some degree. Another feature common to most proofs 1936-42, as well as most dates of the regular coinage, is the "broken nose" phenomenon. Overzealous polishing, or lapping, of the dies was again the culprit in obliterating the bridge of Liberty's nose.

The onset of World War II strained the Mint's capacity to its fullest, causing a sus-

The onset of World War II strained the Mint's capacity to its fullest, causing a suspension in proof coinage. Initially thought to be temporary, this cessation continued year after year through the war's end. Periodic appeals from collectors elicited the sympathy of Mint Director Ross, but little else. This condition was affirmed by H. C. Moore, Acting Superintendent of the Philadelphia Mint: "Facilities of the Mint are taxed almost beyond capacity. Due to this fact no proof coins have been struck in 1943, and none will be struck for the duration of the war at least."[8]

With the coming of peace, it was hoped that the production of proof coins would resume. Instead, the tremendous number of service medals being struck in recognition of the homecoming veterans was said to be overwhelming the Mint's hydraulic presses. In addition, the Mint claimed that it lacked an appropriation to create proof coins in advance of sales. At least, those were the official reasons given. Not stated in print, but known to many in the hobby, was the fact that there were individuals in the Mint's hierarchy who were actively hostile toward coin collecting, and this likely added a few proofless years. It wasn't until 1950 that production of proof coins resumed, and by then the Mercury Dime had been retired. No longer would Weinman's masterwork be rendered in brilliant proof for the delight of collectors.

PROOF DATE ANALYSIS

GUIDE TO USING THIS ANALYSIS:

1. "Ranking" refers to the placement of that particular date's mintage within the overall series from lowest mintage to highest. In other words, the date with the lowest mintage is ranked 1/7, while the issue with the highest mintage is 7/7. As the mintages of proof dimes advanced continually from 1936 through 1942, this ratio turns out to be a direct progression.

2. "Combined NGC & PCGS Population" refers to the total number of proof dimes certified by Numismatic Guaranty Corporation and Professional Coin Grading Service in the respective grades listed. The grades included are the ones most sought by collectors of Mercury Dimes. These figures are taken from the October 2004 editions of the *NGC Census Report* and the *PCGS Population Report*.

3. Values listed for 1945 are taken from *The Standard Catalogue of United States Coins 1945 Edition*, Wayte Raymond, Editor. Values listed for 1955, 1965, 1975, 1985, 1995 and 2005 are from the 8th, 18th, 28th, 38th, 48th and 58th editions of *A Guide Book of United States Coins*, respectively, by R. S. Yeoman, more recently edited by Kenneth Bressett. The earlier editions did not use numerical grading, but it may be assumed that entries described simply as "PROOF" averaged PF-63. Therefore, the values taken from these editions have thus been assigned the PF-63 grade for continuity with later entries. The values for higher grades are more volatile, being subject to changes in the certified population. Readers are referred to *The Coin Dealer Newsletter*, *The Certified Coin Dealer Newsletter* and *Numismedia* for current valuations.

4. The term "choice" in reference to grading describes a coin whose numerical grade would be PF-63 or PF-64. The term "gem" refers to a coin grading PF-65. The term "superb gem" refers to a coin grading PF-66 or higher.

1916

Mintage:
(unknown)

Rarity: The late Walter Breen wrote that as many as five proofs having a satin or slightly matte finish were in existence. Little or no documentation was offered for this claim, and the whereabouts of only a single specimen is presently known. This is the coin illustrated above, found within the National Numismatic Collection of the Smithsonian Institution's Museum of American History. While a portion of this collection was displayed for generations before being put into storage in 2004, it is believed that this lone 1916 proof was never publicly displayed. Its existence is thus little known to the hobby.

Comments: As may be seen in the above photos, a genuine proof 1916 Mercury Dime possesses an absolutely complete strike with not even the hint of weakness. The finest details of Liberty's hair are boldly wrought and there is, needless to say, no question of full bands. All lettering and the monogram stand out in high relief. The borders are broad with partial wire rims, and the inner rims of the borders are deep and sharply defined. As Breen reported, the luster is subdued with a soft, satin finish.

1936
Satin Finish

1936
Brilliant Finish

Mintage:
4,130
(Ranking 1/7)

Rarity: While most of the 4,130 proof dimes minted in 1936 no doubt survive in the hands of collectors or dealers, this is still a remarkably small number of coins. Examples are very scarce and in constant demand. As most proofs of this date have been cleaned at least once, with varying results, top grade pieces are quite rare. Indeed, this is by far the rarest of the 1936-42 proofs at or above the gem level.

No 1936 dimes have been certified as having a cameo finish.

COMBINED NGC & PCGS POPULATION									
PF60	PF61	PF62	PF63	PF64	PF65	PF66	PF67	PF68	PF69
6	10	47	177	643	576	461	85	2	0

Values:		1945	1955	1965	1975	1985	1995	2005
	PF63	10.00	12.50	65.00	185.00	——	——	——
	PF65	——	——	——	——	900.00	1200.00	2000.00

Comments: This date in proof has carried a premium value ever since its sale by the Mint ceased, sometime in 1937. Note the amazing price advance from just 20 cents at issue to $10 in the coin market less than a decade later.

Proofs having a less than fully brilliant finish were coined only briefly, until complaints from collectors led to more generous polishing of the dies. The early proofs have a satin or semi-brilliant finish, but with the extreme highpoint detail, full borders and wire rims not seen on circulation strikes.

The number of surviving satin proofs is quite small, Walter Breen claiming to have seen only eight pieces in his entire numismatic career.[9] The rarity of this issue is such that no separate listing for it appears in any published catalogs, nor have any been certified by the various authentication and grading services. Since silver is among the more reflective of metals, the visible difference between satin proofs and brilliant proofs is too subtle for the hobby to make an official distinction. Thus, just a single table is included here for the entire certified population. This is in marked contrast to the cent and nickel, which are listed and traded at differing price levels for both finishes.

If a satin finish proof dime were to be offered as such, it's difficult to say whether or not it would carry a premium over the more common brilliant proofs. Its great rarity is something appreciated only by a few specialists, and the typical buyer would pass on it in favor of a more conventional brilliant proof. The fact that the Mint did not intentionally produce two different finishes further weighs against the collecting of these coins as separate issues.

Note that the satin proof illustrated retains nearly all of its design elements, including those in lowest relief such as the motto and the monogram. Compare this with the brilliant proofs of this and later years, in which much low relief detail has been polished away in the course of achieving such brilliance.

1937

Mintage:
5,756
(Ranking 2/7)

Rarity: While quite rare in the highest grades, proofs of this date are more likely to be found in popular grades than are the elusive 1936 proofs. Their survival rate in gem condition seems to be higher as a percentage of total mintage.

A single proof has been certified as PF-66 Cameo, this being a very rare coin in which the legends and devices have a slightly frosted texture that contrasts with the brilliant fields. Cameo proofs of the Mercury Dime are extremely rare, and some dates have yet to be certified with this desirable feature.

COMBINED NGC & PCGS POPULATION									
PF60	PF61	PF62	PF63	PF64	PF65	PF66	PF67	PF68	PF69
5	7	39	123	545	726	741	293	37	0

Values:

	1945	1955	1965	1975	1985	1995	2005
PF63	3.25	5.50	60.00	110.00	——	——	——
PF65	——	——	——	——	600.00	450.00	800.00

Comments: Proofs of this date typically are fully brilliant, both in the fields and on the devices. These proofs are subject to over polishing of the die with a resultant loss of low relief elements. Particularly common is the "broken nose," in which the shallow bridge of Liberty's nose is effaced from the die. Other elements sometimes lost to this polishing include the leaves of the wreath and the dangling end of the leather thong that secures the fasces.

Though the hobby was booming in 1937, most of the speculative interest centered around commemorative half dollars, with few collectors taking notice of current proofs. The sharp price advances for the 1936 proofs had not yet appeared, so the 1937 mintage was unaffected by any speculative activity.

The glamour attached to 1937 proof dimes has never applied to this date, so its value has consistently lagged behind the earlier issue. Nevertheless, it is firmly acknowledged as the second rarest entry in the proof Mercury Dime series.

As with all Mercury Dime proofs, beware of well struck currency strikes that have been polished to simulate proof brilliance. These will be lacking the high point detail and broad, flat rims which typify proofs. Such deceptions were commonplace beginning in the 1950s, but the widespread use of third-party certification services has largely eliminated this evil. Caution is still advised when purchasing uncertified, or "raw," proofs.

1938

Mintage:
8,728
(Ranking 3/7)

Rarity: As a strong secondary market developed for the 1936 proofs, this boosted the mintages of proofs in 1938 and later years. While 8,728 pieces is still a ridiculously small number of coins when compared to the millions of proofs sold annually in recent decades, this date is noticeably more available than the 1936-37 proof dimes.

No cameo proofs have yet been certified for this date.

COMBINED NGC & PCGS POPULATION									
PF60	PF61	PF62	PF63	PF64	PF65	PF66	PF67	PF68	PF69
1	8	39	165	731	1183	1060	301	26	1

Values:

	1945	1955	1965	1975	1985	1995	2005
PF63	2.00	3.50	20.00	100.00	——	——	——
PF65	——	——	——	——	525.00	350.00	500.00

Comments: In terms of manufacturing quality, there is little distinction between the proof dimes of 1937 and those of 1938. A higher mintage this year has led to a greater certified population in the most collected grades of PF-63 through PF-66, yet the number of pieces grading higher than PF-66 is roughly similar for both years. This reflects the difficulty in preserving top-grade pieces over the intervening years. While both professional conservation and safe storage materials are now available, these are both fairly recent developments.

Until the 1980s most collectors placed their proof dimes in albums, which were already available in 1938. These offered some protection from contact marks but very little environmental protection; indeed, the albums were themselves made of mildly corrosive materials. Another option, beginning in the 1940s, was the use of rigid, styrene or acrylic holders. These offered good physical protection and somewhat better environmental protection. The widespread use of certified encapsulations since 1986 has provided perhaps the best overall protection from harm, but these came too late to save many proofs.

Easily the biggest deterrent to the survival of proof Mercury Dimes in gem condition has been unskilled cleaning. Most collectors prefer brilliant, untoned coins, but few of the 1936-42 proofs remained in this state, due to the primitive packaging employed by both the Mint and the coins' owners. Clumsy attempts at cleaning proof coins, with their very delicate surfaces, typically left hairline scratches that cannot be removed. Improper rinsing away of cleaning solutions, combined with poor storage options, only accelerated the retoning process, prompting additional cleanings over the years.

1939

Mintage:
9,321
(Ranking 4/7)

Rarity: Though its mintage was only slightly higher than for 1938, the 1939 proof dime enjoys a noticeably higher survival rate in top grades. Quality control was slightly better for this issue, but the growing popularity of proof coins with collectors at this time probably accounts for the greater proportion of carefully preserved examples.

The proof dimes of 1939 likewise have a much greater certified population of cameo examples than for any other date 1936-42. No fewer than 26 pieces have been so certified, with the breakdown as follows: PF-64, 3; PF-65, 2; PF-66, 11; PF-67, 9; PF-68, 1.

COMBINED NGC & PCGS POPULATION									
PF60	PF61	PF62	PF63	PF64	PF65	PF66	PF67	PF68	PF69
1	3	30	110	440	1015	1437	779	64	0

Values:

	1945	1955	1965	1975	1985	1995	2005
PF63	1.75	3.50	17.00	70.00	——	——	——
PF65	——	——	——	——	450.00	325.00	450.00

Comments: The mintages of proof coins continued to rise each year, and 1939's sales of proof dimes reflected this increased interest. While the hobby itself was growing, the price advances for 1936 proofs of all denominations fueled some speculative activity, too.

Proof dimes of this date are distinctive only in that they seem to have been more subject than usual to over polishing of the dies. To achieve the desired brilliance, the Philadelphia Mint's employees sometimes went a bit overboard in the lapping operation. Proof dies that began to show some wear were lapped yet again, each time diminishing some of the low-relief design elements. The majority of proof Mercury Dimes have an interruption in the bridge of Liberty's nose from such polishing, but the more extreme examples have very shallow lettering and incomplete details where the design meets the coin's fields.

1940

Mintage:
11,827
(Ranking 5/7)

Rarity: The proofs of this date are quite comparable to those dated 1939, both in terms of overall quality and survival rate. 1940 proof dimes are somewhat less often seen in the very highest grades.

The big difference between this date and 1939 is the extreme rarity of cameo pieces for 1940. Just two examples have been certified to date, one each in PF-65 and PF-67.

COMBINED NGC & PCGS POPULATION									
PF60	PF61	PF62	PF63	PF64	PF65	PF66	PF67	PF68	PF69
3	8	39	157	760	1307	1466	530	42	0

Values:

	1945	1955	1965	1975	1985	1995	2005
PF63	1.25	3.00	15.00	60.00	——	——	——
PF65	——	——	——	——	400.00	380.00	425.00

Comments: In retrospect it seems amazing that collectors of the time didn't order more proof coins. Clearly, most hobbyists ordered just one or two examples of each denomination, with some ordering additional singles of the cent and nickel, as these denominations were the ones most likely to be collected by date and mint. What was lacking during these years was the speculative urge that became so prevalent after the reintroduction of proof coinage in 1950.

1940 proof dimes enjoyed a fairly rapid appreciation in value, once proof coinage ended in 1942. Even so, this date, along with 1941 and 1942, lagged behind earlier issues in the marketplace for many years. Perhaps the high number of currency pieces coined during the early 1940s dampened collector enthusiasm for the associated proofs of these years.

1941

Mintage:
16,557
(Ranking 6/7)

Rarity: While the mintage of proof dimes rose significantly from the previous year's total, this seems to have affected only the overall number of surviving proofs. In terms of grade rarity, this date is more available in the popularly collected grades of PF-63 through PF-66, yet the number of superior pieces is about the same. Again, the difficulty in preserving top-grade proofs was the determining factor in how many remain for today's collectors.

Cameo proofs are exceedingly rare, just a single PF-67 having been certified.

COMBINED NGC & PCGS POPULATION									
PF60	PF61	PF62	PF63	PF64	PF65	PF66	PF67	PF68	PF69
8	10	56	271	1143	1847	1688	510	38	0

Values:

	1945	1955	1965	1975	1985	1995	2005
PF63	1.25	2.00	15.00	60.00	——	——	——
PF65	——	——	——	——	375.00	275.00	400.00

Comments: As noted above, preservation has played a big role in the survival of gem proofs for this date, but another factor is involved, too. The proofs of 1941 seem to have been made with a little less care than those from the years immediately preceding. The spike in sales this year may have caught the Mint by surprise, as there is a noticeably higher incidence of over polished dies for the 1941 proofs. Of course, the most well known examples are the half dollars lacking the designer's monogram, but this careless die work is symptomatic of 1941 proofs in general.

1942

Mintage:
22,329
(Ranking 7/7)

Rarity: Proof mintages jumped dramatically yet again, though the totals for 1942 across the various denominations are still miniscule by current standards. 1942 dimes are the most common of all Mercury Dime proofs in all grades, due both to the larger number coined and a more consistent emphasis on quality control by the Mint.

Cameo pieces are very rare for this date, with just four having been certified. These include one grading PF-65 and three certified as PF-66. Perhaps needless to say is the fact that no Mercury Dimes of any date have been certified by NGC as Ultra Cameo, nor by PCGS as its equivalent Deep Cameo.

COMBINED NGC & PCGS POPULATION									
PF60	PF61	PF62	PF63	PF64	PF65	PF66	PF67	PF68	PF69
9	13	59	278	1504	2368	2534	1018	97	1

Values:

	1945	1955	1965	1975	1985	1995	2005
PF63	1.00	2.00	10.00	60.00	——	——	——
PF65	——	——	——	——	375.00	275.00	400.00

Comments: While no internal documentation survives regarding the proof coinage of 1942, it is evident that the Philadelphia Mint was better prepared for an increase in production than it was in 1941. The quality of proof dimes, as made, is consistently higher for this date. The severe over polishing of dies, so evident in 1941 proofs, is much less often seen for 1942. It seems that the Mint finally mastered its technique for achieving full brilliance without sacrificing the shallow details of the dies. While one might expect that this emphasis on quality control would have resulted in the production of more cameo pieces, this was evidently never a consideration by the Mint.

---

[1] National Archives, Records Group 104, Bureau of the Mint, Letters Received, Box 305

[2] ibid.

[3] *The Numismatist,* November 1916.

[4] *The Numismatic Scrapbook Magazine,* May 1936.

[5] *The Numismatist,* July 1936.

[6] *The Numismatic Scrapbook Magazine,* October 1937.

[7] ibid, March 1942.

[8] ibid, June 1943.

[9] Breen, Walter. *Walter Breen's Complete Encyclopedia of U.S. and Colonial Coins*

APPENDICES

Glossary

*

Statistics

*

References

APPENDIX A

GLOSSARY

ANACS - Formerly owned by the American Numismatic Association, hence its initials, this is now a commercial grading and encapsulation service located near Columbus, Ohio.

CAMEO - This grading designation refers to a proof coin displaying contrast between its frosted raised elements and brilliant, mirrorlike fields (see also DEEP CAMEO). Cameo Proofs of the Mercury Dime are very rare.

COLLAR - This is the steel ring which surrounds the coining chamber between obverse and reverse dies. Modern coins are struck within a closed collar in which the expanding edge of the planchet is forcefully restrained against the collar's inner surface, imparting the coin's edge device. In the case of Mercury Dimes the edge is reeded.

CLASHMARKS - When a planchet misfeeds and the dies strike one another, each is left with an inverted impression of the other. These ghostlike outlines are then transferred to each coin struck until the dies are repaired by lapping, or polishing.

CUD - A coin variety in which a portion of the die has broken away, usually as the result of a progressive die crack. This missing portion appears as a blank or filled-in area on the coin. A retained cud is one in which the dislodged piece of the die remains in place.

CURRENCY STRIKE - This describes a regular production coin, struck only once and intended for use in commerce. The term "business strike" is also used.

DDO - Doubled-die obverse. When a working die is not accurately in register between multiple impressions from a working hub, a slight doubling or shifting of the image is imparted to the die. This is then transferred to all coins struck from that die.

DDR - Doubled-die reverse (see above).

DCAM, ULTRA CAMEO - Deeply Cameo. These terms are used by PCGS and NGC, respectively, to describe the same condition in which a proof coin displays exceptionally good contrast between its frosted devices and brilliant fields. Mercury Dimes displaying this degree of contrast are unknown (see also CAMEO).

DMPL, DPL - Deeply Prooflike. These terms are used by PCGS and NGC, respectively, to describe a non-proof coin having very reflective fields. These designations are rarely applied to Mercury Dimes (see also PL).

DIE - This is a steel cylinder which bears on one end a negative or incuse image of a coin design. Master dies are used to raise working hubs, while working dies are used to strike coins. In striking Mercury Dimes, the reverse die was used as the upper or "hammer" die, while the obverse was positioned as the lower or "anvil" die.

DIE BURN - While not a widely used term, the author chose this to describe the random, brilliant patches that appear within the fields of some Mercury Dimes as a consequence of the die being vigorously lapped to remove clashmarks or some other flaw.

FB - Full Bands. Dimes having full separation between the two horizontal bands at the middle of the fasces may be designated as FB in the grading process.

HUB - The opposite of a die, this is a steel cylinder which bears on one end a positive or relief image of a coin design. A master hub is used to sink master dies, while working hubs are used to sink working dies.

LAPPING - This describes the mechanical polishing of a coin die to achieve a brilliant finish or to eradicate some flaw in the die.

MECHANICAL, MACHINE OR STRIKE DOUBLING - All three terms describe the same phenomenon. This occurs when one or both dies bounce back against the struck coin at the moment of striking or when one or both dies move laterally as they separate from the coin. The result is a slightly doubled image which is flat and shelf-like, rather than being contoured as with a true doubled-die variety.

MINTMARK - This is a small letter appearing on a coin which indicates its place of manufacture. The absence of this letter on a Mercury Dime reveals that it was coined at the Philadelphia Mint. Dimes coined at Denver and San Francisco bear D and S mintmarks, respectively. These were all applied at the Engraving Department of the Philadelphia Mint, where the dies were made.

NGC - Numismatic Guaranty Corporation of America, located in Sarasota, Florida, is a commercial service which authenticates, grades and encapsulates coins.

ORIGINAL ROLL - Coins are delivered to the Federal Reserve Banks from the Mint in bags or boxes, never in rolls. Thus, rolls are wrapped by commercial banks or, in more recent years, by armored car services from freshly minted and delivered coins. "Original" rolls consist of coins which have been kept together since new and have not been picked through by collectors who then substituted lesser coins for the finer pieces.

PCGS - Professional Coin Grading Service, located in Newport Beach, California, is a commercial service which authenticates, grades and encapsulates coins.

PLANCHET - This is a finished coin blank which has been shaped and cleaned for striking by the coin press.

PROOF - This is a coin made from specially prepared dies, struck two or more times to bring out all details. It is intended for sale to collectors at a premium. Proofs of the Mercury Dime were sold only in 1936-42.

PL - Prooflike. Non-Proof coins displaying reflective fields may earn this grading designation. Prooflike Mercury Dimes are unusual for most dates and are most often encountered with 'S' Mint dimes of the 1940s (see also DPL).

REEDING - This is the series of raised bars which appear around the edge of United States dimes and many other coins. When coins were made of precious metals, this edge device protected against the practices of shaving or clipping metal from the edge.

RPM - This identifies a repunched mintmark variety, an example being D over D, or D/D.

SLIDER - This describes a coin which appears Uncirculated and may be offered as such but which possesses the very slightest wear.

STATISTICS

TABLE 1. The Rank of Non-Proof Mercury Dimes by mintage from Lowest to Highest.

RANK	DATE	MINTAGE	RANK	DATE	MINTAGE
1	1916-D	264,000	40	1940-D	21,198,000
2	1921-D	1,080,000	41	1940-S	21,560,000
3	1921-P	1,230,000	42	1916-P	22,180,080
4	1931-D	1,260,000	43	1938-P	22,198,728
5	1926-S	1,520,000	44	1918-D	22,674,800
6	1931-S	1,800,000	45	1924-P	24,010,000
7	1930-S	1,843,000	46	1934-P	24,080,000
8	1931-P	3,150,000	47	1939-D	24,394,000
9	1928-D	4,161,000	48	1925-P	25,610,000
10	1929-S	4,730,000	49	1929-P	25,970,000
11	1927-S	4,770,000	50	1918-P	26,680,000
12	1927-D	4,812,000	51	1917-S	27,330,000
13	1929-D	5,034,000	52	1927-P	28,080,000
14	1925-D	5,117,000	53	1926-P	32,160,000
15	1938-D	5,537,000	54	1919-P	35,740,000
16	1925-S	5,850,000	55	1945-D	40,245,000
17	1923-S	6,440,000	56	1945-S	41,920,000
18	1930-P	6,770,000	57	1941-S	43,090,000
19	1934-D	6,772,000	58	1941-D	45,634,000
20	1924-D	6,810,000	59	1942-S	49,300,000
21	1926-D	6,828,000	60	1944-S	49,490,000
22	1924-S	7,120,000	61	1923-P	50,130,000
23	1928-S	7,400,000	62	1917-P	55,230,000
24	1938-S	8,090,000	63	1937-P	56,865,756
25	1919-S	8,850,000	64	1935-P	58,830,000
26	1936-S	9,210,000	65	1920-P	59,030,000
27	1917-D	9,402,000	66	1943-S	60,400,000
28	1937-S	9,740,000	67	1942-D	60,740,000
29	1919-D	9,939,000	68	1944-D	62,224,000
30	1916-S	10,450,000	69	1940-P	65,361,827
31	1935-D	10,477,000	70	1939-P	67,749,321
32	1939-S	10,540,000	71	1943-D	71,949,000
33	1920-S	13,820,000	72	1936-P	87,504,130
34	1937-D	14,146,000	73	1945-P	159,130,000
35	1935-S	15,840,000	74	1941-P	175,106,557
36	1936-D	16,132,000	75	1943-P	191,710,000
37	1920-D	19,171,000	76	1942-P	205,432,329
38	1918-S	19,300,000	77	1944-P	231,410,000
39	1928-P	19,480,000			

TABLE 2. The Rank of Proof Mercury Dimes from Lowest to Highest.

RANK	DATE	MINTAGE
1	1936	4,130
2	1937	5,756
3	1938	8,728
4	1939	9,321
5	1940	11,827
6	1941	16,557
7	1942	22,329

REFERENCES

BOOKS:

American Numismatic Association. Counterfeit Detection, Volume I. ANA. Colorado Springs, CO 1983.

Committee on Finance of the United States Senate. *Coinage Laws of the United States 1792-1894,* David L. Ganz, Editor. Bowers and Merena Galleries, Inc (reprint). Wolfeboro, NH, 1990.

Breen, Walter. *Walter Breen's Complete Encyclopedia of U.S. and Colonial Coins.* F.C.I. Press, Inc. & Doubleday. New York, 1988.

Breen, Walter. *Walter Breen's Encyclopedia of United States and Colonial Proof Coins 1722-1977.* F.C.I. Press, Inc. Albertson, NY, 1977.

Bressett, Ken & A. Kosoff. *Official A.N.A. Grading Standards for United States Coins, Fifth Edition.* American Numismatic Association. Colorado Springs, CO, 1996.

Carothers, Neil. *Fractional Money - A History of the Small Coins and Fractional Paper Currency of The United States.* John Wiley & Sons, Inc. New York, 1930.

Fivaz, Bill & J. T. Stanton. *The Cherrypickers' Guide to Rare Die Varieties, Third Edition.* Bowers & Merena Galleries, Inc. Wolfeboro, NH, 1994.

Friedberg, Robert. *Paper Money of the United States, Twelfth Edition.* The Coin and Currency Institute, Inc. Clifton, NJ, 1989.

Gibbs, William T., Editor. *Coin World Almanac, Seventh Edition.* Amos Press, Inc. Sidney, OH, 2000.

Johnson, James G. *Fair to Very Fine.* Published by the author, reprinted from *Coin World.* Sidney, OH, 1978.

Judd, J. Hewitt, M.D., Q. David Bowers, Editor. *United States Pattern Coins, Experimental and Trial Pieces, Eighth Edition.* Whitman Publishing, LLC. Atlanta, 2003.

Pollock, Andrew W. III *United States Patterns and Related Issues.* Bowers & Merena Galleries, Inc. Wolfeboro, NH, 1994.

Stevens, Holly (editor). *Letters of Wallace Stevens.* Alfred A. Knopf. New York, 1966.

Taft, Lorado. *The History of American Sculpture.* Arno Press (reprint). New York, 1969.

Taxay, Don. *The U.S. Mint and Coinage.* Arco Publishing Co., Inc. New York, 1966.

United States Treasury Department. *Annual Report of the Director of the Mint for Fiscal Year Ended June 30. 1916.* U. S. Government Printing Office, Washington, DC, 1916. Also, various additional years through 1946.

Vermeule, Cornelius. *Numismatic Art in America.* The Belknap Press of Harvard University Press. Cambridge, MA, 1971.

Wexler, John A. & Kevin Flynn. *Treasure Hunting Mercury Dimes.* Stanton Printing and Publishing. Savannah, GA, 1999.

Wexler, John A. & Tom Miller. *The RPM Book. Lonesome* John Publishing Co. Newbury Park, CA, 1983.

Yeoman, R. S., Kenneth Bressett, Editor. *A Guide Book of United States Coins.* Whitman Publishing, LLC. Atlanta, various editions.

PERIODICALS:

American Numismatic Association. *The Numismatist.* Various issues as noted.

Carlson, Carl W. A. *"Letters show designer's thoughts on 1916 dime." Coin World.* July 24, 1991.

Coin World. *"Noted Numismatists Offer Comment on Controversial 1923-D Mercury."* October 18, 1963.

Ford, John J., Editor. *Numisma,* July-August, 1957.

Gibbs, William T. *"Poet's wife becomes Weinman's model." Coin World,* June 28, 1991.

Gibbs, William T. *"Winged Liberty Head 1916-45." Coin World,* (seven parts) June 19 through July 31, 1991.

Harriman, Allen. *"An in-depth look at the Mercury Dime series." The Coin Dealer Newsletter Monthly Summary,* March 1977.

Hewitt, Lee F., Publisher. *The Numismatic Scrapbook Magazine.* Various issues as noted.

Risser, John. *"Wallace Stevens." Susquehanna Magazine.* April 1990.

Robinson, Frank S. *"Mercury Dime Questions Unresolved." The Numismatic Scrapbook Magazine,* August & September, 1970.

Sear, Rick. *"A date by date analysis of Mercury Dimes." The Coin Dealer Newsletter Monthly Summary.* April, May 1980.

Wagner, Dick. *"Delay Despoils Denver Dime Debut." The Numismatic Scrapbook Magazine.* September 1973.

UNPUBLISHED MATERIAL:

National Archives and Records Administration, Region II. Records Group 104, "Bureau of the Mint, Letters Received" and "Bureau of the Mint, Letters Sent."

Pacific Coast Numismatic Society. Meeting minutes and other archival documents, 1919-1923.

Coins and currency are history you can hold.
Be a part of their future.

David Lawrence combines traditional value...

- **Quality:** At DLRC, we only sell coins and currency graded by the accepted industry grading houses. In addition to being quite fussy about the material we offer for sale on our Web site, we use our unique color/star-rating system to advise you on a coin's degree of toning and eye appeal.

- **Service:** We have four professional (non-commissioned) numismatists available to help you with all of your collecting questions. Our knowledgeable and friendly support staff is there to help with all other questions, assuring you the highest quality personal service in the industry.

- **Selection:** DLRC offers over 6,000 certified coins, currency and books for sale at all times.

...with the most progressive tools in modern trading.

- **Continuously Updated Web site:** New items are added daily with large, full-color images. Easy, secure online ordering. Our *myDavidLawrence* feature allows you to keep track of orders, want lists, consignments and auction bids. Best of all, it's easy to use.

- **Weekly Internet-only auctions:** These exclusive auctions provide easy, interactive bidding with no shipping charges and full return privileges. Most items are offered without reserve.

- **Online want listing:** Don't miss that key date you've been hunting for years! With our want list service, you are automatically notified by e-mail when a match is added to inventory.

John Feigenbaum & Win Callender, members.

www.davidlawrence.com
800.776.0560

David Lawrence
RARE COINS

Home of the Richmond Collection

The NGC Registry

The NGC Registry is a community of coin collectors which enables you to share your passion for the hobby. Enter your collections and have them ranked alongside other great sets. The goal of The NGC Registry is to foster camaraderie by acknowledging collectors who assemble truly remarkable sets and encouraging beginners as they embark on this fun and rewarding endeavor.

There are many advantages to using The NGC Registry:

- An accurate weighting system assigns a score to each coin and grade, assuring that your collection is ranked according to its true rarity.

- You receive a scoring bonus for coins with the NGC Star Designation (★). This coveted designation, unique to NGC, identifies coins with superior eye appeal.

- Images and descriptions of your coins are automatically entered into a Coin Gallery, creating a vivid graphic showcase of your collection.

- Share your experiences through the Collectors' Journal, a weblog that is fully integrated throughout the Collectors' Society.

- Subscribing members receive regularly updated prices for all of their coins from *NumisMedia*.

- The NGC Registry is the most inclusive system of its kind, allowing collectors to enter coins certified by NGC and PCGS.

Join today and share your passion. Visit The Registry at www.NGCcoin.com.

P.O. Box 4776 | Sarasota, FL 34230 | **800-NGC-COIN** (642-2646) | www.NGCcoin.com

An Independent Member of the Certified Collectibles Group

ABOUT THE AUTHOR

David W. Lange is Director of Research for Numismatic Guaranty Corporation in Sarasota, Florida. A long-time numismatic researcher and writer, Dave has been a columnist for the American Numismatic Association's monthly journal, *Numismatist,* since 1988.

He has also written hundreds of feature articles and columns for a wide variety of numismatic publications, and these have been honored with awards from the American Numismatic Association and the Numismatic Literary Guild.

His other books in this series include *The Complete Guide to Lincoln Cents and The Complete Guide to Buffalo Nickels.* Additional titles by David W. Lange include *History of the U.S. Mint and Its Coinage, The Official Red Book of Modern United States Proof Sets* and *NGC Grading Guide for Modern U.S. Coins,* the latter co-authored with Richard S. Montgomery.